THE POX

AND THE

COVENANT

MATHER, FRANKLIN, AND THE EPIDEMIC THAT
CHANGED AMERICA'S DESTINY

TONY WILLIAMS

Published by Sourcebooks, Inc.
P.O. Box 4410, Naperville, Illinois 60567–4410
(630) 961–3900
Fax: (630) 961–2168
www.sourcebooks.com

Library of Congress Cataloging-in-Publication Data
Williams, Tony.
   The pox and the covenant : Mather, Franklin, and the epidemic that changed America's destiny / Tony Williams.
      p. ; cm.
   Includes bibliographical references.
   1. Smallpox—Massachusetts—Boston. 2. Mather, Cotton, 1663-1728. 3. Franklin, Benjamin, 1706-1790. I. Title.
   [DNLM: 1. Mather, Cotton, 1663-1728. 2. Franklin, Benjamin, 1706-1790. 3. Disease Outbreaks—history—Boston. 4. Smallpox—history—Boston. 5. History, 18th Century—Boston. 6. Religion and Medicine—Boston. 7. Smallpox Vaccine—history—Boston. WC 590 W727p 2010]
   RC183.5.M4W55 2010
   614.5'210974461—dc22

                              2009042649

         Printed and bound in the United States of America.
                  SB 10 9 8 7 6 5 4 3 2 1

To Catherine and Paul—my beloved children, with whom I am well pleased

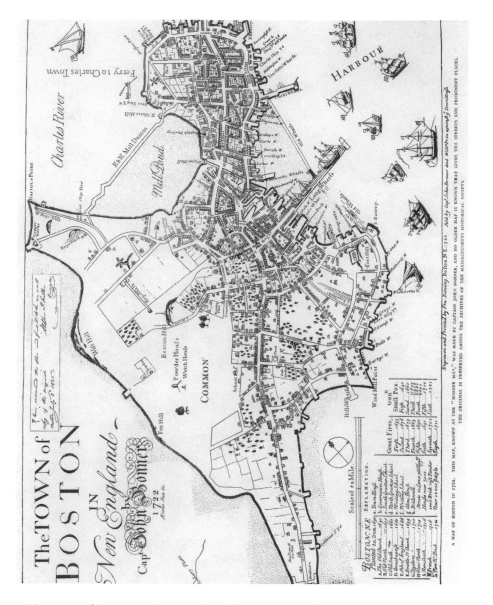

The town of Boston in New England by Capt. John Bonner, 1722. Aetatis Suae 60. Facsimile map by George Smith after map by John Bonner.

Boston: George G. Smith, 1835. Courtesy of the Massachusetts Historical Society.

CONTENTS

ACKNOWLEDGMENTS

This book is dedicated to my beloved children, Catherine and Paul. They are my living proof that historians who used to believe that Puritans were not emotionally attached to their children held foolish notions. They are the light of my life, and I am thankful to live in an age where childhood illnesses and accidents are routinely handled by modern medicine. They enthusiastically interrupt my writing, demanding that we assault imaginary castles in the air. They are great supporters of their father's work, if not quite yet readers of it. I hope their rising generation may develop a passion for history and acquire knowledge of our nation's heritage at a time when this is sadly becoming increasingly less true.

I owe an immense debt of gratitude to my good friend, historian, and public servant, Dr. Jeff Giauque. He was the first to read the manuscript and offered incisive comments, each one surgically noting exactly what changes were necessary. Almost all of his suggestions anticipated those of my editor at Sourcebooks. Jeff's comments improved the manuscript immeasurably.

My other good friend, Dr. Ravi Shamaiengar, lent his expert medical knowledge as well as a sharp editorial eye to reviewing the manuscript. The conversations about the book were a good excuse to go out for coffee. Ruth Douillette offered to read several of the initial chapters early on that put me on track. She reminds me that writers need revising every month for my book review submissions to the Internet Review of Books.

My dearest friends were a constant source of encouragement and diversion. Cliff and Melissa Allen, Mark and Heike Elfendahl, Bruce and Sally Khula, Jeff and Jessica Lavoie, Tom and Suzanne Neely all made us laugh as we exchanged countless hours of fellowship.

I want to thank the librarians at the Colonial Williamsburg Foundation's Rockefeller Library and the Swem Library at the College of William and Mary. These libraries have outstanding collections of colonial history. Special thanks go to director of the Rockefeller Library, Dr. Jim Horn, and his assistant Inge Flester for handling several of my special requests.

Mary Cottrill of Colonial Williamsburg graciously invited me to present a lecture on this book at the DeWitt Wallace Decorative Arts Museum. Harmony Hunter kindly asked me to sit down with her and record a podcast about the book for the Colonial Williamsburg website www.history.org. At the Visitor Center Bookstore, Bob Hill and his friendly staff invited me to do many book-signings over the last two years.

Many years ago, I served as a graduate research assistant to Professor John C. Burnham at Ohio State University. He mentored me informally in the history of medicine. Although I did not formally study under Professor Burnham, he taught me perhaps more than he realized about the history of medicine over many hours of conversation. The seeds of this book were planted in those discussions. I am honored to have known such a towering intellect and scholar.

Peter Lynch, my editor at Sourcebooks, may have a light pen, but he wields it like a sharp blade. His edits were always exactly what were needed. He has exhibited a profound respect for the collaborative nature of a relationship with an author. It was a great privilege to work on my second book with Peter. I would also like to thank my publicist Heather Moore at Sourcebooks, who skillfully promoted my first book with verve and professional charm, while Liz Kelsch cheerfully organized the book tour and made the media contacts for this book.

My special thanks go to my wife of fourteen years. Lynne has daily reflected the love of God in our marriage. We were made for each other, and I look forward to a lifetime together.

INTRODUCTION

The late 1600s saw the flowering of a revolution in science, from the publication of Sir Isaac Newton's *Principia* in 1687 to the development of the scientific method. The critical inquiry ushered in the dawn of a new age of thought in eighteenth-century Europe called the Enlightenment. The philosophers of this "age of reason" held that human reason should be free to examine all questions of the natural world. They believed in progress and had a utopian belief that they would eventually uncover every answer and unravel every mystery. They believed they would sweep aside what they considered to be a thousand years of medieval ignorance and superstition. They apparently ignored the fact that reason had been alive and well before the Enlightenment and that religious faith—as well as superstitions—survived into the Enlightenment, even by the scientists who heralded the new age. Despite their optimistic and progressive view of history, the conflicts of the era were not always neat and often produced curious results.

The events described in this book focus on just such a debate, and they revolve around an individual who was one of the most renowned men of his day. Our figure was an American who made significant contributions to the Enlightenment even though he resided in the colonies, which were considered a provincial backwater. He joined the international, cosmopolitan conversation in letters and journals that defined the Enlightenment, communicating with luminaries in enlightened circles in London, Scotland, and the Continent. European universities offered him honorary degrees for his scientific achievements. He was elected a member of the prestigious Royal

Society, the preeminent scientific body in the world, and he sent many contributions to its journal, which circulated among scientists in European cities. He helped to establish the first scientific society in America, keeping abreast of the latest scientific findings and making lasting contributions of his own, even when other scientists lacked the courage to challenge traditional scientific dogma.

In the supposed backwater of the American colonies, he employed the new instruments of the scientific revolution, observing the heavens through telescopes and the hidden world via microscopes. He readily accepted the heliocentrism of Nicolaus Copernicus that stirred a controversial revolution that riled traditional churchmen and scientists alike. Moreover, he supported the mechanistic world-view of Newton that spawned deism, in which philosophers held that God was a "blind clockmaker" who created the universe and left it alone to run like a giant clock according to natural laws. He even worked out an almanac that had a calendar, astronomical data, and expected eclipses.

This person introspectively examined his own virtues and vices in an Enlightenment project of self-improvement. He recorded his moral failures in his diary and his personal struggle to overcome them. His diary was a kind of autobiography that he self-consciously wrote and edited in order to provide an example of instruction to his own children and the rising generation.

This person transcended merely personal concerns and engaged in many Enlightenment projects for the public good. He improved the life of his city by forming mutual-aid societies, helping the poor, and supporting the education of free blacks and Indians. Taking an even larger, imperial view, he engaged in revolutionary political activity. He argued and fought for Americans to preserve the traditional rights of Englishmen. As rebellious American subjects took to the streets to fight English tyranny, he rallied them despite the threat of arrest as they revolted against royal officials for ruling arbitrarily, seizing them and British warships.

His character could at times be vain and self-seeking. He was after all one of the most famous Americans in the colonies and in Europe, based on his voluminous published writings, correspondence, and scientific activities. He was praised for his discerning and versatile mind, extraordinary industry, and reputation and desire to serve the public good unselfishly. Like many men and women of the Enlightenment, he idealistically sought to serve the "welfare of humanity" generally while personally living according to the ideal of the refrain, "What good may I do?"

The person described above was not Benjamin Franklin. He was a Puritan minister who resided in Boston: Cotton Mather.

If this is surprising, it is due to the fact that the popular portrait most Americans have of the Puritans is one-dimensional. When many think of the Puritans, they think of the people who settled in America, celebrated the first Thanksgiving with Indians, and unknowingly spread diseases. Puritans are seen as religiously oppressive, intolerant of dissenters, and witch hunters. Their social conduct is seen as, well, puritanical. They supposedly wore only dour black and renounced all worldly pleasures and anything that smacked of fun.

History, however, holds a different view of the Puritans. The American Enlightenment is generally dated to the later part of the eighteenth century, when giants such as John Adams, Benjamin Franklin, Alexander Hamilton, Thomas Jefferson, James Madison, Thomas Paine, and other Founding Fathers argued for liberty against tyranny and created a "new order for the ages." Yet while one cannot overestimate the importance of the work of the Revolutionary generation in examining human nature, studying ancient and modern philosophy, and creating a lasting republic, one should not ignore the Puritan participation in the early American Enlightenment.

Puritan science was often used to demonstrate the glory of God's creation. But in this they were hardly different from Galileo Galilei and other churchmen who were in the vanguard of science for centuries. The idea of warfare between science and religion was a nineteenth-century invention that unfortunately clouds our judgment of Puritan science. It is also true that their original contributions and groundbreaking experiments were quite modest compared with some of the better-remembered European scientists of the late seventeenth and early eighteenth centuries. However, to conclude as a result, as many have done, that the Puritans rejected science and reason is demonstrably false.

It is my contention that in the dramatic story that follows, Puritans participated in the cosmopolitan world of science and were leading scientific figures in the American colonies. They made significant and lasting contributions to medicine and science. They would be recognized as enlightened men of science and learning if not for the powerful image that pervades of a people steeped in religion and clad in dour black.

The story of a calamity that struck Boston in 1721 provides the evidence for a reassessment of the Puritans and their relationship to the early American Enlightenment. The disaster led Reverend Cotton Mather to achieve his end of serving the public good when he introduced a scientific innovation to save lives. He did so over the objections of similarly enlightened men who argued against the experiment. The debate, in fact, confounds our typical understanding of men of reason and learning battling dogmatic churchmen who resisted anything smacking of the new science.

Because Cotton Mather was a man of God, his foray into a vicious public dispute over medicine opened the door to attacks on his ministerial role. Mather's enemies censured the cleric for intervening in matters outside the realm of salvation. The hundred-year-old Puritan experiment in establishing a godly society already seemed in danger of collapsing when Mather risked the surviving shreds of ministerial authority on a revolutionary medical procedure in an increasingly worldly and affluent city. The results jeopardized the foundations of the covenant established by the forefathers he revered so deeply.

I hope that the story of the remarkable events in 1721 Boston will help to correct the image of the Puritans in the popular imagination. The sides taken by the different actors in this gripping tale may seem incongruous to our modern ears, but that is what makes it such an important story.

PROLOGUE

On September 6, 1620, the Puritans aboard the *Mayflower* departed on their religious errand into the American wilderness. They were Separatists who fled on their divinely ordained mission to escape persecution and establish a pure church free of the Catholic corruptions of the Anglican Church. As chronicler William Bradford wrote, in England, "religion has been disgraced, the godly aggrieved, afflicted, persecuted…. Sin has been countenanced, ignorance, profanity, and atheism have increased, and the papists have been encouraged." The Puritan church in the New World would recover its ancient biblical purity and be a model for the English Church; the Separatists could then return to their Mother Country.

The *Mayflower* sailed from Plymouth for the New World, Bradford wrote, with a "prosperous wind." The crowded vessel measured roughly one hundred feet in length and was rated at 180 tons. Her sister ship, the *Speedwell*, had proved to be leaky beyond repair and had put in at Dartmouth to be mended. After a great deal of expense of lost time, the pair put to sea again but was forced back to Plymouth when the *Speedwell* sprang more leaks. The ship was clearly unequal to a transatlantic voyage, and some of her passengers boarded the *Mayflower* while others were forced to stay behind. Half of the provisions had been consumed in the weeks spent dealing with the *Speedwell*. It had been an inauspicious start to a voyage blessed by the Lord.

The *Mayflower* sped across the white-tipped waves once the voyage was under way, and the passengers were quickly afflicted with seasickness. The crew took great delight in the sufferings of the landlubbers and tormented them mercilessly. "There is an insolent and very profane young man," Bradford wrote, "who was always harassing the poor people in their sickness, and cursing them daily with grievous execrations." He even laughed that he hoped to "throw half of them overboard before they came to their journey's end." The Puritans believed that a just God punished the young sailor for his cruelty when, halfway through the voyage, "it pleased God…to smite the young man with a grievous disease, of which he died in a desperate manner." He was the first to be thrown overboard.

The favorable winds dissipated, and the *Mayflower* encountered a series of fierce storms and westerly gales that forced the crew to furl the sails and ride it out. They were "forced to hull for many days" and driven back. They surrendered to the will of God and prayed for deliverance to survive their arduous journey. One day a young indentured servant came on deck during a terrible storm and was thrown into the sea. He somehow grasped the rope that raised and lowered the topsail even as he was dragged several feet under the surface. He was frantically hauled onto the deck. The Puritans interpreted his rescue as an instance of God's providence rewarding them for their piety. Unlike many other transatlantic voyages, only one passenger died.

After a two-month trip during which they suffered the dreadful effects of that common seafaring disease scurvy, land was sighted on November 9. There were some disputes about where they would ultimately land because they tried to head southward for the Hudson River but encountered dangerous shoals and breakers that threatened to wreck the ship. The captain resolved on Cape Cod, but not before "discontented and mutinous speeches" were uttered by some of the "strangers" (passengers who were not Puritans) on board. The strangers were Englishmen who vowed that they were free men and would not submit to any authority over their lives.

Given these threatening circumstances to a people plunging into a vast and dangerous wilderness, the Puritans assembled and laid the foundation of their government in the New World. They wrote:

In the name of God, Amen. We whose names are underwritten, the loyal subjects of our dread sovereign lord, King James, by the grace of God, of Great Britain, France, and Ireland, King, Defender of the Faith, etc., having undertaken for the glory of God, and advancement of the Christian faith, and honor of our king and country, a voyage to plant the first colony in the northern parts of Virginia, do by these presents solemnly and mutually in the presence of God, and of one another, covenant and combine ourselves into a civil body politic, for our better ordering and preservation, and the furtherance of the ends aforesaid and by virtue hereof to enact, constitute, and frame, such just and equal laws, ordinances, acts, constitutions, and offices, from time to time, as shall be thought most meet and convenient for the general use of the Colony, unto which we promise all due submission and obedience. In witness thereof we have here underscribed our names as Cape Cod, 11th of November, in the year of the reign of our sovereign lord, King James of England, France, and Ireland the eighteenth, and of Scotland the fifty-fourth. A.D. 1620.

On the face of it, the document is a significant expression of republican government by representatives who govern by the consent of the people. It was a practical attempt to establish law and order in the wilderness for the common good, demanding obedience from all to a just authority. The laws would be drawn with biblical precepts in mind and govern the individual passions among the unruly adventurers.

More important, the Mayflower Compact was a covenant that knitted the people together in a "civil body politic"—a united whole solemnly bound together with each other and under God. This political covenant was a civil agreement that was consistent with Puritan covenantal theology.

The entire edifice of Puritan theology was rooted upon a voluntary covenant between God and man, and it created the framework for eternal salvation. The covenant of grace was God's promise to redeem a humanity fallen since the sin of Adam and later renewed with Abraham and the Jews. God was just, good, merciful, and loving, saving those saints whom he predestined to save from the beginning of time. These elect experienced the grace of conversion and led godly lives.

The Congregational Church was an ecclesiastical community of saints created by a mutual covenant to achieve grace and salvation. They were free of any outside authority and decided upon the admittance and expulsion of its members and chose their ministers. The ministers were beholden to preach on Holy Scripture and actively persuade the unconverted to examine their souls carefully and discover whether they were blessed with divine grace.

Puritan society was also governed by a political covenant in which government would regulate conduct to establish order and control sin. As with most people in the West, they believed in an organic social hierarchy ordained by God. The natural leaders among them would become magistrates who enforced biblical laws. The people gave their assent to be governed by their consent when they voluntarily formed a political compact with each other and their leaders. Likewise, each family was considered a "little commonwealth" in which fathers were sanctioned to govern their wives and children to achieve the covenant of grace.

Their entire errand into the wilderness was itself seen as a covenant with God. The Puritans were charged with, as John Winthrop told a new wave of Puritan settlers a decade later in 1630, being a new chosen people, a new Israel. They received a great commission to establish a "city upon a hill," a perfectly reformed church to set an example for England. If they were pious and obedient to God's will, their endeavor would be blessed. If they strayed from their mission and sinned in their worldliness, they could expect horrible judgments and afflictions from an angry and just God. They voluntarily assumed a grave and awful obligation.

The covenantal relationship of the Puritans with each other and their God was the core and cement that gave meaning to their lives and society. For one hundred years, no event could be understood apart from Puritan covenantal ideas and identity. For that century, the Puritans clung tightly to those beliefs. Although they constantly fretted about any sign of decline from their original covenant, by the time of their third generation, their allegiance to the covenant had remained generally vibrant and faithful. Puritan Boston was not so much in decline as it was simply changing over the course of a century.

Yet there were indeed some worrisome tidings. By the early 1700s, there were challenges to the covenant. Internal struggles within the congregations and larger conflicts within Puritan society were tearing at its foundations. The ministers did not garner the respect from the population they once had. Nor could they look for help from the state, which was more interested in protecting the property rights and the liberties of the people than in enforcing the Ten Commandments. The cleavages that were gradually undermining the covenant would rend the entire social fabric in 1721 when a ship arrived from Barbados and unleashed the forces of physical destruction and social dislocation.

Chapter One

A KILLER LURKING

In early April 1721, the crew of the HMS *Seahorse* had finally been mustered onboard the ship. The vessel had been on-station in Barbados for some time, patrolling the waters of the wealthy sugar island against pirates and French privateers. Sugar was voraciously consumed in Europe to sweeten food and drink or turned into rum. The Royal Navy had been built up the previous century to protect this far-flung empire in the West Indies. With a large enough convoy of trade ships assembled, the *Seahorse* would sail for Boston, America's largest port city, and then on to London.

The men were preparing for this departure by loading on supplies of food, particularly fresh fruits and vegetables. While they were busily working, no one saw the lurking killer even in the crowded conditions on the gun deck. It was probably hiding in some large sea chest among blankets or clothing.

The sailors quickly became models of discipline. They stowed their personal effects in their small sea chests and slung their hammocks. They efficiently completed their tasks without close supervision by their officers.

The men did not have much room on the lower deck. The captain and ship's officers may have had more spacious quarters, but nearly one hundred sailors were crammed into the overcrowded gun deck. The unwashed men emitted a bewildering array of odors, made even more unpleasant by livestock and spilled chamber pots. Vermin and disease thrived in these filthy conditions. The hammocks may have been regularly washed and the top deck scrubbed with vinegar, but these palliatives did little to ameliorate the foul environment. Their diets were not only monotonous but also nutritionally unsound, leaving them susceptible to a variety of diseases, including deadly scurvy. But the disease climate was comparable to that experienced on land.

Soon the *Seahorse* left the crystal-clear waters and warm weather behind as it crested the waves in a northerly direction. The sailors were probably glad to be away from the tropical fevers and the stultifying heat of the Caribbean Islands. Although life at sea was difficult, the men were glad to be aboard the warship instead of a merchant vessel that had many fewer hands and much harder work.

There was a growing sense of pride and patriotism among the Royal Navy sailors as the service became more professional. Most of the sailors enjoyed certain freedoms of a life at sea. They were on a little piece of England amid the great expanse of ocean. They were freeborn men who were earning good wages and traveling to distant places all over the Atlantic.

African sailors experienced an ambiguous life on the *Seahorse*. Slavery was thought improper and was illegal on His Majesty's warships. Some officers may have brought their slaves with them to sea, but they had to disguise that fact carefully. Black seamen were not officially designated in a special way. Despite the difficulties of the work, though, they enjoyed their service aboard the *Seahorse*, for it was a world in which they were usually judged for their professional skill rather than the color of their skin.

Black seamen—or "Black Jacks," as African sailors were known—enjoyed a refreshing world of liberty and equality. Even if they were generally relegated to jobs such as cooks, servants, and musicians and endured their fellow seamen's racism, they were still free men in the Royal Navy. One famous black sailor wrote, "I liked this little ship very much. I now became the captain's steward, in which situation I was very happy; for I was extremely well-treated by all on board, and I had leisure to improve myself in reading and writing." The freedom of life at sea led many slaves to run away from their masters and join ship crews in order to win their liberty. They pretended to be free and were taken up by merchant vessels and royal warships alike.

Free and proud as the sailors may have been aboard the *Seahorse,* there remained an unseen killer aboard the warship when it departed Barbados. The men were ignorant that one of them had brought aboard a mass murderer that could silently wipe them out before it was discovered.

The killer escaped notice because it was microscopic—a virus. It did not yet have a human host, but that did not matter. The virus could survive for weeks outside a human body, such as in a blanket or an article of clothing. Because of the timing of the voyage and the appearance of the symptoms, it is likely that no sailor was infected until about halfway through the voyage. It would not be difficult under such circumstances for a sailor to breathe in millions of infinitesimal viruses from such items.

The virus was of course not conscious of its actions. The organism simply needed a human host so that it could reproduce and endure. In order for a sailor to catch the disease, he needed to have been free of the disease until the moment of infection. Even if it lacked self-awareness, the virus infected one of the sailors at the most opportune time. The voyage to American ports normally lasted two weeks. If a virus infected a sailor too early in the voyage, it would kill several sailors, but the infection would be confined to a single ship, because the captain would not put into port if his ship was full of contagion. A sailor who contracted the disease within a week of his ship's docking would enter a population of susceptible people and spread it without realizing the disastrous results of his innocent actions.

Ships offered the best route for the virus to spread malevolence. The Royal Navy, as well as merchant ships, traversed the Atlantic between Europe, Africa, the Caribbean, and British North America. They regularly stopped at ports for repairs, supplies, and trade. The interconnected, global nature of these imperial trade networks gave the virus the potential to unleash a major pandemic that could kill many thousands.

As fate would have it, one of the Black Jacks aboard the man-of-war became infected with smallpox. Probably midway through the voyage, the brick-shaped virus (one of the largest known viruses) entered the mucous membranes in his nasal passages and quickly multiplied at the site. At this point the virus ingeniously turned the man's body against itself. After forcing the locally infected cells' internal mechanisms to replicate more and more virus particles, the new virus particles then entered his bloodstream. They were easily carried to the man's liver and other internal organs, where they found a bounty of suitable host cells to hasten their replication. The legion of virus particles eventually infected the skin cells where they finally caused an outbreak of visible symptoms.

Spawned in central Africa, the disease originated from an animal poxvirus that crossed the species barrier to humans either from domesticated animals or those that were hunted. It flared among the nomadic hunter-gatherers and small village settlements and began evolving until it was uniquely adapted for human cells. The migrations of people and the advent of the seafaring trade spread the disease to Asia, the Mediterranean, and Europe. European explorers brought it to the New World with devastating impact on the native population.

Chances were good that the warship *Seahorse* would convey the disease to at least one American port. At the same time, there was no known effective means of combating an outbreak once it started and began to run its vicious course through a population. The disease would follow a predictable pattern as it had for millennia.

Most of the people who suffered the scourge would survive, but approximately a quarter of them would die an excruciating death. Those who lived could be blinded, scarred, or horribly disfigured, to say nothing of the psychological scars and grief of losing loved ones. Smallpox was the greatest killer in human history, and justifiably it was one of the most feared.

Contagion caused severe social dislocations in any city where it struck. Anarchy and confusion were the inevitable result of an epidemic. Residents understandably fled for their lives in terror from infected cities. Commerce was interrupted for the duration of the outbreak. Women halted their daily activities with friends and neighbors; children stopped going to school. Religious observances brought comfort, but many people weighed the risk of attending a gathering of large numbers of people even in a church.

The *Seahorse* was headed for Boston, Massachusetts, the center of American Puritanism since its founding almost exactly a century before. Covenantal theology would shape the Puritans' understanding and reaction to the disease. Puritanism would also face its greatest challenge because of the outbreak.

Most of the Bostonians would interpret the outbreak as punishment from an angry and just God, a sign of his divine wrath against them for their collective sin: their pride, their worldliness, their impiety. They would risk their health and their lives by seeking solace from the disease in their churches as they implored their God for mercy with prayers of supplication.

This epidemic would lead the Puritans to assume that supernatural forces were in play. They believed that God allowed the hovering angel of death and his evil minions to ravage humanity according to some hidden divine will. Like the biblical character Job, they would endure the terrible plague as well as the heartrending loss of their loved ones. If they had the audacity to ask why they were made to suffer, they would receive an unsatisfactory answer and be forced to accept the mysterious ways of God.

After several days of skirting the North American coast, the *Seahorse* reached Boston, the largest city in the colonies, with a population of roughly eleven thousand souls. With such a large number of people, Boston rivaled the cities of mother England, save only for London. Boston was moreover one of the great hubs of the Atlantic trade network. It gathered goods from the farms of the New England hinterland and from smaller cities and ports along the American coast. These commodities were shipped all over the Atlantic while other goods were imported into the city and sent elsewhere. For a virus, a better place to contaminate could hardly be found.

The infected seaman blithely went about his duties aboard the *Seahorse*. He interacted with his shipmates as he normally would, ignorant of the deadly corruption that he was carrying. He was not yet contagious, but he soon would be. And the ship sailed closer and closer to Boston. Other ships were arriving and departing from the port with great frequency. A local pilot came aboard and eased the ship through a maze of islands and into the harbor.

Soon the hills of the peninsula were in view. Dozens of ships of various sizes lay in the harbor. The vast majority were merchant vessels whose holds were filled with tons of cargo: cod from the Grand Banks, sugar and perhaps slaves from the West Indies, lumber and masts from New Hampshire, and agricultural goods from nearby farms. The Royal Navy sailors did not look enviously on their mercantile counterparts. Life on the trade ships was characterized by bad rations, harsh and arbitrary discipline, and more demanding work routines.

The British captain knew his men needed leaves ashore after their lengthy deployment in the Caribbean, and he announced which watch would receive leave first. Those who were required to stay aboard did not necessarily mind too much, for their stay would provide a respite from the demanding daily workload. Dockyard workers would handle most of the arduous work of loading supplies on the ship.

The infected sailor was among the shipmates preparing to go ashore. The men grabbed some coins from their sea chests or borrowed against their pay. They intended to have a grand time drinking, whoring, and gambling while staying a few nights at a tavern or boardinghouse. Perhaps some would spend their money more wisely on trinkets for loved ones or items for themselves. Some plotted to leave the ship without permission. The practice of such "rambling" was frowned upon, but the officers usually looked the other way. Their tolerance endeared them to the men and sustained morale.

The *Seahorse* approached the massive wharf that jutted out from the Boston shoreline. By this point, the infected Black Jack probably felt a bit ill. He may have felt feverish and rubbed his temples against a developing headache. If he vomited over the side of the boat, his shipmates might have laughed that he was seasick in the calm waters of the port. They did not realize that as he coughed or sneezed he was releasing millions of germs into the air for them to breathe in. He was fully contagious.

As the sailors made sluggish progress while they rowed *Seahorse*'s longboat toward Boston, the features of the town became clearer. Looming in the distance were the three modest hills—Cotton, Beacon, and Mount Vernon—that comprised Trimountain, from where any enemy incursion by the French fleet could be spotted.

Clearly discernable soaring high above the skyline were the church spires and cupolas. Spires were frowned upon by the early Puritans, for they smacked of "popery." They preferred unadorned, simple wooden buildings, though spires were later added after the first generation of Puritans had passed. The rising spires were a sign of the religious pluralism that had been forced on the Puritans when the king issued a new charter in the wake of the Glorious Revolution. Heretical Baptists, Quakers, and Anglicans had won official religious tolerance and were no longer executed or driven out of town for their beliefs. These sects had built their churches and meetinghouses, worshipping freely according to the dictates of their conscience, to the consternation of many Puritans.

The walls and guns of the South Battery came into view on the waterfront on the left just below Fort Hill. They were reminders that the valuable trade here was part of a larger imperial struggle in Europe. The men rowed past a relic of that international competition. The Old Wharf had been a defensive seawall that was built with funds of publicly minded citizens who subscribed to the effort. It was constructed of stone and ran more than two thousand feet. The wall was a mighty twenty-two feet at its base and narrowed to twenty-two inches at its top. Because no enemy fireships were ever launched against Boston, the seawall quickly fell into disrepair. For the last few decades, outward-bound sea captains had systematically dismantled the wall by robbing its stones for ballast to steady their ships.

Now that the merchant vessels, accompanied by the *Seahorse,* settled into their berths at the wharves, Bostonians came running to claim packages, pick out the best goods to purchase, or welcome home loved ones safely returned home from sea. Besides family members and curious spectators, workers scurried about the seaport unloading tons of imported cargoes.

The townspeople were oblivious to the fact that the *Seahorse* was bringing death to their shores. Bostonians were hardly ignorant of the fact that ships from every possible port regularly brought disease with them. Their forefathers had quarantined ships for inspection at Castle Island in the harbor back in 1647. More recently, because so many ships brought disease from the Caribbean, the town's lawmakers mandated that ships should stop at a newly opened pest house on Spectacle Island. It was set up for the "lodging of sick persons…from beyond the sea" to protect the townspeople from foreign diseases. After any signs of illness had passed, the crews then were allowed into the port. But in this case, the captain of the *Seahorse* did not realize that at least one member of his crew was infected with a terrible disease. Earlier in 1721, a law was passed that ordered all vessels from France and the Mediterranean to halt at Spectacle Island because of an outbreak of the plague in Europe. Boston's legislators chose to quarantine ships from the wrong part of the Atlantic. Thus the *Seahorse*'s crewmen on leave disembarked onto the Long Wharf.

Meanwhile, repairs were planned for the *Seahorse* and then dockworkers would load fresh supplies onto the ship. Captain Thomas Durrell broke the bad news to the crew that he was assigning fifty of them to man a commandeered sloop and chase some pirates reported to be in the area. Their leave would have to wait. A skeleton crew was left on the *Seahorse* while the rest of the crew and officers went ashore. At least one carried an infectious disease.

Chapter Two

WALKING AROUND BOSTON

The *Seahorse* sailors—their pockets relatively full as they entered a city that, despite its Puritan origins, offered a gamut of worldly pleasures—jauntily strolled along the pier. Everyone immediately recognized them as sons of Neptune, and they proudly swaggered as members of the Royal Navy. They did not yet have naval uniforms, but their maritime outfits of tarred, baggy breeches, a checkered shirt, a blue jacket, and a cap were conspicuous even in Boston. They walked with a distinctive swaying that had steadied them at sea.

They passed civilians who were a greatly mixed lot and hardly dressed in the cheerless black clothing and skullcaps that their Puritan ministers donned for the pulpit. Instead, the people wore an array of different colors and fabrics. The wealthy emulated the latest London fashions when their packages arrived. Ladies' fashions were only a few months behind their London counterparts, while their husbands were quite dandy in silver-wrought coats. Gentlemen went abroad bewigged. Young ladies dressed with an eye toward ensnaring a husband, and young men had taken to the foppery of wearing their hair scandalously long.

The Long Wharf was aptly named because the pier jutted into the bay a lengthy and impressive sixteen hundred feet. The pier was crowded with warehouses and shops for the convenience of trade ships that could moor at dozens of berths. Men ran around loading and unloading cargoes from ships with their towering masts and complex rigging. Longshoremen no longer needed to row out in lighters to transport the goods in from anchored ships in the harbor. The Long Wharf was certainly the largest of the wharves at Boston and the center of activity, but more than fifty smaller wharves were crammed along the congested waterfront. Less than a decade old, the facility was necessarily large enough to accommodate the mushrooming trade of the chief port in colonial America. *Seahorse*'s sailors had visited large ports all over the Atlantic and may have visited Boston previously, but the burgeoning port was still an impressive sight.

As the British sailors walked along, they split up into groups of friends. Some of them peeled off to answer the call of one of the dozens of watering holes that the Puritan city had to offer. The rest continued along at a good clip, finally reaching the actual shoreline where the pier turned into King Street. At the intersection of suitably named Mackerel Street, the elegant Bunch of Grapes Tavern beckoned the ship's officers to enjoy its renowned rum punch and fine fare.

In addition to the taverns and warehouses, King Street was lined with a variety of artisan shops where goods were crafted and sold by wives and servants. Dwellings were typically located above the shops. Many of the buildings were constructed of wood and left unpainted and weathered. Signs hanging above the doors signified the trade of the artisan within. Not surprisingly, a variety of crafts—including coopers, glassmakers, masons, silversmiths, shoemakers, and tailors—were represented in the city to meet the local and foreign demand. The artisans were almost invariably connected in some way to supporting the shipping industry. Bakers supplied biscuits for transatlantic voyages, and coopers made the massive barrels for the amazing plethora of goods that were stored inside.

Merchants and shop owners also hawked a bewildering selection of locally made as well as imported goods for consumption in their specialty and general stores. Apothecaries, booksellers, grocers, and tobacconists were some of the businesses that thrived in this commercial city. Innkeepers, tavern owners, and boardinghouse landladies rented rooms and provided drink and a hot, fresh meal for the sailors. In any of these establishments, the crew came into close contact with a great number of people.

The entrepreneurial spirit was alive and well in Boston. Merchants reaped great profits from their foreign investments. William Clark, for example, built an extravagant three-story brick mansion with as many as twenty-six elaborately decorated rooms and numerous sash windows. He and other wealthy homeowners were successful enough to afford to paint or even wallpaper their rooms. Exquisite walled-in gardens and orchards tastefully complemented the interior furnishings of such homes. The mansions were the sites of fancy weddings and lavish dinner parties. John Foster, Samson Waters, and Samuel Sewall all built competing homes in the south and north ends that rivaled Clark's manor.

The mercantile class enjoyed a rising influence over the town. Intricate trade networks throughout the city had shaped its design. The wharves and storehouses, shops and marketplaces, and streets all brought an indelible stamp upon the seaport. The merchants directed the use of its natural resources, investments, and property. They enjoyed a rising influence in running public affairs. The ethic of worldly success and social mobility seemed to crowd out the older

Puritan virtues of order and discipline. A fine line separated the blessings of the Puritan work ethic and a sinful love of money, and Congregational ministers were ever vigilant to warn of its violation.

Middling artisans may not have been as wealthy, but they shared in the benefits from the bustling trade. Both groups risked their savings in various enterprises and to invest in continuing civic development. It was their capital, imagination, and direction that helped to sustain Boston as the leading seaport of the British North American colonies. People may have occasionally railed against the "damnable rich," but the dynamic economy offered many opportunities to the shrewd investors who seized them. There was a leveling spirit in Boston that created a broad equality and comfort to most people.

Nowhere was the relative economic and political equality of the people and their civic-mindedness represented better in the city than in the townhouse that the sailors encountered after walking just a few blocks down King Street at Cornhill (which led to the Neck). The massive two-story building had been the brainchild of wealthy merchant Robert Keayne in the mid-seventeenth century. His bequest created the pivot of political and economic life in Boston and beyond its shores. It housed the representative General Court of Massachusetts as well as the local town meeting that directly expressed the will of the self-governing people. Merchants assembled here daily at eleven o'clock for the mercantile exchange to conduct their most important business deals. The building housed a well-stocked and handsome library.

On the night of October 2, 1711, the wooden structure had been consumed in a terrifying conflagration. The most destructive fire of the colonial era raced through several blocks of wooden buildings, burning down more than one hundred homes in the middle of town. The inferno raged for more than two hours and killed several citizens and sailors who were battling the blaze. Within a few years, an even more elegant (and fire-resistant) brick townhouse was built on the site.

Boston's finest streets were alive with the bustle of urban life. As the British sailors walked the streets, they may have had to make way for a swanky imported carriage driven by a slave footman and occupied by a wealthy merchant and his wife. Slower moving, yet more prevalent, were the "carters" who hauled their wares between the docks and shops. Horses were ridden through town at a slow canter because galloping was strictly forbidden in order to protect the swarms of playing children. Many pedestrians on business known only to them jostled along. Bothersome swine and packs of dogs roamed freely through the streets, mixing with the human traffic.

The streets were motley breeding grounds of filth. Some paving stones had been laid down, but their placement was irregular, and they often broke under the weight of the traffic of heavy carts. Free blacks were required to work on the roads in lieu of military service, but they could not keep up with the sheer volume of traffic. Some shop owners dumped gravel in front of their establishments to give it a neater appearance. Patches of packed dirt turned muddy and mixed with the trash dumped from homes, animal waste, and occasional carcasses. Some streets had a primitive drainage system with a crowned center and lower gutters on the side, but they allevi-ated the disgusting conditions only slightly. Tanneries, butchers, slaughterhouses, curriers, and tallow-chandlers were relegated to specific parts of town and banned from dumping their waste in the thoroughfares, although the law was usually obeyed more in the breach. The regulations were put in place because it was believed that the stench sickened the residents.

Eighteenth-century medicine and people's imaginations accepted the miasma theory that linked disease to noxious air. The fumes from garbage, human and animal waste, carcasses, offal, and even cemeteries were blamed for sickening people. Malaria, for example, was translated as "bad air," which many believed explained its underlying cause. The suspected origins of smallpox, yellow fever, and other major diseases also were attributed to foul smells. Logically, the way to combat disease was to clean the streets and freshen the air as much as possible. The town hired scavengers to remove the offending wastes and garbage from the streets, but funds were routinely short and workers too few to make more than a dent. Try as they might, no town could rid itself of the offensive odors.

The eighteenth century was a smelly era, and disease was rampant. The limited countermeasures probably did help to combat disease, just not in the way that the prevailing wisdom reasoned. Moreover, seamen who lived at sea for months at a time with one set of clothing and in crowded quarters were hardly conscious of the smell.

Unless they were interested in purchasing specific items in the shops, the *Seahorse*'s sailors were less interested in sightseeing than getting drunk at one of the more than eighty drinking establishments around the port. By comparison, four coffeehouses offered the latest seafaring gossip and foreign newspapers while patrons sipped their coffee, tea, or chocolate drinks. A few establishments allowed local captains and mariners to hang a mailbag to collect their correspondence after returning from sea. A number of very respectful taverns, such as the Bunch of Grapes or the King's Arms, served as meeting and dining places for the upscale clientele that included merchants, politicians, and even ministers.

Most sailors preferred the looser taverns along the waterfront that served the mostly seafaring population. The rowdiness was more pleasurable, the gaming more overt, the raucous songs more familiar, and the prostitutes more readily available. A Puritan minister complained about the effects of these on the social hierarchy and godly society: "When drink is got into the brain, then come out filthy songs, and scoffing at the best men, yea at godliness itself in the power of it."

The infected sailor from the *Seahorse* may have run into an old shipmate and swapped stories convivially over a couple of rounds. The drunken men would inevitably get involved in some scrapes and fistfights in which they would defend their shipmates. The town had trouble controlling the frequent brawls caused by Royal Navy sailors and crewmen from the trading vessels.

Boston's Puritan ministers could hardly resist lamenting what they saw as the horrible decline of morality and rise of sinfulness in their worldly and impious city. Cotton Mather railed against the seedy taverns on more than one occasion, even utilizing the animals painted on their signs as the perfect metaphors for the debauchery and the destruction of the souls inside. "I have seen certain taverns," Mather stated, "where the pictures of horrible devourers [lion, bear, etc.] were hanged out for signs and thought it were well if such signs were not sometimes too significant."

Mather's father, the Reverend Increase Mather, and other moralists were concerned that impressionable young people were drawn to the illicit behavior like moths to a flame. Boston was descending into a modern-day Gomorrah. The elder Mather lamented: "A proud fashion no sooner comes into the country but the haughty daughters of Zion in this place are taking it up, and thereby the whole land is at last infected…[by] such like whorish fashion, whereby the anger of the Lord is kindled against this sinful land!"

It was not so much a pint of beer or cider as drunkenness that worried the Puritan clergy. What caused even more anxiety for the pious was that much of the depravity shockingly occurred on the Sabbath or on Thursday lecture days. One minister worried about the "levity and wanton frolics of the young people, who, when their devotions over, have recourse to the ordinaries where they plentifully wash away their remembrance of their old sins and drink down their fear of a fine, or the dread of a whipping-post." When Samuel Sewall, a stodgy merchant, broke up a card game, a rebellious youth mocked him fittingly a few days later. "A pack of cards…strayed over my forehead," he reported. A disgusted Cotton Mather blamed the seafaring folk for spreading much of the vice and crime that seemed to plague Boston: "And now, I begin with seafaring. Oh, what a horrible spectacle have I before me! A wicked, stupid, abominable generation; every year growing rather worse." To the Mathers, such wantonness was stark proof that the original covenant from the days of their respectable forefathers was in decline.

As the evening hours stretched into night, and the sailors from the *Seahorse* lost track of how many drinks they had consumed, they heard the nightly pealing of the town's bells at nine o'clock, signaling the curfew. They likely defied the law and continued drinking. Later on, they stumbled into their boardinghouses or slept in the taverns. Other townspeople, particularly servants and slaves, rushed home during the night to avoid being rounded up, not to mention escape the terrors Bostonians superstitiously believed lurked in the night. The town's watchmen patrolled the unlit and dangerous streets, watching for fires and vainly attempting to control people's unruliness.

By now, the sick Black Jack was probably experiencing the first symptoms of smallpox. Initially, smallpox victims feel like they have a particularly nasty case of the flu. They have difficulty sleeping because of burning fevers, piercing headaches, nightmares and delusions, chills and shivering, and feelings of anxiety. They also feel severe lower-back pain. Nausea and convulsions follow, adding to the misery.

Ashore somewhere in Boston, a malaise took over the ill sailor's miserable body. His disease-infected cells had swollen until they had burst in his bloodstream. His circulatory system began to carry the virus to his skin. He stayed in bed for days and rarely stirred. His shipmates probably checked on him regularly, but he would not take any food or water. They wondered if they should call for a doctor. Smallpox victims usually rallied briefly after a day or two, and their fears were allayed, but then they began to exhibit even worse symptoms. Then, the inevitable and defining characteristic of smallpox appeared on his body.

Spots dotted his chest and arms. These red spots turned into pimples, which in turn bulged into blisters and finally filled with pus. The piteous sailor became a swollen and hideous sight that inspired terror in any who might gaze on him or even hear of his condition.

An experienced Boston doctor described the "speckled monster," as smallpox was called:

Purple spots, the bloody and parchment pox, hemorrhages of blood at the mouth, nose, fundament, and privities; ravings and deliriums; convulsions, and other fits; violent inflammations and swellings in the eyes and throat; so that they cannot see, or scarcely breathe, or swallow anything, to keep them from starving. Some looking as black as the stock, others as white as a sheet; in some, the pock runs into blisters, and the skin stripping off, leaves the flesh raw.… Some have been filled with loathsome ulcers; others have had deep, and fistulous ulcers in their bodies, or in their limbs or joints, with rottenness of the ligaments and bones: some who live are cripples, others idiots, and many blind all their days.

The unnamed victim did not remember exactly where he had traveled in the town or whom he had encountered in any of the establishments he visited, but he surely infected a number of people.

It is impossible to say how many people had inhaled the tiny viruses, but it is safe to speculate that a dozen or more had. They, in turn, carried the disease throughout the city—to its shops, its churches, its homes. A major hub of international trade was poised to suffer a major outbreak of smallpox.

Chapter Three

CONTAGION

In early May 1721, Captain Wentworth Paxton checked on his black servant who had not come down to work. The man was in bed. Wentworth stared in horror when he saw the red marks covering his exposed skin. He instantly recognized the gravity of the illness and informed the authorities that there was smallpox in his home.

When the town's authorities learned of such cases, they followed the pattern of responses established during previous epidemics. They did not understand how the disease was communicated among the population, but they rushed to take measures to contain it. They were reasonable, commonsense actions that held some promise, particularly given the eighteen-century perception of disease. More important, Puritans (and other religious denominations) believed the disease had supernatural causes and therefore required an appropriately pious response. The devout flocked to the Puritan meetinghouses and Anglican churches to implore God's forgiveness for their sins and to appease his wrath, which they interpreted as the cause for the plague. Disease always prompted practical secular and religious reactions.

Smallpox, and disease in general, was an accepted part of life in Europe and the American colonies. In London, smallpox was endemic, meaning that it was always present in the population. Thousands of people died of smallpox there annually. It was a common childhood disease, and most adults were thereby immune. For centuries, Englishmen (and other Europeans) carried the disease with them when they traveled to Newfoundland to fish and established trading posts and permanent settlements in America.

When the first Puritans arrived, they were surprised to find empty fields and no native population. From 1617 to 1619, the pestilence had ravaged the Massachusetts coast, killing an estimated nine out of every ten Indians there. The death rate was consistent with that of virgin populations encountering the disease for the first time. Instead of an estimated three thousand Narragansett warriors, Puritan Miles Standish reported finding "a few straggling inhabitants, burial places, empty wigwams, and some skeletons," when he and the other Pilgrims scouted the area a year later. Massachusetts Bay Governor John Winthrop viewed the epidemic as a sign of God's favor for the Puritans. "The natives, they are near all dead of the smallpox," he wrote, "so as the Lord hath cleared our title to what we possess."

The disease was aboard the ships of the Puritan great migration that began in 1630. In 1631, a passenger reported, "We were wonderfully sick as we came at sea with the smallpox," and fourteen died on that journey. Over the next century, generational smallpox epidemics ravaged the colonial and Indian population. The disease was usually conveyed to Boston by visiting ships.

William Bradford noted the presence of smallpox in Plymouth among the settlers as well as the tragic introduction of the microbes to American Indian populations. In 1634, he described the pitiable scene:

> The Indians…fell sick of smallpox, and died most miserably. A more terrible disease cannot attack them; they fear it worse than the plague, for usually it spreads amongst them broadcast. For want of bedding and linen and other comforts, they fall into a lamentable condition. As they lie on their hard mats, the pox breaks and matters and runs, their skin sticking to the mats they lie on, so that when they turn a whole side will flay off at once, and they will be all one gore of blood, dreadful to behold; and then, what with cold and other hardships, they die like rotten sheep…. Some would crawl on all fours to get a little water, and sometimes die by the way, not being able to get home again.

In 1649, many "were visited with smallpox" when an epidemic struck the Massachusetts Bay Colony and its surrounding towns. One observer noted the hand of God that smote "them with sickness, and taking diverse from among them, not sparing the righteous, but partaking with the wicked in these bodily judgments." In 1666, hundreds in Boston suffered the disease, and dozens died during another major outbreak. In each case, the ministers and town officials declared a day of fasting and prayer to plead for God's mercy.

Michael Wigglesworth lyrically blamed what he believed was rising sinfulness during the seventeenth century for the incidence of disease. He wrote:

> Our healthful days are at an end,
> And sicknesses come on
> From year to year, because our hearts

Away from God are gone.
New England, where for many years
You scarcely heard a cough,
And where physicians had no work
Now finds them work enough.
One wave another followeth,
And one disease begins
Before another cease, because
We turn not from our sins.
We stop our ear against reproof,
And hearken not to God:
God stops his ear against our prayer,
And takes not off his rod.

In 1677, English ships carried the disease to Boston and Charlestown. By June 6, 1678, Puritans spent the day fasting and praying because eighty people had already died. God's wrath apparently was not appeased, and people died throughout the summer. That September alone, more than 150 people suffered horrible deaths. Hundreds died that year in the worst outbreak of the century in the growing colony. Young Cotton Mather wrote in his diary, "Boston burying-places never filled so fast." Perhaps too late, ships arriving in New England ports were quarantined as they had been in the past. The epidemic stirred Thomas Thacher to write a pamphlet, *A Brief Rule to Guide the Common People of New England How to Order Themselves and Theirs in the Smallpox, or Measles.* Although much of the content was directly lifted from the writings of a European physician, Thacher's pamphlet was notable for being the first medical work published in the colonies, and it showed an attempt to grapple with the medical issues associated with the dreaded disease.

In the summer of 1690, an epidemic erupted in Boston when a

West Indian ship brought the disease from the tropics. Several public fasts did nothing to assuage an angry God, and more than three hundred townspeople died. Smallpox raged anew in 1702 and 1703 when it and a simultaneous outbreak of scarlet fever claimed hundreds more.

Additional means of combating smallpox included airing out goods and bedding, "smoking" goods and carriages, cleaning streets, and quarantining the infected in hospitals. Although the various measures and prayers evidently did not prevent the recurrent outbreaks or save many lives, they were the only tools the authorities had at their disposal. These measures were dutifully implemented when smallpox erupted in Boston in 1721.

On May 8, the town's Selectmen met at the Town House. Selectmen were local representatives and men of "property and standing" in a system of town meetings and self-governance inherited from England by "ancient custom." As we shall see, the local representative government assumed primary responsibility for handling the smallpox crisis. The government had its usual agenda of settling land disputes, dispensing licenses to sell alcohol, and granting pensions for wounded soldiers and widows. All of that was set aside for the moment by the public emergency. The Selectmen assembled to take immediate action to halt the spread of smallpox.

After calling the meeting to order and calming down the heated discussion, the Selectmen reviewed what they knew. "A Negro man is now sick of the smallpox in the town who came from Tertudos in His Majesty's ship *Seahorse*." That made it very likely that the "distemper may now be onboard that ship."

The Selectmen also knew about Captain Paxton's infected servant at his master's house near the South Battery. However, it was not known whether "any other person is infected with that distemper in this town." Therefore, they had to decide on measures to isolate the disease and prevent a general epidemic. Fortunately, the town had experience with smallpox epidemics and had a number of actions at its disposal.

Quarantine was the most widely used countermeasure and had been introduced into Boston as early as 1647, when the town required infected ships to drop anchor at least three miles from shore and banned any "persons or goods from the ship to be brought ashore" without permission. Because ships regularly brought smallpox and other diseases that ravaged the population every generation, Boston had erected a public hospital at Spectacle Island. The General Court passed a law in February 1718 requiring all disease-carrying ships to dock there in order to air bedding and clothing while keeping an eye on the crew. During the autumn of 1720, a sloop bearing smallpox had arrived from the Canary Islands. When the crew showed they were "all well and in health" after the quarantine period, they were allowed into Boston with "fresh clothes."

The *Seahorse* slipped through because no one knew that a crewmember had smallpox when she entered Boston Harbor. Now that the source of the disease had been quickly discovered, the Selectmen decided to dispatch a physician, John Clark, to "go onboard His Majesty's ship *Seahorse* and report in what state of health of sickness the ship's company are in, especially with respect to the smallpox or other contagious diseases." Clark descended from a long line of physicians, and his now deceased daughter had been married to Reverend Cotton Mather.

The Selectmen also moved to isolate the smallpox victim from any further contact with other townspeople. They sent a nurse to Paxton's home to attend the sick servant and "suffer no person to come within the room" where the patient lay. With the current state of medicine, they did not expect the nurse to be able to apply a cure. In addition, two "prudent persons" were appointed to stand guard at the doors of the house and prevent anyone from entering or departing. As was customary, a red flag bearing the inscription "God have mercy on this house" flew above the front door. The Selectmen adjourned the meeting satisfied that they had done what they could and prayed for the best.

Doctor Clark was rowed to the *Seahorse* and climbed up a proffered rope ladder onto the deck. He was greeted by the officer of the watch because the ship's captain, Thomas Durrell, was ashore. Clark plied the officer with questions as he conducted an inspection. Clark was not pleased by what he saw. Several sailors were ill, and many were in town, possibly spreading the infection. On the whole ship, he reported, there were "not above ten or fifteen effective men." Clark returned to town and shared the grim news with the Selectmen.

The representatives met again on May 12 to receive Clark's troubling report. They directed Captain Durrell to order his commanding officer to sail down to Spectacle Island to prevent further infection in the town. They arranged for a local captain to "procure a sufficient number of men" to pilot the *Seahorse* because of the dearth of healthy sailors on the ship. Eventually, the town reimbursed Robert Orange to the tune of three pounds and nine shillings for his efforts in piloting the ship.

On May 20, the Selectmen reported no more cases of smallpox and judged their efforts to contain the disease seemed to have worked. The town officials—justices, selectmen, overseers of the poor, and constables—combed through Boston, making a "strict search and inquiry of the inhabitants at their respective houses," to find any additional smallpox cases. They were relieved to report that only two black men in town and sailors on the quarantined ship were sick. The servant at Captain Paxton's was "almost recovered, and will be in a day or two removed to the province hospital at Spectacle Island."

Perhaps the Selectmen were attempting to avert a general panic in the town, or maybe they were just overconfident. Either way, their announcement proved to be premature. They may have known that they were already too late and that many would die in the weeks and months to come. The sick men had come into close contact with several individuals around town, and the virus had been incubating within their bodies, silently invading the asymptomatic hosts. Meanwhile, in several homes around Boston, the residents felt as if they were coming down with a nasty case of the flu.

Just two days later, on May 22, as rumors began to fly that an evil had taken residence in the port, readers of the *Boston Gazette* read in horror as it was confirmed that the Selectmen were indeed wrong. Many more were becoming sick, and most ominously, they could be found in every corner of the town. "There are now eight persons sick of the smallpox," the *Gazette* reported. Two sick people were in the heart of town, on School Street close to the Town House. One sufferer was on the South End waterfront at Battery-March, adjacent to the South Battery. Four were ailing near the Common: three on Tremont Street and one on Winter Street. Another person afflicted with smallpox was in the distant North End on Bennet Street. An observer wrote, "The grievous calamity of the smallpox has now entered the town." The disease had spread like wildfire, and no one knew where it might spring up next. No place in Boston was safe.

Because of the prevailing medical wisdom that many diseases were spread through noxious miasma in the air, the Selectmen on May 24 "voted that the streets and lanes within this town be forthwith cleansed and the dirt removed to prevent the smallpox spreading." They saw this as a preventive measure to contain the disease. They appointed a person to inform "all the free male Negroes, mulattoes, etc., of this town…to work six days" and oversee that "that service be by them performed." Supervisors would be empowered to "impress carts for the carrying away the said dirt." Twenty-six men were then listed so that there could be no mistake.

Requiring free black men to perform public works tasks for the town was nothing new. Less than two years before, the Selectmen enforced a law appointing the free blacks to "diligently attend and perform their labor in cleansing or repairing the highways or other services for the common benefit of this town." The Selectmen justified singling out these men for this special labor because it was to be done in lieu of the watch duty or militia service performed by the free white men of Boston. Northern black codes were more lenient than southern ones, but they had excluded militia service decades before.

Seeing the free blacks cleaning the streets may have inspired some measure of confidence among the people and their leaders. For a week the measures the Selectmen ordered seemed to be working. On June 3, the *Boston News-Letter* reported, "We have had but one person taken sick of the smallpox since Saturday last, and those that were then visited with that distemper are all in a likely way to recover, most of them being up and about their chambers." The town government was doing everything in its power to halt a general outbreak. The measures were soothing to their fears, but they proved a fleeting hope that the spread of the virus was contained. Every day, more and more people were catching the disease. It would not be long before the death toll skyrocketed.

Despite the small bit of good news, the first instinct of many Bostonians was to flee for their lives. And that is exactly what one thousand souls (nearly 10 percent of the population) did. In the best-case scenario, their flight across the Neck to the mainland to stay with distant family members saved their lives. This was particularly true for those who had not previously survived a case of smallpox and therefore had no immunity. Usually, this number included the young people who had been born since the last epidemic.

The town politicians gave the citizenry an example of flight. The members of the General Court opted to flee and conduct the town's business elsewhere. It was adjourned on June 1 and reconvened across the Charles River at "Cambridge, to sit there June 6." The bicameral General Court of the colony usually met in the capital and was comprised of an upper house—the governor's council— that was selected by the popularly elected lower house, called the assembly. The royal governor had a veto over its legislation and in turn appointed the judiciary. The charter granted after the Glorious Revolution had given the colony's government a separation of powers and maintained the basic character of its self-rule.

Of course, any flight from Boston risked causing a major pandemic throughout New England and beyond. When sick persons went abroad or carried infected items, they were as great a threat as a ship arriving from the West Indies. As residents fled from the disease and normal trade and travel continued by land and sea, the disease proliferated widely. Bostonians, however, were understandably interested primarily in their own safety. Fleeing to the environs of an isolated farm was a good idea because practically 100 percent of those at risk usually caught the disease in a crowded city such as Boston.

With their belief in divine Providence, the Puritans and other Christians of the town interpreted the smallpox scourge as a sign of divine wrath. God was either directly punishing Boston for its collective sin or allowing the devil to ravage its inhabitants to test their faith.

Signs of decline from the original piety of their forefathers who settled in Massachusetts to establish a pure church were rampant in the eyes of many. Fewer people were converting and becoming church members, requiring questionable innovations such as the Halfway Covenant, which allowed children of church members to be baptized as halfway members. Moreover, many were tempted by the worldliness and pursuit of profit in the cosmopolitan city and failed to attend the two sermons on the Sabbath or Thursday lectures. The sermons were simple and readily understood in order to provoke a steady movement toward conversion. Because those who failed to attend services did not have the benefit of hearing the sermons, Puritan ministers assumed that there would be a concurrent rise in immorality. Many townspeople spent their nights drinking and visiting prostitutes, as well as swearing, carousing, and dancing. They were more interested in fashionable clothes and wigs than in the condition of their souls. A Reform Synod met in 1680 to combat these evils, but it failed to produce the expected reformation, and many people remained unregenerate and indifferent. As a result, Puritans believed they suffered affliction for their sins as divine punishment because they failed to preserve the covenant passed on to them from their fathers.

For all the perceived evidence of a decline in observing the founding covenant, the third-generation Puritans were a devout bunch, and fears of the decline were grossly exaggerated. They found their deepest expression in the preachers' use of jeremiads—sermons bearing the message of the Old Testament prophet Jeremiah to restore the covenant and renew the promises of a chosen people with God. Jeremiads were a favorite topic in sermons on public occasions, such as days of fasting and prayer, days of thanksgiving, artillery company ceremonies, and election-day gatherings. Cries to turn from sin and restore the broken covenant had been common since only a few years after the *Mayflower* landed.

The outbreak of smallpox encouraged the same rigid soul-searching of the jeremiads. Because few of the countermeasures against smallpox worked, an outbreak usually sent people to their meetinghouses and churches. They went to listen to sermons that focused their thoughts inward and to pray for God's mercy. The terror of those who gathered in meetinghouses and churches for the first time in a long while might be stirred to live a more godly life. In addition, even the godly were sinners and needed to seek absolution.

Cotton Mather, the most esteemed minister in Boston at the time, wrote in his diary: "The entrance of the smallpox into the town must awaken in me several tempers and actions of piety relating to myself, besides a variety of duties to the people." He specifically mentioned the prospect of preaching to young people and mariners, two groups he viewed as in special need of reform.

Mather had a ministerial concern about the souls of his flock as well as all townspeople, imploring them constantly over the previous decades to repent of their sinful lives. But he was also a scientist who sought to advance the good of mankind with scientific and medical discoveries to improve and save lives, starting with his fellow Bostonians. Previous outbreaks of measles and smallpox had claimed the lives of several Mather family members, and he felt compelled to do something about the incipient epidemic. The responsibility might have weighed down any man except for the fact that Mather saw himself as doing the Lord's work and joyfully assumed the burden. Just how much he could bear remained to be seen.

Chapter Four

ORDINARY AND EXTRAORDINARY CONCERNS

In the spring of 1721, Reverend Cotton Mather enjoyed the comforts of his spacious home on Ship Street overlooking the North End wharves and Boston Harbor. It was not constructed of brick like the mansions of the wealthy merchants in the town, but it was an imposing three stories high. The great chamber could host many congregants for prayer meetings from his North (Second) Church, which was a short walk away, and the church where his father, Increase, had preached. His grounds had lovely gardens for strolls and quiet meditations with the Lord. As the harsh New England winter was finally giving way to spring, Mather exulted: "The time of year arrives for the glories of nature to appear in my garden. I will take my walks there on purpose to read the glories of my Savior in them. I will make it an emblem of a paradise, wherein the second Adam shall have acknowledgements paid unto Him."

During the month of May, Mather learned of the smallpox outbreak. He probably sat often in his favorite room—his book-lined library, which housed more than three thousand volumes, making it the largest private library in the American colonies—contemplating how he might make a difference in the emerging public health crisis. The library was primarily his personal retreat and sanctuary where he lost himself in the classics, religious tracts, and latest scientific books. It was a place of refuge to lose himself for hours writing an incredible number of sermons and a prodigious number of tracts and books—an outpouring that rivaled the combined writings of all the other ministers of Massachusetts. Besides the quiet hours spent in contemplation, he conducted discussions about divinity in his study with Harvard students who were lucky enough to be tutored by one of the greatest minds in the colonies.

Cotton Mather was born on February 12, 1663, with the burden of grand expectations and tradition on his shoulders. Even his name revealed the inheritance descending from the renowned founding ministers Richard Mather and John Cotton. This firstborn son of Increase Mather and Maria Cotton felt the manifest obligations of his heritage. Six family members were ministers; all the adults were full church members. Mather nevertheless managed to be an uncommonly precocious youth.

Prayers were among the first words the boy uttered. He could write before he entered school, and he sat on the wooden meeting-house bench transcribing his father's sermons. His learned father also taught him to read, and he voraciously consumed fifteen chapters from the Bible daily. He also combed through volumes on church history in his father's library and practiced his Latin under Increase's tutelage. The exceptionally pious boy took breaks from his study to pray six times daily. He traveled all the way from the family home on Cotton's Hill to the South End for schooling under the poet Benjamin Tompson and then the distinguished schoolmaster Ezekiel Cheever (except during the freezing winter months when his father kept him home). By the time he was eleven, he was more than able to pass the Harvard entrance exam in which he had to demonstrate a mastery of ancient languages. He was thoroughly prepared for Harvard with an exacting study of ancient languages and such classics as Homer, Ovid, and Virgil in their Greek and Latin originals.

Because Harvard College's mission was to train Congregational ministers as well as educate Christian gentlemen who assumed civic leadership in the colony, Mather received a broad education in Greek, Hebrew, Latin, logic and rhetoric, moral philosophy, and natural philosophy (as science was then called). The college library abounded in classical and modern authors for a curious young man such as Mather to delve into. In the environment of the Enlightenment, students learned to turn a critical eye on the ancient learning of Aristotelian science and Galenic medicine. They engaged modern scientific texts that included the scientific method of René Descartes and Francis Bacon, the ideas of circulation by William Harvey, and the physics of Nicolaus Copernicus.

The young man was smitten by modern science and read as widely as he could in the Harvard library and Mather home. Although Harvard offered little formal instruction in medicine, Mather tapped into those libraries to study the subject extensively. Indeed, his reading in medicine was comparable to the instruction that any physician would have received as an apprentice reading medical texts. In fact, only one doctor in Boston had earned a degree in medicine. All others had "read" medicine just as Mather did. He was largely self-taught in the subject, but this placed him squarely in the mainstream of current medical training.

Mather had another motivation for studying medicine. He developed a stammer while at Harvard that threatened to dash all his hopes for a ministerial career. Because the center of Puritan worship was hearing exhortations by ministers in two ninety-minute sermons every Sunday, a stammer would effectively disqualify Mather from following his father and forefathers into the ministry. So the young man studied medicine for an alternative career while learning techniques for mastering his speech impediment. He had fits of melancholy and hypochondria from studying medicine, but they were significantly easier to overcome.

There was one more obstacle to conquer if he were to become a minister. Mather could hardly become a minister, let alone a church member, if he did not experience God's transforming grace. Puritan ministers exhorted the individual members of their congregation to examine their eternal souls to discover the signs of whether they had been elected for salvation. This led to a painful process of soul-searching for many young adults. Those who felt God had elected them would be subjected to a public inquiry in most Puritan congregations. They were admitted only if they provided the proper responses to their questioners. Having been bombarded with the idea of man's depravity, many were sure their impurity and imperfect faith were evidence they were damned. Even for those who believed they had experienced grace, the lack of certitude led even the pious to consider themselves to be hypocrites or to wail on their deathbeds that they were uncertain as to whether they were saved. Ministers actually had to counsel their saints not to be filled with distraction and despair. One minister warned that a saint should not spend his time "daily plodding upon his own misery." However, church members were constantly reassured by their ministers that God welcomed their childlike faith and imperfect exertions and offered them mercy.

Mather finally felt the Lord's presence in his soul after intense searching the year after he graduated from Harvard. He began a lifelong habit of private fasts and intense prayer. He would prostrate himself on the floor and harshly abase himself before God as a sinner who pretended to feel his grace. He mortified himself as a hypocrite to wash away any sign of pride when he felt Christ's saving grace. When the harsh and unrelenting feelings of unworthiness threatened to plunge his soul into an abyss of despondency, he finally consulted with his wise and loving father. Increase reminded his son that Jesus would forgive a truly penitent sinner.

The reassured young man then felt the stirrings of grace that signaled his conversion, receiving "strange, and strong, and sweet intimations." At one point, the "unaccountable cloud and load" lifted from him, and he felt transformed "by a new light, and life, and ease arriving to me, as the sunrise does change the world, from the condition of midnight." In typical Puritan fashion, Mather resisted feeling certitude regarding the eternal state of his soul, for he could have been deceived by the devil or duped by his own pride.

In 1679 the North Church admitted the sixteen-year-old Mather as a member. Having learned to control his stammer, he started preaching informally. A New Haven congregation invited him to become its pastor, but he preferred cosmopolitan Boston, which he called "as great a place as any in these parts of the world." He felt destined for greatness, not obscurity in a backwater.

By 1685 Mather was ordained a minister at the North Church alongside his father. But unlike his reclusive father, who spent the majority of his hours in his study, Mather graciously assumed the burden of catechizing young people and shepherding the sick. He was married a year later to Abigail Phillips and started a family.

Ironically, the former stutterer soon become the most popular preacher in Boston and received weekly invitations to give sermons at neighboring churches and on public days. In time, the North Church congregation grew to more than fifteen hundred attendees, including four hundred members. Because of the equality of their souls, members included rich and poor, men and women, white and black, old and young.

Increase and Cotton Mather were not simply men of the cloth. The Harvard president and his son were at the vanguard of American intellectual life. Science in particular was of great interest to both of them. As Puritan ministers, they readily accepted the new learning of the scientific revolution and Enlightenment that was brewing in Great Britain after the Restoration of Charles II. Religiously they wanted to reestablish a pure church modeled on ancient Christianity that was free of what they perceived to be its medieval Roman Catholic corruptions. Scientifically they embraced the discoveries that challenged ancient Aristotelian science and medieval scholasticism.

It was Cotton Mather who stated that "we are born in an age of light" because of the advances that were made in knowledge during the Age of Reason. Many European intellectuals used the same metaphor of light to celebrate the rediscovery of learning after a thousand years of darkness and superstition. They were wrong, for learning had never truly been lost, and many innovations were made during the Middle Ages. Nonetheless, they believed themselves and their exciting age of discovery to be the dawn of a new age.

The English philosopher George Berkeley described the Enlightenment as "that ocean of light, which has broke in and made his way, in spite of slavery and superstition." Poet Alexander Pope penned a fawning ode to Isaac Newton and the Enlightenment with the following verse:

> Nature and nature's laws lay hid in night.
> God said, let Newton be! and all was light.

Mather was no less enraptured by the joy and possibilities inherent in discovery. "Ideas," he delighted, "like the sands on the seashore, for the vast variety of them!"

The new science of the seventeenth century altered man's conception of the universe and its workings. Two main ideas emerged from the discoveries of Nicolaus Copernicus, Galileo Galilei, Robert Boyle, and Isaac Newton. First, heliocentric theory placed the sun, not earth and humans, at the center of the universe. Second, the mechanistic worldview held that the universe operated like a giant clock, that ran according to the regular, fixed, and orderly workings of universal natural laws. These laws were discoverable by the use of experimental observation and measurement in Francis Bacon's and René Descartes's scientific method and by human reason rather than Scripture.

In the late seventeenth and early eighteenth century, Puritans reconciled science and religion into a coherent whole. Cotton Mather believed that God gave humans reason so that they could discover the natural laws in God's creation, thus science would glorify God. But it would be wrong to say that science was simply put in the service of religion, for Mather studied the natural world for its own sake as well. Moreover, when Mather harmonized the study of nature with religion, he was not out of step with most scientists of the age who did not see the spheres in conflict.

For example, the Mathers studied comets with telescopes as an exciting regular and predictable force of nature as well as for their metaphysical influences. Increase Mather was fascinated with astronomy and wrote three books on the subject in the mid-1680s. Mather understood what the new science revealed about the comets and natural law, but he also believed that there was a supernatural dimension that was an omen of impending disaster. In 1684, he called the appearance of Halley's comet "Heaven's alarm to the world." Many prominent scientists were interested in both the astronomical and astrological significance of comets and other heavenly phenomena.

Superstitions were consuming passions for many of the most

learned men of the scientific revolution. Newton was obsessed with alchemy for years. Harvey, Newton, and Galileo practiced experimental science alongside astrology. Scientists believed in the existence of witches and their malevolent practices. Modern science would eventually undermine many of these beliefs, but those who stood at the apex of the scientific revolution did not themselves immediately offer a challenge.

Mather (and other scientists) believed the mechanistic operations of the natural universe worked according to certain laws. But Mather posited that God could intervene in the natural world via supernatural forces that could not be readily explained by science. God acted providentially in the world for good or to chastise sinners, while the devil and his minions acted for evil. Hence, miracles, divine signs, and "special providences" occurred while nature otherwise followed predictable laws. These special providences included comets, dreams, earthquakes, eclipses, fires, floods, lightning, tempests, and other phenomena. As science progressed and led to a greater understanding of nature, the natural causes of special providences were more easily explained. However, they were also interpreted for their supernatural meaning.

The Mathers were in a unique position to participate in the cosmopolitan and international spirit of learning. They were both educated at Harvard, and during Increase's presidency there, the college continued to adopt new texts and became the leading center of the new science in America. As the core of American trade with the great cities of Europe, Boston became the center of the Atlantic book trade, as dozens of booksellers set up shop there. The public houses in the city also carried the latest newspapers and journals from Europe. Moreover, the first American newspaper· was the *Boston News-Letter*. The *Boston Gazette* appeared only a few years before, and in August 1721 another would be published.

Not content that intellectuals alone should be aware of the

scientific discoveries, Mather avidly popularized Copernicus's helio-centrism for a lay audience by preaching on the subject from the pulpit. The ideas were embraced by the clergy and their congregations as proof of God's majesty in the order and design of the universe and its natural laws. Members of the Mathers' Second Church were instructed by two devout ministers who were arguably the most learned men in America.

The clearest evidence that Cotton Mather held a colonial-wide and international reputation as a scientist was his election to the British Royal Society in 1713. The auspicious formation of this group centered on Gresham College and included such London illuminati as Robert Boyle, Robert Hooke, and Christopher Wren. Their first meeting in 1660 followed the restoration of the Stuarts to the monarchy and was a voluntary association of scientists into an academy to advance learning and experimental philosophy. They received a royal charter a few years later with the immodest goal of using experiment to "shape out a new philosophy." There studies were to be "applied to further promoting by the authority of experiments the sciences of natural things and of useful arts."

The Royal Society soon drew up its method of advancing the sciences:

> The business of the society in their ordinary meetings shall be, to order, take account, consider, and discourse of philosophical experiments and observations; to read, hear, and discourse upon letters, reports, and other papers, containing philosophical matters; as also to view, and discourse upon, rarities of nature and art; and thereupon to consider what may be deduced from them, or any of them; and how far they, or any of them, may be improved for use or discovery.

In short, the society was to compile "a complete system of solid philosophy…and rendering a rational account of the causes of things.

The reach of the Royal Society was worldwide as it encouraged and welcomed contributions from all over the globe. It sponsored voyages by the astronomer Edmond Halley and later Captain James Cook. It sent the invaluable instruments of the scientific revolution—barometers, clocks, microscopes, telescopes, and thermometers—to scientists in the corners of the world to measure natural phenomena. Most important, it was a cosmopolitan body that welcomed foreign members onto its rolls and encouraged their correspondence. In turn, the society sent out its journal, *Philosophical Transactions,* which was the world's single-most important scientific publication.

It would not have been a surprise to those who corresponded with or read the works of Cotton Mather that he would be elected into that illustrious body. He was only the eighth American colonist to win that honor. This allowed him proudly to place FRS—Fellow of the Royal Society—after his name. And he was not a mere passive reader of the *Transactions* from across the Atlantic, but rather an extremely active contributor to the body of knowledge the Royal Society was building. He sent as many as eighty-two scientific letters to London in the decade after he was elected. The impressive array of topics he dealt with included astronomy, botany, medicine, meteorology, zoology, and like many members, natural curiosities. The Royal Society was "well-pleased" with his papers and considered it "extremely acceptable" to receive future correspondence from him.

In 1683 the Royal Society had inspired Increase and his son to organize the Boston Philosophical Society, the first scientific society in the American colonies. Its purpose was to establish a "conference upon improvements in [natural] philosophy and addition to the stores of natural history." The membership remains relatively obscure, but it was comprised of those Boston intellectuals who wanted to form a voluntary society dedicated to a broad spectrum of scientific topics. Dr. William Avery, one of the town's first physicians, was involved and corresponded with European scientists, including Robert Boyle. Avery's letters were transcribed by a young and eager Cotton Mather. The society also exchanged letters with a professor at the renowned University of Leiden. Americans were not unsophisticated colonists but participants in the dynamic explosion of scientific discovery.

Just a few months before the *Seahorse* weighed anchor, a ship arrived at Boston from England bringing one hundred copies of Mather's book *Christian Philosopher*. Its title was somewhat deceptive because it was the first general book on science written by a colonist. It summarized the recent findings of his European colleagues and did not contain any revolutionary experiments or ideas, but it was an important synthesis nonetheless. Mather had high hopes for "getting our colleges filled with them." He wrote to another highly respected American scientist, John Winthrop, about the book, informing him that a complimentary copy would be coming as a "small acknowledgment unto an invaluable friend, unto whose generosity I have been indebted." The scientists of America kept one another aware of the latest scientific tracts and disseminated them, even their own works.

As spring became summer in 1721, the number of smallpox cases increased. Cotton Mather had a dual burden ministering to his congregants who were facing their own mortality in addition to his usual theological sermonizing. He was also considering some way that he might be of public service. Moreover, his personal life was often far from harmonious.

Although his gardens and library normally offered Mather respite from his daunting workload, they offered little solace at the moment. Mather struggled not only with the outbreak but with the usual concerns that he had as a minister. Sometimes the two were conflated and threatened to swamp him under the burden.

Mather was embroiled in a divisive struggle within his own North Church. He was shocked by the "numbers…swarming off into the New Brick meetinghouse in the neighborhood" from North Church. It was a battle created by the very nature of Puritan congregationalism. Congregationalists voluntarily joined together to worship based upon a covenant of members, who then elected a minister. It was devoid of any overarching church hierarchy. Congregations could, in theory, fracture indefinitely. A faction had split off from North Church before. In 1712, a sizable minority of the congregation separated and formed the New North Church only a few blocks away. A disgruntled Increase Mather hoped, "A blasting from God will be upon them."

Cotton Mather's response in the spring of 1721 was, if anything, more severe. The Mathers had encouraged Reverend Peter Thacher to leave his congregation to come to New North. After finally winning his release from his angry congregation who did not wish to see him go, Thacher's installation at New North effected an even greater uproar. Those who opposed his election formed a third church, which was called New Brick in the North End. Even though Mather had withdrawn his support, many of his congregants flocked to New Brick. Mather was scheduled to preach the first sermon in their meetinghouse and vindictively planned to "take my farewell of them with a most solemn warning unto them."

With a metaphor of startling effrontery that none could miss, Mather stood at the pulpit and compared the departing congregants to "the withdrawal of the Disciples from our Savior a little before He died." Mather may have tried to show "how easily and cheerfully we endure their departure," but his heart was filled with malice. Even as the smallpox epidemic was beginning, he penned furiously in his diary: "The wicked spirit manifested by them, who for the pride of pews, and such vile motives, are gone out from us."

The greater immediate danger of smallpox finally allowed him to put the issue to rest. Mather focused on praying for the remaining members of the flock who "fear the contagion (as people generally do) to continue with earnest and constant prayer to the glorious God at such a time." Congregationalism allowed for new churches to be formed, but the separations engendered competition and envy, which diminished the unity of the original covenant.

Perhaps his greatest personal affliction was his son Increase, who tormented his father. When Increase was born in 1699, Mather joyously received divine intimations that his first surviving son would be a servant of God like the last three ministers of the Mather line. His name, just like his father's, was a symbol of that inheritance. At first, Increase seemed to live up to his name and showed great promise in his early education and piety, but he soon revealed a base character. Mather lamented: "I am full, full of distress, concerning my little son Increase…My poor son Increase! Oh! The distress of mind with which I must let fall my daily admonitions upon him!"

Increase utterly failed to live up to the expectations that were placed upon him. He did not attend Harvard and was scarcely cut out for the ministry. Mather apprenticed Increase to a merchant to pursue that respectable profession, even if it meant the pursuit of profit over godliness. However, the wild tales he heard along the waterfront stirred the young man's imagination and sense of adventure. Increase seemed bent on a life at sea as a son of Neptune. His father was worried that he had "been too willing to indulge and follow the genius of a child in the choice of a business for him." The shiftless young man traveled to London, where he plagued his uncle for months.

If Mather was anxious over his son's career path, he went absolutely apoplectic over his dissolute actions when Increase returned to Boston. The irresponsible youth apparently had impregnated a "harlot" who was "big with a bastard" (to use his father's outraged description). Mather bewailed to his diary: "Oh, sorrow beyond any that I have met withal! What shall I do now for the foolish youth!"

Just as the *Seahorse* was sailing toward Boston, Increase was in more trouble. As if getting a whore pregnant were not enough, Increase was now raising hell with some "detestable rakes" at night for some drunken rioting. "My miserable, miserable, miserable son Increase!" was all his father could say. Where had he gone wrong? Had he not prayed enough for his son? Mather blamed himself for the indiscretions of his "incorrigible Prodigal."

Mather promised to "cast him and chase him out of my sight, forbid him to see me, until there appear sensible marks of repentance upon him." He also begged God to "cast out the Devil that has possession of the child." Mather, however, would no more reject his son than the biblical examples. Instead, he would continue to suffer, complaining to his diary, "My bowels are troubled for him."

Another son, Sammy, took up the banner that Increase had dropped and followed a path much more pleasing to his father. Eight-year-old Sammy, along with his siblings, acquired measles during a 1713 outbreak, but he never contracted smallpox because he was born after the last major epidemic. Living an almost inverse life of his brother, Sammy was a somewhat troublesome boy, but he matured into a bright and responsible young man. His father shifted his dreams to him and even addressed an instruction booklet in the form of an autobiography to him on how to live virtuously. Sammy entered Harvard in 1719 and was there when smallpox materialized during the spring of 1721.

His beloved daughter Eliza, or Liza, was also away from home. She was taken in by Mather's former father-in-law, the same John Clark who investigated the sickness aboard the *Seahorse*. She might have been chased there by Mather's abrasive, and probably mad, third wife, though apprenticing out children of both sexes was commonplace in the colony. Although destined to become a Puritan wife and mother, Liza's education was not neglected by her father, who taught her science and Hebrew, among other subjects. She may have been immune to witnessing the unhappiness in her father's home, but she had no more resistance to smallpox than her brother Sammy.

Sammy and Liza were understandably petrified of dying from smallpox. Mather related their fears to his diary, "My two children have their terrors of the contagion breaking in upon us." Uncertainty added to their fear as more were reported sick every day, even in the North End. Moreover, it was plain that sooner or later they would be infected. By the end of June, Mather reported, "Oh! What shall I do, that my family may be prepared for the visitation that is now every day to be expected!"

Mather was gravely concerned for his two susceptible children, but he was paralyzed with fear trying to decide whether to send them out of town with the increasing numbers who were fleeing. "I have two children that are liable to the distemper; and I am at a loss about their flying and keeping out of the town." He indecisively looked above for the proper course; "I must cry to heaven for direction about it." His anguish over their safety in the coming months might have made him wish he had sent them away.

Nevertheless, the minister saw an opportunity in the descending scourge that threatened his family with death to improve his own faith and that of his children. Mather was a man of faith and placed his entire trust in the Lord. If he were "on this occasion called unto sacrifices—that if these dear children must lose their lives, the will of my Father may be duly submitted to." His two children had not yet felt the ecstasy of coming through a rigorous and painful conversion experience to know that they were saved according to their Calvinist beliefs as Puritans. Their father hoped that the fear of impending death would prod their self-examination of the state of their souls. "My two children that have their terrors of the contagion breaking in upon us," he wrote, "I must lay hold on the occasion to quicken their effectual flights unto their Savior."

In early June, Sammy raced home from Cambridge to escape the infection there, but he arrived just as "the smallpox begins to spread in the neighborhood." Mather was beside himself with worry, and he did what he always did: he retreated into his study for a day of private humiliations and supplications. Several times in the coming weeks, he lay down in the dust and prayed "especially on the behalf of my two children, that are exposed unto the dangers of the smallpox." He asked humbly for "a direction of heaven, what I may do for their welfare in that, and (for all of them) in all regards." The answer soon came.

Mather was not just concerned for his children, however. He cared for the handful of slaves that he owned. He considered them "in some sense my children." Mather, like most other Massachusetts' slave owners, owned only one or two slaves. In early 1721 his black servant sought baptism. "I must use my best endeavors to prepare him for it," Mather promised.

The small family farms and maritime trades of New England were not conducive to the flourishing of black slavery, and there were fewer in Massachusetts than any other colony (despite the fact that the number of slaves had increased to almost two thousand). Slaves often lived in their master's attics or backrooms and worked alongside them as servants or farmers. Many helped out in artisan or merchant shops.

They were rented out in the same shops or on ships, and often they were allowed to work in those trades for extra money or to buy their freedom. In such close proximity to their masters, slaves were treated much more leniently than in other parts of the country.

Mather and other New Englanders (though by no means all) believed that the Bible sanctioned slavery. Their Christianity nonetheless provided a framework for servitude that upheld the basic humanity of slaves as well as the equality of their souls. It also shaped the mutual duties of both slave and master. Slaves were required to obey their masters. Christian slave owners had a grave responsibility to care for the material well-being of their slaves and an even more important obligation to convert the African heathens. In his essay *Negro Christianized,* Mather explained the solemnity of this charge: "You deny your master in heaven if you do nothing to bring your servants unto the knowledge and service of that glorious Master."

The conversion of Africans to Christianity presupposed the equality of their souls and their natural ability to be catechized in its tenets. Mather brushed aside the idea that Africans were inferior because of their skin color:

> Their complexion sometimes is made an argument why nothing should be done for them. A gay sort of argument! As if the great God went by the complexion of men, in his favors to them! As if none but whites might hope to be favored and accepted with God!... Away with such trifles! The God who looks on the heart, is not moved by the color of the skin, is not more propitious to one color than another.

Many colonists accepted the fact that Africans had equal souls but argued that they were too ignorant to learn the doctrines of the faith. Not so, claimed Mather, who thought them perfectly capable of attaining the same knowledge if they were treated as persons rather than beasts: "They are kept only as horses or oxen, to do our drudgeries, but their souls, which are as white and good as those of other nations, their souls are not looked after, but are destroyed for lack of knowledge. This is a desperate wickedness. But are they dull? Then instruct them the rather; that is the way to sharpen them." Blacks must first be educated and taught to read so they could be properly catechized and able to read Scripture. Then they could be baptized so they could examine their souls for the presence of grace. By experiencing a conversion to Christ, they became full members of a congregation (even if they sat in segregated seats—as did many groups in the hierarchical society).

Although Mather's slave desired to be baptized earlier in 1721, the smallpox epidemic was the additional impetus to save his soul before a tragedy befell him. "My African servant stands a candidate for baptism, and is afraid how the smallpox, if it spread, may handle him," Mather noted on June 6. "I must on this occasion use very much application to bring him into a thorough Christianity," he resolved. But the chaos of the epidemic and the town's response to it would delay the baptism well into the next year.

While he considered in his study how to frame a letter to the town physicians, Mather also continued to work on the demanding number of sermons he had to deliver. He probably decided that a smallpox epidemic was no time for the usual sermons and exhortations based upon unrelated scriptural passages. Indeed, as he scrutinized the pages of his well-worn Bible, he turned to passages that might have a particular relevance to the public crisis. He was still attempting to save souls but would tailor his message to meet the needs of the moment. He had plenty of material to choose—there were no shortage of calamities, healing miracles, and calls for repentance and faith in his Bible.

Chapter Five

AT THE PULPIT

Mather confronted smallpox for the first time publicly as a minister of North Church. His private concerns had to be set aside, for his congregation looked to him to assuage their fears and console them. They clung to that reassurance during these apprehensive days. Mather's larger purpose, however, always transcended such temporal fears and guided their immortal souls heavenward to contemplate their salvation.

On Sunday, June 4, the members of North Church were summoned to the morning service by the clanging of the meeting-house bell. Their children and servants were in tow as they walked inside. Despite the cases of smallpox that had been reported, it would probably never rage sufficiently to keep people home. Indeed, the threat to their lives compelled people to attend services in droves as they pondered the state of their souls.

The exterior of the austere building was covered with unpainted clapboards, and the interior was unadorned. There were no stained-glass windows, saints' statues, icons of the Virgin, or anything that would detract from the centrality of the word being preached. A simple table stood as an altar. No one would mistake the meetinghouse for a European Catholic cathedral or even an Anglican sanctuary.

The Geneva Bible was the accepted translation of God's word. It avoided what Puritans saw as the corruption and pomposity of the King James Bible, which one Puritan derided as written in the language of "fat and strutting bishops, pomp-fed prelates." The Puritan Bible, like their meetinghouses and services, was simpler.

The congregants sat in rows of benches according to carefully delineated arrangements that all understood and respected. Their places were positioned to reflect the natural hierarchy of society. Men went to one side; women to the other. Age, wealth, and social rank further determined the seating order with the wiser, richer, and better bred toward the front. Children, servants, and Africans sat in the balcony, along with the unconverted who were there to have their hearts and wills swayed by the word (although they could not participate in the Lord's Supper).

Reverend Cotton Mather and his family entered grandly, the minister dressed in a black preaching gown and skullcap. The parishioners stood out of respect and deference. He passed by the elders of the church who were seated on a bench under the pulpit facing the congregation. Painted on the pulpit above the elders' heads was a single staring eye. The great eye signified the ever-vigilant, all-seeing eye of God, who saw their naked souls and judged their sin.

Mather climbed several steps to make his way to the pulpit. Following standard practice, he quoted the text as he began his sermon and expounded upon the context. John 4:54 read: "This second miracle did Jesus again, after he was come out of Judea into Galilee." He avoided what Puritans insultingly labeled "dumb reading": reading the scriptural verses first and then talking about them.

Sermons were spoken in plain terms that were readily understood by the congregation, but they were still complex and not vulgar. They were restrained and deliberate, lacking the emotional appeal of later evangelical revivals. Tightly woven in their logical and rhetorical design, Puritan sermons were meant to stir the knowledge of the saving power of Christ and render biblical doctrines intellectually convincing. Devoid as they were of needless ornamentation and Latin quotations from ancient authorities, the surgical delivery and undeniable truths were intended to work on the hearer's heart and affections. There was little that was abstract. Particular sins were condemned, and congregants could not shrink back from the truth of the ministers' words or the eye of God. Their power was able to "astonish and shiver the heart of the sinner all in pieces."

One minister summed up the purpose of Puritan sermons: "While we are thus speaking to you, God many times conveys such a spirit of grace into us, as gives us power to receive Christ.... The word that we speak conveys spirit and life into [you]."

Mather was known for a few flourishes that were welcomed by most Puritans, if the number of invitations he received to preach at other meetinghouses around town and the numbers of people who attended attest to his popularity. He did, however, have an inclination toward an ornamental style and citations that displayed his learning a bit vainly. He was one of the ministers who came closest to breaking with traditional sermons and gnawed on the nerves of a few traditionalists. One listener was disgusted that Mather included such phrases as "sweet-scented hands of Christ, Lord high treasurer of Ethiopia" in his sermons. His parishioners' attention was nevertheless held rapt by the deep import of Mather's words. They bore straight into their minds and hearts as surely as the eye of God staring down at them.

For this first sermon of the day, Mather described the second sign of Christ's divinity: the healing of a nobleman's son. The man asked Jesus to heal his son who was deathly ill with fever. Jesus complained, "Except ye see signs and wonders, ye will not believe." The father learned that the boy's fever abated as soon as Jesus promised he would live. Mather explained the logical implications to his audience and reasoned through the central relevant doctrine. Examples, similes, and comparisons helped his flock to understand his ideas. He reminded them to have faith and not depend upon signs to believe. Yet, in this case, the people of Boston did have a sign of divine wrath—a special providence—testing them in the form of smallpox. The sermon was the first of many that Mather would select related to his Savior's healing people due to the crisis at hand.

Prayer followed the sermon, again with distinct differences from Roman Catholic and Anglican traditions. The congregants stood instead of kneeling or genuflecting, listening closely to the ministers' supplications imploring God's mercies on undeserving sinners, particularly during a time of judgment under smallpox. Moreover, none of the prayers that were said for the duration of the emergency sought the intervention of any patron saints of illness and healing. The Protestant reformers had swept them aside for the "priesthood of all believers" and did not believe in intercessory prayer. They prayed directly to God. The Puritans believed in "visible saints" who were admitted as church members but would not be prayed to when deceased. The prayers were followed by the singing of psalms, usually led by a deacon. Because the importance of the words superseded the quality of the tune, one observer amusingly described the effect as, "Everyone sang as best pleased himself," and hopefully God, with a confusing disharmony.

After the conclusion of the first service of the day, the congregants gathered for restrained conversation befitting the Sabbath. Men and women passed along vital bits of information or gossip. News and rumors associated with the smallpox was the topic everyone discussed this Sunday. The families retired for some rest and contemplation of Mather's sermon before they returned in the afternoon. Every time they assembled, there was a greater and greater chance that the *variola* was communicated to people, who would then spread it around the neighborhood.

On Thursday, June 8, the congregation was called together for the weekly lecture. The number of shirkers, who were special objects of Cotton Mather's concern about the general religious and moral decline of the Boston community, was probably fewer than normal because the lecture seemed a better choice this evening than the tavern. Another change from the usual Thursday lecture was the fact that that day was an unofficial fasting and prayer day in the meetinghouses. While the people were hungry, they were famished even more for a spiritual renewal and the cleansing of their sin.

Their minister had consulted with his brethren the previous Friday and jointly appointed Thursday as a day of prayer. "Because of the destroying Angel standing over the town, and the grievous consternation on the minds of the people, I move the ministers who are the lecturers of the city, to turn the next lecture day into a day of prayer, that we may prepare to meet our God," Mather wrote.

When Mather ascended the pulpit stairs, he delivered a sermon titled "Preparation to Meet Our God Coming to Us in Ways of Adversity and Mortality." He wrote in his diary that the "lecture turned into a day of prayer because of much calamity by the smallpox impending over us." The parishioners did not expect a sermon that would cheer them up amid the growing disaster, and they were not disappointed. The moment was rife with an opportunity to remind the worshippers to remember their mortality because time flew, and they knew not when their hour would come.

Mather chose Amos 4:12 as the Scripture to lecture on. The entire chapter relates how God had sent Israel numerous plagues and draughts to punish his people for their sin, but over and over again, "Yet have ye not returned unto me, saith the Lord." For their willful disobedience and refusal to read the signs, the chosen people received a stern rebuke. In the chosen line from Amos, God warns them: "Therefore, thus will I do unto thee, O Israel: and because I will do this unto thee, prepare to meet thy God, O Israel."

The congregation must have emitted wails and wept openly to hear such warning words of an angry and righteous God. They were the new Israel and were bound to the Lord in their new covenant. Their sin and worldliness had led them astray, and they were to be punished like the ancient Hebrews. This admonition, however frightening, was a gift to the people because it was a chance to repent and save their souls before it was too late. First they would have to suffer divine judgment.

Mather appreciated the "opportunity of speaking many things in a sermon this day, for the good of the inhabitants, and for the advancement of that piety, to which the judgments of God should awaken them." The topic dovetailed perfectly with his understanding of the decline in Puritan New England. The smallpox epidemic might provoke a restoration of the original covenant and the piety of the first generation of settlers.

Yet there was one more possible measure to take besides quarantine and prayers, the minister thought. This other option had never been tried before, at least in the American colonies. It was not actually a cure for smallpox, but it might nonetheless save many lives. He had been waiting a half dozen years for smallpox to sweep through Boston for him to make the attempt. First he would have to persuade the physicians to consider trying it. With that in mind, Reverend Cotton Mather sat down in his spacious study in his North End home to compose a letter to the doctors of the town. He knew the import of what he was doing; he knew he was changing history.

Chapter Six

A CONSULT OF PHYSICIANS

The contagion of smallpox clasped Boston in a lethal grip. Cotton Mather the father was angst-ridden over the health of his children, despite his prayers and professions of sacrifice. In his role as a good shepherd, Reverend Mather was also distressed for the physical and spiritual well-being of his flock. As an important public figure and citizen, Mather had trepidation for his fellow townsmen and the effect that a smallpox epidemic would have upon Boston. He hoped it would result in their flight into the meetinghouses and churches throughout the city, but he was smart enough to recognize that panic would probably result in social dislocation, economic collapse, and widespread personal grief.

Cotton Mather, FRS, however, would offer not only consolation for the stricken or prayers for the faithfully departed. As a scientist, Mather was interested in the public's welfare. "We all came into the world upon a very important errand," he declared, "which errand is, to do and to get good." Upon the first sign of general infection, the father, minister, public servant, and scientist with a particular interest in medicine sprang into action.

Mather had nothing less in mind than a revolutionary design on how to combat smallpox. It had never been attempted before in the colonies, but his character did not mind innovation if he thought it might benefit people. Nevertheless, he did not plunge headlong into a foolish and rash course of action. Rather he formulated a deliberate plan based upon his extensive reading of the latest findings in scientific journals and made further investigations into the matter to formulate his hypothesis. Moreover, this plan would demand a rather lot of pluck and courage to overcome any opposition. His idea was several years in the making, waiting for this opportunity in late May 1721 to be implemented.

The story of how this idea germinated in Cotton Mather's mind takes us back to a couple of flashes of insight stretching into the previous decades. His moments of inspiration were animated by some heady reading and a discussion with the most unlikely person.

In December 1706, Mather needed a household servant, and so several parishioners purchased a slave for him. Mather thought the strong young man was "of a promising aspect and temper." The day he was presented to Mather, the new owner "put upon him the name of Onesimus," after the runaway slave in the Bible who converted to Christianity. Mather, true to his principles regarding slaves, taught Onesimus to read and write and labored for his Christian conversion. Mather allowed Onesimus to work for an income and marry another slave, by whom he had a son (who died in his youth).

In 1716 Mather asked his slave "whether he ever had the smallpox." Onesimus answered with a confounding "yes and no." When Mather only stared back blankly at him, Onesimus explained that "he had undergone an operation which had given him something of the smallpox, and would forever preserve him from it." He added, "It was often used among the Guramantese, and whoever had the courage to do it, was forever free from the fear of the contagion." Onesimus went on to explain the procedure and then "showed me in his arm the scar which it had left upon him." With his own eyes, the minister saw evidence that a smallpox inoculation could work to prevent the deadly threat. He later wrote, "I was first instructed by it, by a Guramantee-servant of my own, long before I know, that any Europeans or Asiaticks had the least acquaintance with it."

Mather was not content with the testimony of just one person, however, and he questioned other Africans around Boston. They all agreed on the essentials of inoculation: "It is now become a common thing to cut a place or two in their skin, sometimes one place, and sometimes another, and put in a little matter of the smallpox. After which, they, in a few days, grow a little sick, and a few smallpox break out, and by-and-by they dry away.... Nobody ever died of doing this, nor ever had the smallpox after it."

Mather's study of science combined with his willingness to listen to his slaves in order to save lives from the deadly virus. Few others in the milieu of race relations in the American colonies would have been so open-minded as to accept their stories. Additionally, Mather always credited his slaves with providing key information, even when it damaged his arguments for the procedure.

Only months after discoursing with Onesimus, Mather met a physician named William Douglass. The two were perfectly suited to strike up an intellectually invigorating acquaintance—or so it seemed. They shared an interest and broad reading in medicine. Douglass had studied medicine at the most prestigious centers of medical learning and training, including the universities of Edinburgh, Leiden, and Paris. He was the only physician in Boston who had actually taken a medical degree rather than read and apprentice with a practitioner who had been trained in the same way. He also was a fellow member of the Royal Society. Douglass was an intellectual and a man of cosmopolitan tastes and travels.

Mather and Douglass, however, never really struck up a friendship, whatever their similarities. If Mather struggled at times to rein in his vain and caustic character, Douglass was haughty and markedly disdainful of the backwater provincials he encountered in Boston. "You complain of the practice of physick being undervalued in your parts and with reason," Douglass later wrote to colonial scientist Cadwallader Colden, whom he considered respectable and worthy of communication. "We are not much better in that respect in this place. We abound with practitioners though no other graduates than myself. We have fourteen apothecary shops in Boston, all our practitioners dispense their own medicines, myself excepted being the first who hath lived here by practice without the advantage of advance on medicines."

Douglass apparently thought enough of Mather to lend him one of the latest issues of *Philosophical Transactions*. When Mather sat down to pore over the volume, he found an article chronicling an inoculation method that sounded conspicuously similar to the one he learned of from Onesimus. The printed correspondence was from Dr. Emanuel Timonius, who had studied medicine at the prestigious medical faculties at Padua and Oxford universities. To show the distant reach of the Royal Society, Timonius was a fellow of the society writing from Constantinople in December 1713. He described the process of smallpox inoculation as it was practiced in Turkey. It was not the first time that authentic reports of the procedure had been received by the Royal Society; a decade earlier Dr. Clopton Havers had described the practice as it was done in China.

Mather read and digested the Timonius article that summarized how patients were inoculated against smallpox. During the winter or spring of a smallpox outbreak, doctors would find an otherwise young and healthy person who had come down with the virus. With a needle they would prick a larger pustule and extract some of the emission into a clean glass, which was stopped and kept warm. The extract was then carried by another person to a warmed chamber where a patient was waiting. The patient's arm would be lanced several times until small drops of blood appeared, then a drop of the extract was placed atop the wounds. The blood and extract were mixed together and covered with half of a walnut shell for a couple of hours to prevent its being rubbed off. Patients were advised to abstain from meat and broth for twenty days while they suffered the outbreak of the virus.

Then Timonius conveyed the most important information about the procedure. The patients had a variety of responses, but they generally suffered a milder outbreak than those who were ill with smallpox in the "common way," as a natural case was called. They usually only had a dozen or two pustules on their body, and these rarely left a pockmark, except at the place of the incisions. Those who were inoculated gained the same immunity as those who already had smallpox and had developed a natural immunity by suffering the disease and producing antigens.

The information in *Transactions* dovetailed nicely with Mather's theory of disease, which was strikingly modern. Mather had read the works of Antoni van Leeuwenhoek (and would soon read Benjamin Marten's *New Theory of Consumption,* which confirmed Leeuwenhoek's findings). Van Leeuwenhoek was a Dutchman who uncovered the secrets of the microscopic world by grinding his own lenses to peer through these new instruments of the scientific revolution. He corresponded frequently with the Royal Society and had his researches published in the *Transactions.* His microscope revealed infinitesimal bacteria, hydra, protozoa, and spermatozoa, which he collectively labeled "animalcules."

Based upon his reading, Mather argued that a disease resulted from "millions of billions of trillions" of invisible, pathogenic "animals" or "insects" swarming around and invading human hosts. These tiny creatures entered the human body through food and drink, respiratory passages, and even skin pores. Once in the body, they "multiply prodigiously" and spread in the blood to the vital organs. Animalcules were transmitted from person to person through common towels and casual contact, resulting in an epidemic when enough people were sickened.

Mather saw a direct causal link between animalcules and smallpox. He wrote, "It begins now to be vehemently suspected that the smallpox may be more of an animalculated business than we have been generally aware of. The millions of [blank] which the microscopes discover in the pustules have confirmed the suspicion." The best methods of eliminating smallpox were to destroy the invisible enemies or to make the population resistant to them so that they had no effect—namely, through inoculation. Mather was one of the earliest proponents of the germ theory of medicine that would fundamentally alter medicine.

Mather was certainly intrigued by Timonius's writings. He had had smallpox himself as a young man during the epidemic of 1678, which killed roughly seven hundred Bostonians out of a population of four thousand. Later, he experienced great anguish when several family members were almost destroyed in the "fiery furnace of the smallpox" that consumed Boston in the last great outbreak in 1702–1703. Mather and other colonists were intimately aware of the fragility of life due to crippling accidents and deadly disease. His own children were disfigured when, as toddlers, they fell onto a burning hearth. His newborn infants and older children were swept away in a 1713 measles epidemic. He knew the abyss of grief caused by the loss of two loving wives. He compared losing a child to "the tearing off of a limb." Mather investigated the prospect of averting illness and death in the hope of one day easing the pain of death.

Mather collected some American curiosities to send to Dr. John Woodward of Gresham College and a leading member of the Royal Society. On July 12, 1716, Mather sat down in his study and composed a letter to Woodward comparing the smallpox inoculation that he had read about in Timonius's correspondence with the conversation he had with Onesimus, whom he described as "a pretty intelligent fellow." Mather wondered, "How does it come to pass that no more is done to bring this operation into experiment and into fashion in England?" He hazarded a guess that Londoners might be willing to pay physicians for this course of action that would save their lives. Mather had the audacity to write, "I beseech you, sir, to move it." With a grandiose hope for doing good and winning lasting fame, Mather thought they could "save more lives than Dr. Sydenham."

Thomas Sydenham, acclaimed as the "English Hippocrates," was an excellent modern medical authority to aspire to. Educated at Oxford, he practiced in London and investigated smallpox and other diseases. Building on the work of the Renaissance doctor known as Paracelsus, Sydenham was one of the first doctors to advocate that diseases were specific entities outside the human body, questioning the idea held by followers of classical authorities such as Galen who believed they resulted from an imbalance in the four humors and were generated within the body. In other words, diseases were independent of the victims. Disease had a uniform character affecting all people the same way. Sydenham wrote, "Nature, in the production of diseases, is uniform and consistent... and the selfsame phenomena that you would observe in the sickness of a Socrates you would observe in the sickness of a simpleton."

Mather knew and respected the modern work of Sydenham and looked to build upon it.

Then Mather revealed his own resolve to act the next time smallpox reared its ugly head in Boston. He vowed, "If I should live to see the smallpox again enter into our city, I would immediately procure a consult of physicians to introduce a practice, which may be of so very happy a tendency." But Mather then equivocated: "Could we hear that you have done it before us, how much would that embolden us!" He might be able to muster more courage to introduce the innovation if it were successfully carried out in Europe's largest city by its most respected scientific authority.

Mather later confirmed his reading of the Timonius letter and his learning about African inoculation in another letter describing inoculation that was published in the *Transactions.* This one was sent by Dr. Jacobus Pylarinus, the late Venetian consul in Smyrna, and printed in 1716. Mather either read it soon after he sent his letter to Woodward or sometime after 1718, when Douglass returned from a stay in Barbados and permanently "took up his abode" in Boston.

The process that Pylarinus passed on did not significantly differ from that described by Timonius or the Africans. A few more incisions were made on the forehead, chin, cheeks, wrists, and feet. Both descriptions included taking secretions from a healthy person and restricting the patient's diet, and both results closely resembled what Mather had learned of elsewhere.

Two independent articles published in the world's foremost scientific journal and practical evidence that variolation was efficacious in granting immunity to the deadly disease was proof enough for Mather. By an unusual combination of factors, a minister who was very well read in medicine read about a procedure practiced thousands of miles away and spoke with others in his own home about a folk remedy that was about to join with the modern enlightened age.

He did not forget his pledge when the 1721 smallpox epidemic was widening its grip on his hometown.

Curiously, during the years between his conversation with Onesimus and his reading and communication with others on the promise of inoculation, Mather did not discuss the matter with any of Boston's physicians or apothecaries. He did not share with them Timonius's published letter nor share the revelations of Onesimus. If he did, he left no record of it. Instead, he waited until there was an outbreak of smallpox five years later to act on his promise to himself. If he had shared his thoughts and plans with anyone in Boston earlier in order to feel them out and win them over to attempting smallpox inoculations, he might have shaped a consensus among the medical community and saved himself (and the town) much trouble. They could also have agreed on a very limited plan to test inoculations carefully on willing volunteers.

As it was, Mather did not communicate his idea to the doctors of Boston until June 1721. And he did not receive an agreement to attempt inoculation. Perhaps he imagined they would share his enthusiasm for action in order to benefit the population. He might advocate science accomplished through "Experience! Experience! 'Tis to thee that the matter must be referred after all," but he did not foresee that doctors might be hesitant to administer smallpox virus to their patients during an outbreak. They would clearly need more proof before they took medical advice from a minister.

Chapter Seven

DR. BOYLSTON RESPONDS

Armed with his knowledge and fortified by his courage, Mather acted immediately on his plan. He composed a letter as promised and shared the knowledge that he had guarded for five years. The reaction of Boston's doctors, however, was hardly one that Mather anticipated. He was perhaps blinded by his own enthusiasm and egotism that he was right and assumed that all reasonable men would be easily persuaded to act on his suggestion.

In late May 1721, he wrote in his diary that the "grievous calamity" of smallpox had entered Boston. In the same breath, he wrote, "The practice of conveying and suffering the smallpox by inoculation has never been used in America, nor indeed in our nation." He wondered, "How many lives might be saved by it, if it were practiced?" He then confidently asserted that he would "procure a consult of our physicians, and lay the matter before them."

On June 6, Mather prepared an "Address to the Physicians of Boston," exhorting them to meet and consider the practice of inoculation. He included an abstract of the Timonius and Pylarinus letters and began circulating it. "Gentlemen," he wrote, "My request is, that you would meet for a consultation upon this occasion and to deliberate upon it, that whoever first begins this practice, (if you approve that it should be begun at all) may have the concurrence of his worthy brethren to fortify him in it." Mather insinuated that there might be some opposition to this untested method of combating smallpox and pledged to use his authority and that of the other ministers (no small consideration in Puritan Boston) to rally the public.

Mather added some careful cautions with his recommendations. He predicted that the practice in Boston should have the same results as in other parts of the world, but he admitted, "I durst not engage that the success of the trial here will be the same that has been in all the other countries where it has been tried." Moreover, inoculation should not be attempted but "under the management of a physician." The minister might commend the procedure to the physicians but surely did not intend to practice it himself. Finally, he conceded that this untested procedure should be "warily proceeded in."

The physicians of the town summarily ignored Mather's injunction to try smallpox inoculations. Mather never revealed any letters or heated conversations that explained their opposition. Instead he was answered with stony silence. Dr. William Douglass was highly respected by the same medical community that he had privately scorned and may have persuaded others to brush aside the minister's appeal.

Mather was dismayed that the physicians had not concurred with his desire to begin testing inoculation. For the moment, he had to settle on writing about it. On June 22 he recorded that he was working on a "little treatise on the smallpox." He broke it down into three parts: "First awakening the sentiments of piety which it calls for; then exhibiting the best medicines and methods which the world has yet had for the managing of it; and finally, adding the new discovery to prevent it in the way of inoculation." It was part of a book-length treatise on medicine entitled *The Angel of Bethesda* that he had begun in 1720. He comforted his wounded pride by writing, "It is possible that this essay may save the lives, yea, and the souls of many people." It was almost ready for publication, so he mused, "Shall I give it unto the booksellers? I am waiting for direction."

The following day, Mather was absolutely convinced that he was right and wrote the physicians again: "I write a letter unto the physicians entreating them to take into consideration the important affair of preventing the smallpox in the way of inoculation." One of the letters was to Dr. Zabdiel Boylston. "You are many ways, sir, endeared unto me," Mather began intimately. There was a hint of resignation in the minister's voice as he issued this one final plea to try inoculation: "I now lay before you, the most that I know (and all that was ever published in the world) concerning a matter, which I have the occasion of its being much talked about. If upon mature deliberation, you should think it admissible to be proceeded in, it may save many lives that we set a great store on. But if it be not approved of, you will have the pleasure of knowing what is done in other places."

Clearly, he favored the former. For if Boylston, too, rejected Mather, then he had no other alternatives, and the smallpox would run its course as it always had. And history would have been very different.

While Mather nervously waited for an answer from the physicians, he continued to preach to his congregation that they might relieve their fears of the smallpox by turning to Christ. On June 11 he completed a series of eight lectures on 1 Peter 2:9, in which he reminded his flock to be faithful to the covenant they had made with God in their "errand into the wilderness." The apostle had written: "But ye are a chosen generation, a royal Priesthood, an holy nation, a people set at liberty, that ye should shew forth the virtues of him that hath called you out of darkness into his marvelous light."

The following Sunday, June 18, Mather continued his thoughts on the healing of the nobleman's son from the Gospel of John that he had previously offered on June 4. On Thursday, June 22, after working on his "little treatise" about smallpox inoculation during the morning, Mather went to the lecture and delivered a sermon, "Walking Through Darkness by the Light of God." He chose to speak on the book of Job because of "a dark time coming on the city." Fear was mounting in the community, the number of smallpox cases was growing, and many were privately questioning God's judgment. Like Job, they were wondering why they were made to suffer God's trials as he loosed the destroying angel upon Boston.

In Job 29:3, the afflicted tells of his utter dependence upon the Almighty: "When his light shined upon mine head: and when by his light I walked through the darkness."

Mather's congregation might be tempted to question the ways of the omnipotent, omniscient Lord, but they must instead have faith that his ways are just and that he would care for his chosen people.

Readers of the *Boston News-Letter* that day scanned an item relating that the Harvard commencement was to be held privately because of the contagion around Boston and nearby towns such as Cambridge. The college had largely emptied as students, like Sammy Mather, had fled to the reassuring comfort of their families at home. The commencement exercises would be bereft of the usual pomp and circumstance this year. The anticipated crowd, traditionally dressed in their finery and traveling in carriages over land and by ferry, would stay home this year. The students were relieved of the typical burden of publicly reciting Latin perorations. Instead, they quietly received their diplomas from Harvard's president and were graduated, their futures disquieting rather than seized with youthful exuberance. However, because there was smallpox at Harvard, whatever prudence was exercised in canceling the commencement ceremony was negated by the administration's sending the students traveling through the region.

During June, there was but one death reported from smallpox in Boston. The residents of the town were not duped by either the *variola* or by the devil. Bostonians were afraid to go out because they feared both were everywhere in the town ready to seize their bodies and souls. Certainly the virus was breeding and contaminating the entire city— bedding, churches, clothing, homes, shops. Their fear was more than justified. Meanwhile, Mather waited for word from Dr. Boylston.

Zabdiel Boylston read Mather's letter and was at last convinced.

Boylston was a third-generation American who was born in 1670 in the tiny frontier hamlet of Brookline. His father was a physician and apothecary who ministered to his widely dispersed rural patients and taught his son medicine. His father died when Boylston was fifteen, and the young man then apprenticed under the best surgeon in New England, John Cutler of Boston. Boylston married in 1706, and moved to Dock Square in the South End. He set up Boston's largest apothecary shop, where he sold a variety of herbal folk remedies.

Boylston was a rather adept (and quite lucky) surgeon. He performed a lithotomy on a young man, removing an egg-sized bladder stone. He also successfully performed a mastectomy on a woman suffering with breast cancer. Both somehow miraculously survived in a day before antisepsis and anesthesia. Usually, however, he mundanely dispensed his remedies at his shop.

Boylston carefully examined Mather's letter and accompanying evidence. There is no record of their meeting to confer, but it is hard to imagine that they did not. Boylston later wrote in his clinical study of the epidemic, "Upon reading of which I was very well-pleased, and resolved in my mind to try the experiment." Based upon his surgical record, he was an enterprising physician who took risks to save people's lives particularly when threatened by a deadly illness. He stated that his memory and experience of the "destruction the smallpox made nineteen years before" during the 1702–1703 epidemic influenced his decision. He remembered the suffering all around him and how "narrowly I then escaped with my life." Moreover, the townspeople in 1721 were in "great consternation and disorder." Hope within the town of "preventing the further spread of it" was being lost as evidenced by the fact that on the next day, June 24, guards were ordered away from infected houses as a useless measure.

Boylston hesitated because of the time of year. The innovative practice was usually performed during the winter because of some ancient medical beliefs. The Galenic body of medicine proposed that four humors governed one's health: blood, yellow bile, black bile, and phlegm. These humors corresponded to the four primary qualities of hot, dry, cold, and wet as well as the four seasons: spring, summer, autumn, and winter. Fevers and disease developed inside the body because the humors were out of balance, especially when the weather of the season enhanced one of the humors.

Unfortunately for Boylston, the smallpox epidemic hit during the spring, when hot weather increased the quantity of "hot" blood and there was an attendant rash of fevers. The yellow bile of summer was also "hot and dry," which contributed to severe fevers. Thus it was an inauspicious time of year to attempt inoculation of a hot disease like smallpox. Boylston did not know if the weather would combine with hot blood and yellow bile to imbalance his patients and produce deadly fevers. Nevertheless, he decided to risk it.

Because he was naturally immune, Boylston could not test the safety and efficacy of inoculation himself. So to attest to his faith in the method, he inoculated his six-year-old son, Thomas, and his two African slaves: an adult, Jack, and Jack's two-year-old son, Jackey. Boylston wrote that he "chose to make it" on them and did not indicate whether his dependents had any option to refuse.

Boylston did nothing special to prepare his subjects, and he undertook the experiment in the heat of the summer despite the advice from the Royal Society's *Transactions*. He made incisions on the arms, leg, and neck, applied some *variola*, and waited. He followed his instructions, placing a nutshell over the sites.

Following the time-honored traditions going back to Hippocrates, Boylston observed his patients carefully. The leading authority of the day, Dr. Thomas Sydenham, had advised doctors to observe patients so as to determine "the remedial measures that should be employed." In this case, Boylston was looking for patterns in how his patients responded to the remedy itself as well as using the necessary remedies for the disease that he induced. He monitored them and took notes on their responses.

Boylston learned the difference between reading about inoculation in a journal and actually practicing it. After a week, the two boys became febrile and lethargic for a few days. His son experienced some convulsions and had difficulty sleeping. Boylston felt "a very great fright" but could do nothing but wait. As the hours agonizingly passed, neither his "fears nor the symptoms abating," he took recourse in traditional Galenic medicine and induced Tommy to vomit. The fever subsided naturally (although Boylston thought he had made it pass sooner) as roughly one hundred pustules appeared on the boys. This was a greater number than Boylston expected, but they were not enough for great concern. Jack experienced only a few pustules at the site of the incision, inclining the physician to believe that his slave had forgotten he had already been inoculated. The pocks ran their course and dried up within a week. The patients were all presently as "hale and strong as they were in their lives." Inoculation had indeed worked.

In the coming week, Boylston inoculated seven individuals. The doctor never recorded how he persuaded them or whether they came of their own accord when they heard that it was being practiced. He did, however, carefully observe and record how each patient responded to the procedure, and he even altered it slightly, according to his own hypotheses. Still, amid the changes made to an already innovative practice, Boylston could not escape from much of his received medical wisdom. His methodology was a curious mix of old and new.

Joshua Cheever willingly endured the operation on July 12. He suffered a slight fever after the first week from which he quickly rallied, leading Boylston to believe the treatment had not taken effect. On the ninth day, while Cheever was still wondering if he had been successfully inoculated or not, fire bells clanged through the still night, drawing men from all around to fight it. The town was a model of early firefighting due to the experience of earlier horrific conflagrations, particularly the blaze in 1711. The town purchased axes, buckets, hooks, ladders, and even a primitive engine. There was communal responsibility for extinguishing the flames because a law had been passed: "Not only the person in whose house the fire first breaks out, but the neighborhood are concerned to employ their utmost diligence and application to extinguish the fire and prevent the progress thereof."

Cheever raced "with others to help put out the fire" without delay—and without thinking of the consequences to his health and that of everyone with whom he came in contact. He labored mightily, passing the heavy buckets and wielding an axe. He reportedly worked up a heavy sweat. He then paid for his exertions when smallpox hit him with a vengeance. He suffered a high fever, and his pulse pounded uncontrollably. His whole body was wracked with pain, so much so that Boylston thought his patient "would have the confluent smallpox." The confluent form of smallpox was particularly lethal and characterized by pustules that ran together and spelled almost certain death for its sufferers.

Boylston resorted to the traditional medical cures: he bled Cheever copiously, induced vomiting, and blistered him. The basis of ancient medicine was to maintain a balance of the humors for good health. When the blood was raging and heated dangerously, doctors bled patients in order to drain the excess blood and cool the body. Even though the Enlightenment doctor William Harvey had revolutionized the understanding of the circulatory system, most doctors throughout the eighteenth century were loath to challenge traditional practices and continued to bleed their patients. Boylston felt vindicated when his patient developed the less virulent form of smallpox and recovered. The truth was, Cheever endured a great deal of agony for nothing.

Two days after Boylston inoculated Cheever, John Hiller and a female slave of Boylston's, Moll, underwent the procedure. Hiller followed the normal course, while it did not seem to take with Moll. Boylston again concluded that the slave must have been previously inoculated in Africa.

Boylston was confident enough in his abilities that he inoculated another of his sons, John. The thirteen-year-old did not suffer anything unusual except for several nosebleeds, which Boylston connected to the boy's consumption of milk. Important to his cross-sample of different persons, he then welcomed three older townspeople ranging in age from forty-three to sixty-seven years old and found they came out well, even though he labeled them "weak and infirm persons." In mid-July, there were as many as seven patients in Boylston's home. He soon judged that the operation worked well for varied ages, sexes, and races. Most important, no one had died.

Even as America's largest city, Boston was still small enough at not quite eleven thousand souls that people knew each other's business and had few secrets. Add that Boylston did not seek to hide what he was doing, and truth and rumor flew through the town with dizzying speed in early July.

Most people definitely did not like what they heard. At first, they expressed disapproval in their homes and then more publicly as they gathered in shops and increasingly at meetinghouses for lecture days, Sabbaths, and fast days. Private doubt quickly gave way to clamorous public disapproval and fear.

It is impossible to recreate these hushed conversations, but we can say for sure that people were shocked that Dr. Boylston was adding to the cases of this contagious disease. The dreaded judgment of an angry God was upon them, and this doctor was testing a new medical procedure. They just wanted to escape the judgment of the Almighty and of the smallpox rather than have a lone doctor tinker with forces beyond his control (and their understanding).

Rumors that business owners or their workers and family members had smallpox crippled businesses and friendships because their homes and shops would be avoided like the plague. Shopkeeper Thomas Phillip was a victim of such rumor mongering and lost all of his business. He wrote a letter to the editor complaining of his treatment. "Whereas it has been very scandalously reported by some envious persons, that for certain truth the smallpox was at Thomas

Phillip's…and that it was concealed by them, which has been and is now a great detriment to…trading." He declared unequivocally: "The said report is a scandalous and ridiculous falsehood (for by the blessing of Almighty God), the smallpox is not, nor has not been in my house these several years."

Cotton Mather noted that the mood of his congregation and the townspeople he saw while lecturing at other meetinghouses was apprehensive. "Some under grievous consternation from the smallpox spreading," he wrote. A few days later, he added, "The various distresses come upon the flock, in the grievous disease now beginning to distress the town."

Mather assumed the burden of their concerns as a good shepherd. They "must be suitably considered by me; my prayers and sermons must be adapted unto their condition," he resolved. His flock must be "directed and comforted."

Mather retreated into his study on July 7 for a private day of fasting and prayer. The devout minister supplicated himself on his floor that he might "obtain from a reconciled God, and a powerful and merciful Savior, the blessings of goodness and his gracious presence with me in my ministry." He prayed to be a rock of piety and a pillar of strength for his people.

For a suitably consoling prayer in the time of sorrow, Mather naturally turned to the book of Psalms. He relished the occasion to preach on one of them when the General Court ordered a public day of fasting and prayer for the colony on Thursday, July 13, because of the "judgment that has in his Providence brought on this land by sending the smallpox among us."

Puritans observed days of fasting as much as they celebrated days of thanksgiving, which was not an annual event but a time of thanking God for his benevolence and mercy. Afflictions and natural disasters were considered God's judgment, and they were sent to chastise his chosen people who had a greater responsibility for piety under the covenant on which the colony had been founded. God's people followed days of fasting by setting aside their worldly callings and gathering at church, where they listened to sermons, prayed for deliverance, acknowledged their sins, and promised to reform their ways and obey God in the future. God's mercy would follow for the truly regenerate, and he would lift the affliction.

On the appointed day, Mather preached "The Lifting Up of the Soul unto God under Distresses" from Psalm 86. Although his discourse focused on verse 4, the song of King David began with these words:

> Incline thine ear, O Lord, and hear me: for I am poor and
> needy.
> Preserve thou my soul, for I am merciful: my God, save
> thou thy servant, that trusteth in thee.
> Be merciful unto me, O Lord: for I cry upon thee
> continually.
> Rejoice the soul of thy servant: for unto thee, O Lord, do I
> lift up my soul.
> For thou, Lord, art good and merciful, and of great kind-
> ness unto all them, that call upon thee.
> Give ear, Lord, unto my prayer, and hearken to the voice of
> my supplication.
> In the day of my trouble I will call upon thee: for thou
> hearest me.

The *Boston News-Letter* printed another sermon, which was preached before the governor and General Court. Reverend Nathaniel Appleton opened by saying, "We are here met to humble ourselves before Almighty God, and in a most devout and solemn manner to implore his protection, blessing, and favor to avert all those judgments which our manifold sins have deserved, and to perpetuate the enjoyment of the Protestant religion." Puritans enjoyed spiritual and temporal blessings as God's chosen people, but they were being judged for their collective sins. "If we look round this nation with an impartial eye, we shall have reason to think that all things considered, we are as ripe for judgment as they could well be." He advised his listeners, including a number of politicians, "It will therefore very much become us, when God's judgments are moving about us, to awake out of our spiritual lethargy." But God was merciful and would release his people from the grip of the affliction. "We have seen that there is a gracious and merciful God to fly to in the greatest distress. Him, therefore, let us seek while he may be found; on him let us call while he is near; both to avert this terrible calamity with which we are threatened; and to continue to us those spiritual and temporal blessings we now enjoy."

Those who listened to the calming words of Cotton Mather and the other ministers around Boston were reminded that God's mercy exceeded his judgments. Their tranquility was only a brief respite, because they unwittingly contributed to the spread of the *variola* virus that day by attending the sermon. But they instead blamed a certain doctor who was intentionally infecting his patients.

On Saturday, July 15, Zabdiel Boylston met the criticism of his experiments by publishing an initial account of his success with inoculation with his slaves and child in the *Boston Gazette* and *Boston News-Letter*. He carefully justified the procedure by describing what he had done and appealing to the scientific authority of the letters in the Royal Society's *Transactions*. He then sent an unmistakable signal that he meant to continue the practice. "In a few weeks more," he promised, "I hope to give you some further proof of their just and reasonable account," for he had patients in his home at that moment.

Boston erupted in a fury of outrage. Their ire was clearly understandable. The town was experiencing a smallpox epidemic that was killing loved ones and neighbors, and Boylston was fanning the flames of an extremely communicable disease by purposefully injecting it into more people. Within days, some of them would see Joshua Cheever in the crowd that fought the fire and later discover to their horror that he was Boylston's patient.

For his part, Cotton Mather was quite pleased and called it "an unspeakable consolation" that a Boston physician had assented to his injunction to attempt "the new method used by the Africans and Asiaticks, to prevent and abate the dangers of the smallpox, and infallibly to save the lives of those that have it wisely managed upon them." But as someone committed to reason and the public good, Mather was at a complete loss to understand the reaction against it. He wondered how people could be so irrational and perversely biased against a new procedure that might save their lives during an epidemic. He decided the devil was responsible, stirring up the people's hatred in his indignation at being robbed of the souls he would have consumed had it not been for inoculation. "The Destroyer, being enraged at the proposal of anything that may rescue the lives of our poor people from him, has taken a strange possession of the people on this occasion," he wrote. "They rave, they rail, they blaspheme. They talk not only like idiots but also like frantics. And not only the physician who began the experiment, but I also am an object of their fury—their furious obloquies and invectives."

Mather was disturbed for the important reason that the popular fury might be used to put an end to the practice in democratic Massachusetts. That turn of events would rob him of his role in this self-consciously revolutionary moment in the history of medicine and his role in saving lives in the town. He asked God for help in repelling the "hellish assault" that the "great Adversary" was making upon his attempt to "do good." It would also endanger the lives of his children. They would be susceptible to the disease in the common way if they did not undergo inoculation. "The cursed clamor of a people strangely and fiercely possessed of the Devil," he regretted, "will probably prevent my saving the lives of my two children from the smallpox in the way of transplantation." All he would have left in his arsenal to save his children would be "my continual and importunate cries to heaven for their preservation." A silent majority (or sizable minority) might have agreed with him.

Mather and Boylston had good reason to worry about the future of their experiment. On July 21 the Selectmen and some justices of the peace ordered Boylston to appear before them for a third time to call him to "account for using this practice." Many townspeople were present as well in this self-governing town. Boylston dutifully appeared and saw that most of the doctors of the town were also present—although not in his defense. Upon questioning, Boylston defended his practice and explained that he presently had seven additional patients under his care who had been inoculated and almost symptomatic. "I then gave a public invitation to the practitioners of the town (who were then present) to visit my patients…and to judge of and report their circumstances as they found them."

The assembled officials and physicians then heard the testimony of a French physician, Dr. Lawrence Dalhonde, who related the dangers of inoculation that he had heard of in Europe. He testified that, a few decades before, thirteen soldiers had the operation, but four died of it. "When they were opened," he explained, "horrid things were found in them." Six others survived but were afflicted with tumors and inflammations. It even failed to work on the final three. In other instances in Flanders, Italy, and Spain, the story was the same, with unsuccessful inoculations and crippling infirmities. There was a fair amount of murmuring among the crowd in the wake of Dalhonde's testimony.

The "enraged physicians" who "raised a storm" against Boylston smugly felt vindicated. It is surprising to find doctors who refused to look at evidence of the practice only blocks away. It was poor medical practice on their part to refuse to read the scientific literature, witness the experiment themselves, examine the patients, and draw their own conclusions, as Boylston had done. They were thinking within an existing medical paradigm that limited their ability to conceptualize the possible success of an innovation. Boylston's report, they trumpeted, was dubious at best (and possibly fabricated due to the wild accusations), though welcomed as obviously highly prejudicial against inoculation. The doctors published a warning to Bostonians that inoculation was a highly lethal procedure and "tends to spread and continue the infection in a place longer than it might otherwise be; and that continuing the operation among us is likely to prove of most dangerous consequence." The records indicate a certain amount of dogmatic thinking among most of the doctors and speak to the modernity of Boylston and Mather.

Dr. William Douglass's animosity toward Boylston and Mather and his hidebound reaction to inoculation were further substantiated by his adamant refusal to lend out his copy of the Royal Society's *Transactions.* Boylston and Mather wanted to consult the journal to ensure that they were practicing the method safely and to justify their innovative practice with an air of authority. Instead, Douglass asserted that Boylston was practicing inoculation incorrectly, without showing the articles to anyone else. More to the point, Douglass was so prejudiced against the procedure, he did not want anyone to examine the evidence or attempt additional experiments. If he were educated in the new scientific method of the scientific revolution,

Douglass did not show it during the proceedings of the early summer. A Puritan minister called on him to allow his copy of the book "to come aboard, and be published word for word, that impartial men may *see with their own eyes*, the true state of the case."

Dalhonde's testimony and the joint authority of the town's doctors overwhelmingly convinced the town officials of Boylston's malfeasance. They "severely reprimanded him for spreading smallpox...and with high menaces warned him against proceeding with his practice any farther."

The decision surely met the approval of the gathered citizens for surely no one would contradict the will of the Selectmen, particularly during an epidemic already signaling divine judgment. The social covenant was the collective Puritan covenant with God that bound the entire community. Each member was part of the whole in which one's sins brought down the wrath of God on everyone. Obeying the just authority of the state was an extension of the fifth commandment's injunction to obey one's parents. Puritan children were catechized to believe that, "All our superiors, whether in family, school, church, and commonwealth" were included in God's law. Disobedience to the commonwealth and the resulting social disorder would incur God's punishment. "Whatever is done against the order that God has constituted is done against God."

Thus the belief was that the beginning of the smallpox epidemic was God's test of the faith of the Christian commonwealth of Boston, and Boylston's disobedience might bring greater punishment. Perhaps God would send an additional plague or withhold his mercy of ending the smallpox outbreak. Either way, it was a risk that no reasonable people would want to take.

Boylston barely restrained his anger and frustration as he left chastised. The wild claims of the French doctor were so ridiculous, he might as well have said that inoculation caused patients' heads to fall off or turn men into women. Boylston did not reveal whether he planned to obey the Selectmen or forge on under the threat of prosecution. If he stopped performing inoculations, he would miss a golden chance to make great progress in colonial medicine. If he continued, he might land in jail. His fortitude in even attempting inoculation in the first place boded that he might very well persist.

In late July, while Boylston was battling public officials and fellow doctors, Cotton Mather was worried about the youth of the community. There were "several societies of young people," he wrote, "meeting for the exercises of religion on the Lord's Day evenings, and they generally lying obnoxious to the danger of the smallpox." He decided, "As far as I can find strength for it, [I will] visit them, and entertain them with prayers and sermons that shall be suitable for them." Confused and anguished by the loss of friends and family, the young people were the most frightened among any of the groups in Boston. Mather saw himself charged with a special ministry to comfort them and turn their eyes heavenward.

Mather turned his Bible to Psalm 78:63 and wrote out a sermon for the young people—"The Fire of Divine Wrath, Consuming Our Young People"—because smallpox was "beginning to carry off our young people." Mather warned them about the judgments of God when his chosen people had rebelled against God even though he had delivered them from slavery in Egypt. As a result, "The fire devoured their chosen men, and their maids were not praised."

The haunting words took on special meaning when one of the young people in North Church lost his battle with *variola* and died. Mather thought it appropriate to use the young man's death to shore up their faith and face their own mortality courageously. "A young man in the flock has made a very hopeful and joyful end, and has gloriously triumphed over death!" Mather extolled. "To animate piety, especially among the young people in the flock, especially now the fire of God is consuming them. I preach a sermon on this occasion."

Mather spoke at length with his own children about their faith because their fears were aroused by their friend's death. He carried a great burden, ministering to his family, his relatives, his congregation, his neighbors, his ally in inoculation (Boylston), and public officials. His yoke became more difficult to bear when he himself became an object of hate for his efforts.

Mather nevertheless recognized that others were suffering worse than he. In July eleven Bostonians died of smallpox. Fear and the number of smallpox cases were growing in the port city. Incidents of disease and the death toll would only continue to increase—and everyone knew it. They just did not know whether they would be next.

Chapter Eight

SOCIAL DISHARMONY

In the wake of the Selectmen's pronouncement against Boylston's experiments with inoculation, Boston was in a state of fear and chaos. Boylston, however, continued his work with the seven inoculations already in process, and the townspeople were still in great terror of the disease. Cotton Mather wrote in his diary that some of his kinsfolk "languish under great fear of the contagion that is now spreading among us." People were afraid to go abroad in town, and the disease crippled other social interactions and normal buoyancy. Business was grinding to a halt. The town was being destroyed just as surely as if it were under siege.

Nor was the anger aroused by the first inoculations subsiding. If anything, it was growing worse. Mather continued to feel like an aggrieved victim of ungodly and wicked invective. "The monstrous and crying wickedness of this town (a town at this time strangely possessed with the devil) and the vile abuse which I do myself particularly suffer from it, for nothing but my instructing our base physicians how to save many precious lives."

Mather's involvement in Boylston's inoculation experiment was a well-known fact. His own diary is evidence that people knew he was one of the driving forces behind inoculation. Additionally, Mather himself had approached all of Boston's doctors initially, and their public opposition sought to implicate Mather in the affair as well as his trusted ally, Dr. Boylston. Dr. William Douglass overtly went on the attack against the minister in the newspaper to sway public opinion against inoculation. One can only imagine what he said about Mather in private conversation.

As a minister, Mather readily understood the social covenant and the danger of the social disorder that was tearing Boston apart. The chaos obliged him "in the fear of the divine judgments to fall down before the Lord with most earnest supplications for his pity and pardon to a people so obnoxious to his displeasure."

The town doctors could not leave well enough alone after scoring their victory over Boylston with the Selectmen. Douglass wrote an anonymous piece for the *Boston News-Letter* that assaulted Boylston's character and judgment. Mather also came in for some special abuse. It was the opening salvo that loosed a civil war of words in newspapers and pamphlets for months. And like most civil wars, it would be hard to determine if anyone emerged victorious.

On July 24 Douglass ridiculed Boylston as a "certain cutter for the stone" because of his successful kidney stone removals. Douglass thought his nemesis was an illiterate and ignorant fool who had not properly understood the writings of Emanuel Timonius and Jacobus Pylarinus. Boylston had negligently failed to prepare his patients for inoculation with certain bodily treatments. Moreover, he was an unskilled surgeon who was "unfit to manage any of their symptoms." Worst of all, Douglass warned the readers of the *News-Letter,* Boylston was "propagating the infection in the most public trading place in the town" at Dock Square. Openly predicting disaster, Douglass called for criminal prosecution for murder should any patient die as a result of Boylston's felonious practices.

After attacking Boylston's professional credentials and knowledge, Douglass then had the nerve to delve into the religious arguments associated with inoculation. He went after Mather, whom he considered a busybody with "a pious and charitable design of doing good." The doctor then made the religious argument that inoculation contravened the will of God because it interfered with the normal course of the disease and who was meant to get it. Douglass wondered how Boylston could believe that "trusting more the extra groundless machinations of men than to our preserver in the ordinary course of nature may be consistent with that devotion and subjection we owe to the all-wise Providence of God almighty." Douglass contended that doctors must allow the smallpox to run its natural course as determined by the will of heaven or risk incurring God's righteous anger for not enduring the test of their faith. This was a reasonable view of Puritan faith of which many would have concurred, although Douglass did not have any degrees in theology or ministerial authority.

Reverend Cotton Mather, the man who prayed often for a still tongue in the face of adversity, posed a question to his diary and God: "What should be my conduct under the outrages and obloquies of a town which Satan has taken a most wonderful possession of? I must exceedingly rejoice in my conformity to my admirable Savior, who was thus and worse requited when he saved their lives, and came to save their souls." Mather was equating his suffering with that of Christ as well as seeing him both as a healer and a savior. Mather believed he, like his model, was saving souls as well as curing bodies. He continued his prayer to "give me to see my opportunities to do good strangely multiplied" even amid the "Satanic fury" that was raging uncontrollably.

Mather and other ministers refused to turn the other cheek at that moment and penned a strong response to Douglass's attacks. Mather's father, Increase, was also a man of science and joined forces with his son (although this was not always true for the pair of independent thinkers and characters). More surprisingly, though they differed on their religious opinions, the medical question brought the liberal Benjamin Colman over to Mather's side. Reverends William Cooper, Thomas Prince, and John Webb also sprang to Boylston's defense. On July 27 their rebuttal was printed in the *Boston Gazette.* It was primarily a defense of Boylston's character because the contention over inoculation had already turned personal. But in doing so they stumbled into questions of medicine and specifically inoculation.

The ministers defended Boylston's credentials. It was true that he did not have "the honor and advantage of an academic education, and consequently not the letters of some physicians in the town," but he was trained just as well as any other physician in Boston except for his antagonist. Boylston had built up a great store of expertise and a successful practice, they argued, through "considerable study, expense in travel, a good genius, diligent application, and much observation." If the other doctors of the town similarly trained should not suffer Douglass's denigration, neither could the town "endure to see Boylston thus spit at."

The ministers were on surer footing when they addressed Douglass's accusations that inoculation contravened the will of God. They offered their theological expertise, positing that God gave human beings reason and the means to make scientific and medical discoveries for their benefit. "It may be a means of thankfulness and joy as the gracious discovery of a kind Providence to mankind for that end," they wrote. The ministers revealed that Puritans had largely accepted the natural law arguments of the scientific revolution and the Enlightenment. There was no fatalism of a predetermined character to events that refused to countenance any idea of works. The doctors were correctly using a discovery to save lives, the ministers contended, rather than passively accepting the idea that anything bad that happened must be submitted to idly.

The ministers held that they should use all the means at their disposal that a benevolent and merciful God had provided them, including inoculation, and be humbly thankful. "Can't a devout heart depend upon God in the use of this means, with much gratitude, being in the full esteem of it?" they asked. Additionally, in a sense, doctors contravened the will of God every time they healed someone. The ministers asked why inoculation was any different from the normal medical practices that were performed on patients. "What hand or art of man is there in this operation more than in bleeding, blistering, and a score more things in medicinal use?" The ministers flatly maintained that the innovation was perfectly consistent with a "humble trust in our great preserver, and a due subjection to his all-wise Providence."

The gauntlet had been thrown down, and the challenge accepted. Neither side would back down over the coming months, even as hundreds died. The discordant struggle over inoculation ripped Boston apart just as the virus spread through the town randomly claiming more and more victims.

The clash assumed a peculiar and unexpected shape. The town doctors refused to examine any evidence for a new practice that might save thousands of lives. Moreover, they argued that it contradicted God's will. Contrarily, the ministers were the main proponents for a pioneering procedure that could be tried now that an epidemic threatened the port.

The governing authorities had to sort out these arguments and initially sided with the doctors. The representatives also refused to consider whether the procedure worked as they understandably erred on the side of caution. If it had been offered at a less dangerous time under more stringent precautions, they might have given their approval and dampened public fear and outrage.

While the various governmental, religious, and medical authorities attacked each other vehemently, Zabdiel Boylston simply ignored the order prohibiting inoculation. He violated the will of the Selectmen because he was a physician who had seen that it worked and wanted to save "the precious lives of his poor neighbors." Moreover, there was great popular demand from some frightened townspeople who saw loved ones and neighbors dying around them in the common way and wanted to protect themselves. In spite of the general fear associated with the start of inoculation, there were those who were willing to undergo the procedure. So, without much fanfare, he "took little notice of the inhibition that had been given him."

On August 5 he took on four more patients at his home. Over the next month, Boylston inoculated a total of seventeen patients, including another teenaged son. The doctor continued to mix the new with the old: bleeding patients, blistering their bodies, and administering quantities of anodyne. For now, everything was going more or less according to plan, and Boylston felt vindicated in moving forward regardless of what the Selectmen ruled.

But blatantly disobeying the law posed a grave threat to the social order and social covenant. Rarely was there such a need for law and order as during the chaos triggered by an epidemic. With one of the town's most respected citizens openly breaking the law, others further down the social hierarchy might decide to follow suit. Tempting God so openly could only bring disaster upon the heads of all. Boylston complained that many started ignorantly crying that

inoculation "would bring in the plague among us" as they thought
it had at Constantinople. They may have been duped by false information, but what Boylston ignored is that they were so credulous
because they believed God was sending additional plagues upon his
defiant chosen people.

Boylston saw things differently. Much like the ministers who
marshaled religious arguments in his favor, Boylston thought
himself an instrument of God's grace of discovery. He also
employed the sixth commandment and its prohibition on killing,
stating that it "ordered them the use of means to preserve and
prolong their lives."

During normal times, the ministers had generally been able
to enforce their orthodoxy upon deferential believers. However,
over the course of the seventeenth and early eighteenth century, a
decline of orthodoxy had followed religious disputes, pluralism, and
declining practice. The authority of the ministers was also in retreat.
The smallpox controversy created a morass of religious arguments for
and against inoculation. Rival points of Scripture were applied very
differently to the question at hand. The ministers' endorsement of
Boylston and his novel technique was repudiated as the only possible
perspective. The Puritan encouragement of literacy and individual
interpretation of the Bible led to a multiplicity of arguments about
exactly what the will of God was regarding inoculation. Each side
believed it was right and continued to demonize its opponents. It is
also significant that the Selectmen did not automatically support the
ministers in the debate. The government was no longer an enforcer
of the Ten Commandments or the ethical mores of the people. It
mostly defended public property and liberties and took measures
to protect public health. The ministers were generally limited to
railing against sin but could do little else. The increased grumbling
and open defiance of the ministers was never more blatant than in

1721. In any event, every important authority in town was being questioned. The social covenant was in tatters. Tension would only build in this explosive situation.

And build they did. The day after Boylston resumed his inoculations, the town erupted in opposition to the gross breach of the law as Cotton Mather himself attested in his diary. He retreated into his study for comfort. "It is the hour and power of darkness on this miserable town, and I need an uncommon assistance from above that I may not miscarry by any forward or angry impatience, or fall into any of the common iniquities of lying, railing, and malice, or be wary of well-doing and overcoming evil with good."

Into this division stepped an inflammatory set of characters all too willing to fan the flames that engulfed Boston. Benjamin Franklin and his brother James were young men struggling to make their way in the world. During normal times, probably few would have stooped to take notice of them. However, James seized upon the controversy to launch a provocative newspaper to sell copies and make a name for himself in publishing. Meanwhile, his younger brother joined the attack on Mather and the Puritan ministers and issued some of the most devastating critiques upon their authority.

Chapter Nine

THE BROTHERS FRANKLIN

At the very moment that Dr. Zabdiel Boylston was resuming inoculations, the Franklin brothers were preparing a printing press. Under the watchful eye of his older brother, Benjamin Franklin used his broad shoulders on an impressive six-foot frame to heave the heavy lead type into position. Having both carefully proofread the handwritten text and set it in type, Benjamin was placing the cast-metal letters in rows. The lines of text were held together within rectangular metal frames. With everything ready, the type was inked and paper laid on them. The paper was pressed and the printed text amazingly appeared on the page. Inspecting their handiwork, the brothers might have smiled at each other pleased. They hung the sheets to dry and repeated the process. Printer James Franklin and his apprentice, brother Benjamin, had inaugurated the first edition of the *New England Courant*.

James and Benjamin Franklin were the fourth and eighth child respectively of Josiah Franklin by his second wife, Abiah Folger of Nantucket. Josiah had migrated to Boston from England in 1683 and eventually fathered a total of seventeen children, with Benjamin being the fifteenth child and last son.

Josiah was a nonconformist who was welcomed as a member at South Church. He became a tallow chandler, rendering animal carcasses into candles and soap. It was an unenviable craft because of the hot, reeking work conditions. Nevertheless, Josiah labored hard and had good character, winning some level of respectability. His acquaintances included the highly reputable merchant and judge, Samuel Sewall.

Josiah supported his family with the help of a contract to supply candles for the town watch. He himself served the public by enforcing the Sabbath as a tither and the nine o'clock curfew as a constable. The family rented a house across from South Street but bought a larger home in the center of town at Hanover and Union streets, a brief walk from the Town House.

Like all Bostonians, Josiah apprenticed his children around the town in shops and homes so that his sons might learn a craft and his daughters gain essential skills to be good Puritan wives. James was a relatively easy son to guide into a career and expressed some interest and showed some aptitude for printing. After a few years of education, James was sent to England for training in his chosen vocation.

There was no better place in the British Empire than London to learn about printing. The printers there churned out massive amounts of print ranging from Grub Street ballads to broadsides to government and church pronouncements to books ranging in subject matter from Enlightenment philosophy to trashy novels and pornography.

As a child, Benjamin Franklin was a much more difficult nut to crack, testing his father's Christian forbearance. The youth was sent to be educated at the same school where Cotton Mather had practiced his ancient languages and read the classics. Josiah had the same motivation Increase Mather had for sending his son to Boston Latin: to train him for Harvard College and the ministry. Benjamin was just as precocious as Mather, but he directed his energies to irreverent and skeptical ends. Seeing that his son was not cut out for the ministry, Josiah withdrew him and put the young man to work in the candle shop to replace an older brother who was going to follow his father's trade and set up shop in Rhode Island.

Benjamin did not have the stomach for his father's trade. Living and working within sight of the Long Wharf and its omnipresent ships, hearing stories from worldly sons of Neptune, and dreaming of adventure, he clearly heard the call of the sea. Josiah had already lost one son, his namesake, to a vessel that went down, and he was not about to lose another. He patiently walked his son around the town so that he could see different craftsmen at their trades and spark an interest in one of them.

In 1718 James returned from London with a press and type and was ready to open up a printshop. The town had several printers, but it also had an insatiable appetite for the written word as Puritans were encouraged to read Scripture and New Englanders generally enjoyed almost universal literacy. He could easily begin by printing small jobs, such as turning out sermons and pamphlets. James would know success if he eventually printed books or newspapers or was hired to print government records.

Back in 1704, John Campbell launched the town's first newspaper, the *Boston News-Letter.* It was primarily a compilation of republished news stories from Europe, but the publication was voraciously read aloud in taverns, coffeehouses, and homes nonetheless. Campbell also served as the town's postmaster, so he could distribute his books and papers for free. Unfortunately for him, he lost the postmaster job to William Brooker, who started a competing newspaper, the *Boston Gazette,* in 1719. James Franklin's timing was perfect, for the enterprising printer eagerly agreed to print the *Gazette* for Brooker, which also helped him to secure other lucrative printing jobs.

Josiah Franklin clearly saw that his son Benjamin was a bookish lad. Benjamin read his father's small collection of books that included John Bunyan's *Pilgrim's Progress,* Plutarch's classic *Lives,* several works on divinity, and some books on civic improvement, notably Daniel Defoe's *Essay on Projects* and interestingly Cotton Mather's *Essays to Do Good.* "All the little money that came into my hands was ever laid out in books," Benjamin wrote. He subsisted on a lean vegetarian diet of potatoes, rice, and handfuls of raisins for "an additional fund for buying books." He ate the small meals quickly in order to have more time for reading while his brother and friends seemingly frittered away their hours lounging at a table.

With such bookish inclinations, twelve-year-old Benjamin was apprenticed to his brother to learn the printer's craft when twenty-two-year-old James opened his shop. Benjamin bristled under what he considered an unfair contract and "stood out some time." The contract called for an unusually long nine-year indenture instead of the traditional seven, although the apprentice was to be given a journeyman's wages during his final year. Under pressure from his father to choose a career path, Benjamin "at last was persuaded" and signed the contract. James was to teach him printing and provide his brother with boarding. Benjamin had to submit to the will of his master and be a diligent worker. He bridled under his overbearing older brother.

The inquisitive reader put his hands on as many books as he could. He naturally struck up acquaintances with other printers' apprentices and had them furtively slip books to him from their masters' shops. "Often I sat up in my room reading the greatest part of the night when the book was borrowed in the evening and to be returned early in the morning lest it should be missed or wanted," Franklin wrote in his autobiography.

Benjamin trained his pen as well as his mind. He bought an odd volume of Joseph Addison and Richard Steele's *Spectator*. He was very much impressed by the writing style and sought to emulate it to improve his own. He read the words over and over with an eye to capture their structure and sentiment. He "laid them by a few days, and then without looking at the book," tried to depict the original style. The painstaking work of continually wrestling with his prose began to pay off, teaching him some "method in the arrangement of thoughts" and delighting in words. His talented and clever use of language would be employed in the coming months.

Franklin's youthful exuberance for the intellectual life led him to engage in disputations with some similarly inclined friends. Reading in logic and rhetoric as well as Xenophon taught him the Socratic method of argumentation. Some deistic thinkers also drew out his inherent skepticism and contrariness in their books. Thus armed for debate, he employed Socratic questioning to win arguments and embarrass his foes by forcing them to entangle themselves in concessions and lines of reasoning from which they could not extricate themselves.

The haughty young man learned in time that he was acting the gadfly and won arguments but rarely friends. He was becoming disagreeable, his combativeness "souring and spoiling the conversation, is productive of disgusts and perhaps enmities."

With growing maturity, Franklin resolved to practice the classical virtues of moderation and prudence in his speech. He began "expressing myself in terms of modest diffidence, never using when I advance anything that may possibly be disputed, the words, *certainty, undoubtedly,* or any others that give the air of positiveness to an opinion; but rather say, I *conceive,* or I *apprehend* a thing to be so and so, *it appears to me.*" This habit allowed him to persuade others affably. He might have taught his older brother the same lesson, but it would be some time before either Franklin habitualized such moderation into their characters.

The newspaper that the brothers were drying and cutting that hot August day was decidedly not an example of prudent and cautious judgment. In an age when printers wanted to win profitable government printing contracts and truth was not a defense in trials for libel, most newspapers were relatively dull affairs with a few pages of international news from the empire, shipping data, advertisements, and a smattering of local announcements. James sought to break free of this mold and publish a strikingly original newspaper driven by antiestablishment fervor.

The inoculation controversy provided a context for him to jump blindly into the fray. As the printer and editor of the *New England Courant,* he let loose the dogs of war on Zabdiel Boylston and Cotton Mather, who came in as special targets for heaps of abuse. The anti-inoculation forces gained an important ally and forum in their struggle. Neither James nor his prolific brother left any clue as to why they launched this particular crusade. Perhaps James had picked up a bit of irreverence from his cosmopolitan London printer colleagues and friends; perhaps he wanted to break the mold of stodgy newspapers; perhaps he wanted a bit of fame and fortune. Whatever his motivation, his brash attacks rent the social fabric in Boston and in many ways drove a stake in the heart of the Puritan mission and covenant.

On August 7, copies of the first edition of the *Courant* were sold and distributed by the printer's apprentice even while more and more houses held new victims of smallpox. James Franklin invited some friends and Dr. William Douglass to write pieces lampooning the ministers and Dr. Boylston. The more brazenly impertinent, the better. His friend John Cheekley concluded his piece with a cheeky rhyme: "Who like faithful shepherds take care of their flocks, by teaching and practicing what's orthodox, / Pray hard against sickness, yet preach up the Pox!"

Douglass lost all sense of personal and professional propriety and launched a vicious attack. He scoffed at Boylston for being "the bold undertaker of the practice of the Greek old women." Douglass then pounced on the ministers for meddling in medical affairs. "Six gentlemen of piety and learning, profoundly ignorant of the matter, after serious consideration of a disease one of the most intricate practical cases in physick, do on the merits of their characters, and for no other reason." They should stick with preaching and attending to people's spiritual needs, which they were trained to do—never mind that he freely expressed his religious opinions. By getting involved in the medical controversy, the ministers were foolishly opening themselves up to criticism. "I think their character ought to be sacred, and that they themselves ought not to give the least occasion to have it called into question," Douglass advised. When the ministers praised Boylston and commented on his professional qualifications with lavish praise, Douglass thought it was a joke. "At first reading of this composure, many were persuaded that it was only a piece of humor, banter, burlesque, or ridicule on the inoculator." Less funny was the danger that Boylston was exposing to the community because he was not "proceeding farther to consider seriously the evidences of its dismal consequences."

Another piece in the opening edition of this "opposition" newspaper was a biting satire of inoculation. Because all that inoculation was perceived to do by its enemies was to spread smallpox, a writer cruelly offered that it might be a very effective way to kill Indians on the frontier. Reading of a planned expedition against the Indians and the inoculations, the writer put the two "together in the same apartment of my brain, and by next morning formed themselves into the following project: 'A Project for reducing the Eastern Indians by Inoculation.'" The Puritan soldiers would be "completely armed with incision-lancet, Pandora's Box, Nut-Shell, and Fillet," and led by "General Timonius." The volunteers would be allotted their usual pay, travel expenses, and "a gratuity of 10 Pounds per head of each Indian who survives, conveys, and spreads the infection amongst his tribe, and of 5 pounds per head for those who blow up too soon (or die) before they reach the places where execution is intended." Either way, the inoculated soldiers were a great danger to the natives. In an undisguised attack on the imprudent implementation of the procedure in the summer when the blood humor was "hot," the expedition would set out during that season so as to produce the greatest number of deaths among the enemy. "Ours shall be in summer as in all probability like to do the most execution in that season." This sarcastic piece openly mocked inoculation and its practitioners, containing a not-so-subtle warning that they were spreading the disease to Bostonians.

In the same edition, James printed a poem "On the Distress of the Town of Boston, occasioned by the Smallpox." Although it generally related the suffering of the people in verse, it took a few underhanded swipes at the authorities who were not acting judiciously during the epidemic.

> Long had the rulers prudent care
> (Which Heaven kind vouchsaf'd to bless)
> From quick infection kept the air,
> And sav'd the town from deep distress.
> But cursed sin with rapid feet,
> And quicker flight spread thro' the town,
> Taints every soul in every street,

And calls the hov'ring vengeance down.
Endeavors now no more succeed,
Tho' justice long had shook the rod;
Our crying sins for vengeance plead,
And dare to blows an angry God.
Repeated deaths the town within,
With fearful crowds the country fill;
Some with their fear th' infection bring,
And only shun the doctor's skill.
Ye Pious father mourn the loss
Of youths, whose undisguised truth
Copy'd your own; who did engross
An age of virtue in their youth.
Sinners secure you peace with God,
Accept your Savior's kind relief;
Nor let your guilt (a heavy load)
Oppress you with unbounded grief.
Saints are secure of life above
And only mourn the sinners doom:
They know their Savior's dying love
Will save them here, or call them home.

The poem was not perceived to be an innocent piece of doggerel that poked fun at Boylston, Mather, and their allies. They considered the pieces in the *Courant* to be gratuitous attacks upon their authority. They expected deference and were met by jeers and condemnation at every turn. The criticisms would get a lot more vicious in the ensuing months. They only provoked Mather to push back harder and climb into the gutter in a malicious war of words.

Chapter Ten

FOR AND AGAINST INOCULATION

The late autumn and early winter was a time of publication for a great many pamphlets as well as numerous editions of three newspapers in which a host of arguments were made for and against inoculation. On the surface, all this print was evidence of a lively and open debate in an outpost of free English society. The broadsides were addressed to a literate and educated Puritan audience who had been taught to read and encouraged to critically analyze what they read. The respective sides in the debate sought to persuade their readers and win over public opinion.

Many issues were freely raised in the public forum whether people had expertise or not in this intellectual free-for-all in an age before academic specialization. Orthodox Puritan beliefs were put on trial and employed by both sides in the dispute. Rival interpretations of Scripture filled the pages of the publications. Writers engaged the medical issues as they related to spiritual matters as well as scientific merit. Other peoples such as Muslims and Africans were drawn into the debate by both sides, though not given a voice in it. The arguments formulated by each faction shaped a debate that often took bewildering turns that confounded expectations.

Underlying the overt issues was the basis of authority in colonial Massachusetts. Popular will and rules laid down by the representative government were frequently ignored during the public crisis. Medical authority was another contested area engaged in freely by practitioners, ministers, and laymen alike. Above all, the public authority of the clergy on matters of religion and generally as respected leaders of the community was called into question. The Satanic furies and clamors that Cotton Mather continually alluded to in his diary and other writings were proof that the disputants were able to stir up a great deal of controversy and division that in the end only worked to undermine authority in Puritan Boston.

Unfortunately, the serious and fruitful debate that might have occurred descended into personal attacks, invective, rivalries, and name-calling. James Franklin and Dr. William Douglass succeeded in a withering attack upon Mather and the other ministers. Meanwhile, Mather became reactionary and adamantly demanded obedience to his position rather than offer evidence of successful inoculations. However, Mather and Zabdiel Boylston were not the only ones dueling with words, and others entered the debate. Printers who rolled off sheets in Boston and London seemed to be the only winners.

Few other incidents in the history of the colony offered such striking evidence of the breakdown of the social covenant. No public opinion polls were taken to show how many people were for or against inoculation. But it became obvious that the social covenant was in tatters and arguably dead.

The opponents of inoculation argued that its supporters and practitioners were outrageously and deliberately infecting healthy people with the disease. Contrary to reason, healthy people were made sick. John Williams, a person who dispensed tobacco and other home remedies for illness, wrote a pamphlet against inoculation because he knew someone who had died of it. He demanded to know how one was supposed to "save life, by giving death for it." It was a "very dear" and ill-advised bargain. "Suppose the bloody flux [dysentery] prevail in the town where I live, and a physician goes to one of their houses, and takes a bottle of that fluxical, bloody excrement and puts it into a man, and gives him the bloody flux, which whosoever takes, is delivered in an ordinary way from the danger of that distemper," he reasoned, arguing it would be remarkably imprudent to believe and foolish to attempt. With mocking humor, Williams stated, "Sir, your argument do stink."

Williams blamed the procedure for contributing to the severity of the epidemic in Boston. He declared, "By inoculation, the smallpox hath been carried and spread almost if not quite over this town." Greater mortality was the result of inoculating patients and was supposedly provable by Galenic medicine. The fevers of smallpox were supposed to rage in the hot spring and summer, but the epidemic took the most lives during the cool months of October and November. "In the hot weather, even in the dog days, there were few [who] died, when inoculation was little in use; but since inoculation hath been much in use the weather hath been more temperate, neither hot nor cold (which I know is best for that distemper) yet the mortality hath much increased." He argued that if the dangerous procedure had not continued, the virus would have expired and hundreds of lives would have been saved.

Without examining the evidence by visiting patients and recording their reactions, the opponents simply fabricated facts that the patients suffered more extreme forms of smallpox. Getting smallpox in the common way was described as an almost benevolent experience in which the virus "grows gradually, [and] dies gradually."

Compared with this, inoculation was a "different malignity." The incision was the sight of the terrible "putrefication," and victims had just as many pustules and were just as sick as the common way. The smell of the disease was "worse than ever they smelled it elsewhere." It was "more raw and contrary unto nature, and penetrating on the organs of the body of man." The conclusion was inescapable: smallpox inoculation was a deadly and virulent practice that needlessly and recklessly put "many in the grave."

Mather, Boylston, and their allies spread the disease contrary to the law and without anyone's consent but their own will. An anonymous author warned: "One single apothecary, without consent of his brethren, without asking the civil power, without consent of the neighbors; yea, against their fears, their cries, and clamors, to infect his family with a disease very mortal and very contagious!" For such transgressions of common sense and the law, they deserved to hang from the gallows at the town gate, as would any murderers. "To spread a mortal contagion, what is it but to cast abroad arrows and death? If a man should willfully throw a bomb into a town, burn a house, or kill a man, ought he not to die? So if a man should willfully bring infection from a person sick of a deadly and contagious disease, into a place of health, is not the mischief as great?"

Many were afraid not only of Boylston's currently spreading smallpox and taking lives but what would happen in the future. Instead of immunizing the population against a future outbreak, antagonists claimed that no one knew exactly what the results would be. Unforeseen consequences would result with horrifying effects no one could predict. Inoculation, it was claimed, could facilitate the spread of additional diseases. "Two or three years hence you will see the dreadful effects of this wicked practice; you'll see what happens to the people that are under it," they warned ominously.

Opponents claimed that the practitioners were meddling with

forces they did not understand, which was essentially true. Boylston, Mather, and doctors outside of Europe around the globe (and in later centuries) did not understand why inoculation worked. They just knew that it did. The opponents would have none of this, arguing that it was a deadly failure.

Against this litany of criticisms, Mather, Boylston, and their allies presented evidence of inoculation's efficacy. They had to admit that they were "yet but learners." The experiment was being successfully tested and confirmed the previous findings in scientific journals. They invited other doctors to observe the procedures, and their results were openly published. Although they did not have the support of thousands of documented trials to bolster their case, it seemed to them "beyond all doubt that they who have had it once thus in this way are as well secured from having it again." In other words, the patients had acquired an immunity.

Mather openly stated that the practitioners could not explain the underlying reasons, but those that were inoculated endured the smallpox infection "more safe and easy than that of the common way." The procedure was performed in admittedly the "worst season of the year" and on a variety of persons—"old and young, on strong and weak, on male and female, on white and black"—and none of these factors produced different results.

The supporters used an analogy for reasons they believed made it work. "The smallpox, being admitted in the way of inoculation, their approaches are made only by the outworks of the citadel, and at a considerable distance from it. The enemy, 'tis true, gets in so far as to make some spoil, even so much as to satisfy him, and leave no prey in the body of the patient, for him ever afterwards to seize upon, but the vital powers are kept so clear from his assaults, that they can manage the combat bravely." And if the theory of animalcules were true, "there is less of metaphor in our account than may be at first imagined."

Their opponents even called into question the entire Enlightenment and scientific revolution. The dawn of an age of reason and discovery was not as great as its proponents believed. John Williams mocked: "Sir, you say, our age is favored with a wonderful…discovery, more worth than a world! What world do you mean, sir, that which is in the moon?"

This line of reasoning was anathema to Cotton and Increase Mather, Boylston, and other Puritans who celebrated the Age of Reason and the dawn of the new science. Several defenders hailed the new discoveries of science as a gift from God. "Every age of the world produces some new and useful discoveries…. And if this discovery be reserved for our day, why should it not be accepted in all places with all thankfulness. In a word, I cannot but think its original derived elsewhere because my Bible teaches me that every good and perfect gift comes down from the Father of Lights."

In a stunning contradictory admission, one opposing writer stated that the efficacy of the procedure was irrelevant. Its success was beside the point. That was merely a utilitarian argument that argued the ends justified the means. "The question is not," John Williams asserted, "whether it may save their lives or not." Rather what mattered was "whether it may be lawful." Inoculation, its enemies argued, violated God's natural law and revealed word in Scripture.

Douglass and his allies were not men of science battling the forces of religious dogma with experimental proofs. They referred to Scripture and God's will in fighting their opponents on religious grounds. Although the ministers were specially trained to understand and expound upon the complexities of Scripture, it is also true that Puritans believed the meaning of the Bible was so plain as to be readily understood by any person of reason. Therefore it was quite natural for laypersons and scientists to have religious grounds for their arguments against inoculation.

For Puritans, the Bible was the inspired word of God that revealed his will. As Protestants, they accepted the central tenet of *sola scriptura,* that the Bible was the only source of authority for Christians. They constantly cited Scripture in any disputation, including a debate over a medical practices. Generally, the opponents of inoculation asserted that the practice was not in the Bible and therefore not to be countenanced. "If there is no rule in the word of God to found inoculation upon, then it is not according to his will." Inoculation was not mentioned in the Bible, but passages could still be assembled against it. It was held to be a "horrid violation" of Matthew 9:12, "They that are whole need not a physician, but they that are sick." Implicitly, inoculation breached one of the basic rules of the Hippocratic oath to "do no harm." Besides, the power of healing was held to be the monopoly of the Lord's as shown in Deuteronomy 32:39: "I kill, and give life; I wound, and I make whole." The fact that the passage seemed to negate having any physicians at all was passed over.

The opponents did not only refer to the authority of Scripture, they averred that inoculation violated natural law. God was sovereign over all things, and all that happened was done according to his will. The smallpox epidemic was a sign of God's disfavor, whether he punished Boston or allowed the devil to run amok. It was an unmistakable sign from heaven—a "special providence"—that the inoculators were seeking to avoid. "Question One. Whether the smallpox be not one of the strange works of God," one pamphleteer queried, "and whether inoculation of it be not a fighting with the most high, and a vying with the Holy One of Israel?" They were like the "Pharaoh's magicians who did works of wonders with their rods." Their hardened hearts would surely "bring greater judgments upon them till he had consumed them." Averting the stroke of smallpox through inoculation would provoke the Almighty into greater punishments.

The right answer would be to trust in the Lord and his judgments. Humility and meekness, not pride, were the true postures to hold in the face of divine wrath. The inoculators should join the rest of the population in sinking to their knees and pleading for God's mercies instead of defying his will. One writer penned an appropriate prayer: "Lord, we have sinned, and are afraid of the judgments which are out against us. Say unto thy destroying Angel, it is enough. Stay now thine hand. Lord, if it be thy holy will, let not this sore disease spread further among us!"

Satan and his minions had tricked the fools into following their vanity and acting like God. Inoculation was a "delusion of Satan" and a "temptation from the Devil," by which men were sinning. The procedure was known by its fruits, and it bore "every evil work—strife, hatred, back-biting, and lying." Another noted that the "lawless, unguarded" practice had invited a "state of war, sin, and contention" that rent the social fabric of Boston. It divided covenanted churches against themselves. The punishment would be even greater for God's chosen people, who were "called by God's name" to obedience. Violating the covenant would anger a "jealous God." If Bostonians "walk contrary to God, so God walks contrary to us."

The opponents conceded that it was lawful to prevent the spread of smallpox through natural means, such as quarantine or posting guards at people's doors. The problem, John Williams explained, was that inoculation was an "artificial purge to stop a natural plague." The opponents of inoculation did not elaborate on how both sought to stem the advance of the disease and hinder God's judgment, but only one was lawful.

The supporters of inoculation answered that these charges blasphemously violated the divine will. Cotton Mather probably had a hand in writing a *Vindication of the Ministers* in early 1722 in which the authors wrote that it was "very strange and ridiculous to see the satirists play the divine" with their "saucy" and ill-informed religious arguments. They referred to Scripture occasionally in framing their rationale but generally argued according to their understanding of Providence and natural law. They contented themselves with arguing that their enemies were engaged in a "gross abuse" of God's holy word, as Mather wrote in another pamphlet.

The defenders thanked God for the good providence that was granted. Christians should "humbly give thanks to God for his good Providence in discovering to it to a miserable world." Why could they not "lawfully make use of the best human help the Providence of God affords them?" they wondered. They were hardly deluded by Satan because he could not produce good. "If it be a method of safety and a benefit to mankind, as hitherto it appears to be, how came the Devil to be the author of it? Was he ever a benefactor to mankind? No. But he is a murderer from the beginning."

There was consensus among the Puritans that smallpox was sent as a desolating judgment against sin. But the supporters of inoculation conceived that God was working through the secondary causes of nature with this special Providence rather than directly with his hand. Humans could thus use natural methods to relieve the suffering and death among them. The key point of this argument was to see that God had sent a righteous punishment against his chosen people but was now mercifully delivering them with the discovery of a cure. In addition, the Puritan God had predestined the course of everyone's life and determined whether they would be eternally saved or damned—and inoculation could be part of that plan. God decided "how long we shall live, [and] has also determined that by such and such means our lives shall be continued to that period of time. And how does anyone know but this is to be the appointed means of their preservation in life?"

Faithful Christians were to submit to God's will and trust in the Lord. The inoculators maintained that they firmly surrendered to that will, just like the farmers in the fields. "What is there of the hand or power of man in this work, after the incision is made, and the matter applied? The work is still left with God, and we must wait upon him for his actual influence and blessing, even as the husbandman does for the rain and sunshine of heaven after the seed is thrown into the earth."

Their adversaries would deny the omnipotence of the Almighty. "As to the divinity, they would limit God in his blessing of some one or other particular part or particle of his lower creation, used by the physician or surgeon to prevent, moderate, alter, or cure a disease in their patient." They were accused of breaking the law and deserving death as murderers, but the opponents would be the ones who would answer for their position. "What will they have to answer for, that by their menaces and outrages put a stop to such a general benefit?" Their judge would not be the General Court, but God who granted the remedy.

More modestly, the inoculators argued that Christian physicians had combated illness lawfully for centuries. Their foes were Christians and physicians themselves who regularly healed sickness without scruple. They utilized bloodletting, sweats, purges, Jesuits' Bark or cinchona, Spanish flies, powder of toads, salivations, tooth extractions, cold baths, and any number of remedies to stave off or cure disease. But there was "nobody so impertinent as to call this a tempting of Providence." Moreover, many thousands had in fact died from these cures, yet they continued, while smallpox inoculation was savaged by its enemies. "To bring sickness upon one's self for its own sake," Mather's allies argued, "as may probably serve my health and save my life…is certainly fitting and reasonable, and therefore lawful."

The inoculators were shocked that their antagonists believed that people should forgo the procedure and wait and watch while their neighbors sickened and died of smallpox in the common way. Expecting God to grant them an "extraordinary preservation" was nothing short of "presumption" and put the Lord to the test.

As if it were not bad enough that the inoculators violated the will of God and introduced a dangerous innovation, the knowledge of inoculation had been acquired from Africans and Muslims—both seen as heathens by the Puritans. The anti-inoculators made blatantly racist arguments in disparaging these groups as much as their fallacious theories and erroneous practices. The Africans who shared their knowledge of inoculation from their homeland were ridiculed as "the good people of Guinea," "those judicious people called Africans," and "African gentlemen." Dr. Douglass disreputably held the greatest scorn for Africans: "There is not a race of men on earth more false liars, etc." He wondered why they had not previously shared their knowledge and why it was "never depended upon till now for argument's sake." He believed them to be a blundering and inferior race of men who were deceptive by nature.

Douglass continued his attack on Africans and their gullible minister. He stated: "You have at length in two of their little books a silly story or familiar interview and conversation between two black gentlemen and a couple of the reverend promoters, concerning inoculation. O rare farce!" He went on to deride Mather for following "an army of half a dozen or half a score Africans, by others called

Negro slaves." The same credulous minister argued that Africans had an equal soul and were children of God.

The opponents of inoculation disdained Muslims as much as Africans, calling the Muslims the "faithful people of the prophet Mahomet," "Turks and pagans," and "heathens." A medical innovation that saved lives was suspect and rejected because it came from heathens. The "Mahometan missionaries" were duped by the heathens to spread mischief and death. To show how much the inoculators were tricked by the devil, they listened to the "history of other places" and learned "the manners of the heathen" and scorned Scripture as the true source of knowledge.

Cotton Mather and Zabdiel Boylston based their daring venture in large part on the information provided by Africans. The Puritans open-mindedly defended learning truths from any reasonable people, whether Africans, Indians, or pagans of any stripe. God even taught the other peoples knowledge that he had not shared with Christian Europeans, even his chosen people. "A merciful God has taught [Africans] a wonderful preservative." Mather stated, "I don't know why 'tis more unlawful to learn of Africans how to help against the poison of the smallpox, than it is to learn of our Indians how to help against the poison of a rattle-snake." In his eyes, both were perfectly acceptable.

Was it unlawful for Puritans to learn from heathens, as Douglass and his friends accused? Mather retorted with a series of rhetorical questions: "I inquire, whether our Hippocrates were not a heathen? And whether our Galen were not a heathen? And whether we have not our Mithradate from the heathen? And whether the first inventor of our Treacle were not Nero's physician? And whether we have not learnt some of our very good medicines from our Indians?" Douglass would have to give up his practice if he could not employ all the knowledge he learned from heathens while studying at prestigious European universities.

Simple personal attacks and name-calling rounded out the opponents' critiques. The rival substantive medical and religious arguments became a contending battle of wits to see who could spew the most venomous tirades. Both sides called the other liars. The people who practiced inoculation were "very foolish and very wicked." Mather was a "peevish mongrel" and compared to "dunghill cocks." He was even called a "baboon." When Sammy Mather recovered and jumped into the war of words to defend his father, he was called an "ill-bred school boy" and "a young scribbling collegian" who was a "chip off the old block." Cotton Mather said that James Franklin and his cronies were members of a "Hell-Fire Club" that praised the devil. Williams was a "sorry tobacconist, who could barely spell a word of English."

Cotton and Increase Mather, Zabdiel Boylston, William Douglass, James Franklin, and Benjamin Franklin were some of the public figures who took sides in the war of words over inoculation. Although there was a public side to their debates, it masks the personal anguish they all experienced in the controversy. In the midst of the public anguish over inoculation and smallpox, Cotton Mather wrestled with his personal angst about his own children, their illnesses, and whether to risk their lives on the medical innovation he so desperately sought to introduce.

Chapter Eleven

"MY DYING CHILDREN"

Cotton Mather was an embattled man in early August. The Selectmen had voted against the practice he knew would save lives. The doctors of the town followed the opposition led by Dr. William Douglass, who also overtly insulted the minister. The people were raging against Mather, and now that upstart and disrespectful pup abused him publicly in the pages of the *Courant*.

But it was more than public vilification that aggravated the minister. He had the burden of his official duties, writing and delivering sermons that called on members of different churches to examine their souls in the face of death. He consoled bereaved, crying parents, trying to assuage their grief. Meanwhile, his own children needed him during this desperate hour.

Mather spent many hours in his study, not rubbing his eyes and sore temples while he took a short respite from the cares of the world, but rather fasting and laying on the floor, pleading with the Almighty for strength.

On August 1, his son Sammy entered his father's study and

sat down. He was a bright young fellow and followed the heated controversy in print and conversation. His father was the main proponent of inoculation and had probably explained how it worked. Moreover, the North neighborhood where they resided had been the scene of "no less than ten remarkable experiments." Because his son lacked a natural immunity to smallpox, Mather undoubtedly wondered when this day would come. Probably with tears in his eyes and a broken voice, the young man begged his father "to have his life saved by receiving the smallpox in the way of inoculation." Mastering his quivering voice, Sammy expressed his fear of dying. His father comforted him, prayed, and told him he would think over the matter.

Mather considered the request in the solitude of his study. Of course he did not want to lose another of his beloved children. He wondered, "If he should after all die by receiving it in the common way, how can I answer it?"

Although his son feared for his life, Mather could not help thinking of his leadership position and how he would be perceived in Boston. "On the other side, our people, who have Satan remarkably filling their hearts and their tongues, will go on with infinite prejudices against me and my ministry, if I suffer this operation upon the child." This argument showed Mather's courage in the debate at its nadir. He was frightened for several reasons and responded in a very human way. But there was another side to the argument. Zabdiel Boylston had initially inoculated his own son and since performed it on two of his other sons. Indeed, the anger against Mather might even be mitigated if he were to have Sammy inoculated, because people would see that Mather was not just a minister blathering in the abstract about some new medical procedure. Nevertheless, although he cared for his son very much, he could not help thinking of his own reputation: "If I should suffer this operation upon the child, and be sure, if he should happen to miscarry under it, my condition would be insupportable."

It was all too much for Mather to decide on his own, and he sought the counsel of his sagacious father, Increase. When he brought the matter to the aged minister, Increase thought it over for a few moments and then advised his son to "bring the lad into this method of safety." But he understood his son's fears about the consequences of the treatment failing and urged Mather to "keep the whole proceeding private." That middle way allowed him to save Sammy's life and deflect any criticism, at least for a time, for Sammy's death would be a very public one and would arouse intense public comment. Still, Cotton remained undecided, complaining in a resigned manner to his diary, "I know not what to do." He looked heavenward and prayed for answers.

Mather mulled over this thorny dilemma for several miserable days, yet the answers did not come. He persisted in prayer and avoided a rash decision. Of course, that was little comfort to Sammy, whose panic mounted with every reported new case of smallpox in the neighborhood.

Mather set aside August 4 for more "secret supplications" in his study. He cried to heaven "for the lives of my children," but he did not gain any divine assistance. Four days later, he prayed the same question: "What further shall I do for my Samuel?" Still, he was uncertain and settled for praying "that he may be prepared for what is every day to be looked for!" With his children, kinsmen, and parishioners worried about their mortal lives, the Puritan minister encouraged them to seek the transcendent.

At some point, Mather relented to his son's wishes and had him inoculated. By August 15, Mather wrote in his diary, "My dear Sammy is now under the operation of receiving the smallpox in the way of transplantation." He explained his reasoning: "The success of the experiment among my neighbors, as well as abroad in the world, and the urgent calls of his grandfather have made me think that I could not answer it unto God if I neglected it. At this critical time, how much is all piety to be pressed upon the child!"

Sammy was at risk of dying and very relieved to be undergoing the procedure. His desire to receive the treatment was confirmed (although he was greatly saddened) when he learned that his college roommate had died that day of smallpox "taken in the common way." Mather had great confidence in the procedure and hopes for its success. Curiously, Dr. Boylston was not the physician who transplanted the *variola* into the incision on Sammy's arm or tended him.

When Sammy became feverish as expected on August 22, Mather could not dispel his anxiety about the personal ramifications of his son's death: "If he should miscarry, besides the loss of so hopeful a son, I should also suffer a prodigious clamor and hatred from an infuriated mob, whom the Devil has inspired with a most hellish rage on this occasion." He set aside his selfish inclinations to pray for his son's recovery "accompanied with suitable instructions to the child" about his soul.

If Mather merely was concerned for the survival of his son, it would have been burden enough. But his hyperbolic representation of division in Boston reached biblical proportions: "The town is become almost a Hell upon earth, a city full of lies, and murders, and blasphemies, as far as wishes and speeches can render it so. Satan seems to take a strange possession of it in the epidemic rage." He wondered what he could do to exorcise the demon from the city. "What besides prayer with fasting for it?" he wondered. The answer came quickly this time: he thought that assisting Boylston in publishing an account of the successful inoculations would pacify the outcry.

Significantly, the minister conceded that his private religious supplications had not thus far achieved the ends he wanted. Nor was his diminishing and beleaguered ministerial authority enough to calm everyone's fears. His last resort was to produce scientific evidence to prove to the doubting Thomases that inoculation was the best course of action against the epidemic.

Meanwhile, Sammy was not doing well. The anxious father went in often to see his son and pray by his bedside. It was a "time of unspeakable trouble and anguish" for Mather. Sammy had many more pustules than expected—or at least it seemed so to a worried father. His fever was much higher than reported in any of the other subjects. "The eruption proceeds, and he proves pretty full, and has not the best sort, and some degree of his fever holds him. His condition is very hazardous," Mather wrote on August 25.

Sammy did not improve, and his father was gripped by fear. "The condition of my son Samuel is very singular." Mather blamed the doctor, believing that the "inoculation was very imperfectly performed." Perhaps Mather was duped by Boylston's success and his own enthusiastic promotion of inoculation that no one would die. He was now personally confronting the dangers of a risky medical innovation.

During the next evening, Sammy's fever rose to a "height which distressed us all." The patient was agitated and delirious. They obliged his demands to be bled, but it did not provide immediate relief. Mather flew into his study the following day for hours of prayer and supplications while he fasted. He prayed for faith while his family was "threatened with desolations."

By September 5, Sammy was on the mend and recovering his strength. His father was certainly relieved that the young man's physical survival was ensured. Mather undoubtedly offered prayers of thanksgiving to God. However, with his son now safe, Mather again raised the issue of Sammy's eternal self. He prayed that Sammy may "come gold out of the fire" and sought guidance from above on what he should do, "that Sammy in his new life may live unto God?" Mather sought to guide Sammy's conversion experience to which God and the Puritan faith called him.

But Cotton Mather was not out of the woods quite yet. As Sammy was recovering from his induced bout with smallpox, his sisters—twenty-seven-year-old Abigail and twenty-five-year-old Hannah—were deathly ill with unknown maladies.

On lecture day, Thursday, September 7, Mather wrote a sermon entitled "The Wonders Attending Our Sacrifices," for that very day was "a time of sacrifices" for the beleaguered minister and father. He preached on Judges 13:19–20. The following words resonated with him as he considered his family's condition:

> Then Manoah took a kid with a meat offering, and offered it upon a stone unto the Lord: and the Angel did wondrously, while Manoah and his wife looked on. For when the flame came up toward heaven from the altar, the Angel of the Lord ascended up in the flame of the altar, and Manoah and his wife beheld it, and fell on their faces unto the ground.

Mather was stricken with fear for the safety of Abigail and Hannah. The 1703 smallpox epidemic had given them immunity, but both were now ill, which added significantly to their father's worries. Although smallpox was directly affecting the town, there were any number of other mortal diseases that could strike anyone at any time.

The sisters enjoyed very different circumstances. Hannah (or Nancy as she was known) was unmarried, probably due to the fact that she had fallen into a fireplace as a toddler, which disfigured her face and right side. She had survived a variety of other illnesses, such as a bowel ailment and a bout with the measles during a 1713 outbreak. As a single woman, she remained in her father's home, sharing responsibility for its upkeep especially when he was widowed for a time. Puritans frowned on single people residing alone, for they would be more easily tempted to fall into sin. It was particularly rare for women to live alone and not fall under the patriarchal care of a male family member.

Abigail, nicknamed Nibby, had married attorney Daniel Willard only a month after her widower father had remarried in 1715. She likely never moved into Mather's new home on Ship Street but lived nearby with her husband. She presented her father with his first grandchild, a daughter, the following year. Unlike Nancy, who did not expect to bear children, Nibby was pregnant again during the summer of 1721. She was uncomfortable carrying the child in the summer heat and shared her motherly concerns on more than one occasion with her husband about their children catching smallpox. The disease did not imperil her life, but childbirth in colonial Massachusetts was a dangerous endeavor even in normal times.

Childbirth was one of the central experiences of women's lives. The natural rhythms of pregnancy and lactation meant that they generally bore children every twenty-four to thirty months. Roughly 3 percent (and possibly more) of women died in childbirth, the risk increasing with every delivery. Almost one in four children died immediately at birth, and the chances of surviving until their first birthday was a mere one in two. Puritan women believed that Eve was made to suffer the travails of childbirth for her sin and experienced those pangs. But they concurrently felt great joy at birthing a baby and fulfilling their God-appointed and natural maternal role.

Her pregnancy progressed smoothly into August, and Nibby expected the support of a network of women—including Nancy—to help with the delivery. Unfortunately, disaster struck toward the end of the month. On August 25, Mather reported, "I have other children also at this time, sick and weak and languishing, and in my affliction." Pregnant Nibby had a "violent fever upon her, which extremely threatens her life." Her husband could not tend her because he was "not only languishing under an unknown fever, but also grown delirious with it." Meanwhile, Nancy was "very hazardously circumstanced with several infirmities" of an unknown nature.

Mather prayed for them as well as himself. His emotions were strained by the prodigious tests of the Lord: "My Savior seems to multiply very many and heavy loads at once upon me. Oh! May he help me to carry it well under them! Oh! May my carriage yield him a grateful spectacle!" The burden would only get worse over the next few weeks, making him feel like Job.

On the first of September, as Sammy was hovering near death, Mather cried for his "two dying daughters!" He dramatically howled for "dear Nancy, in the very jaws of death!" He again lamented his current lot: "My God keeps my faith in continual exercise!"

Mather spent his days praying in his study and attending to bedridden Nancy. On September 3 the distraught father watched as physicians examined her and told him that "she has not many hours to live." Scripture and prayer was his only refuge. He found the strength to preach twice that Sunday, choosing Matthew 9:2 for himself, his daughter, and his congregation: "And lo, they brought to him a man sick of the palsy lying on a bed. And Jesus seeing their faith, said to the sick of the palsy, Son be of good comfort; thy sins are forgiven thee."

Nancy's body valiantly fought off her ailments, and her soul was succored by her father's prayers. She faded for three more days but did not give in. Her father tried to stand up under the pressure:

"I am called unto repeated sacrifices. I must go through the duty of a sacrificer. But shall I not exhibit unto the people of God, the conduct of a sacrificer, in such a manner that my trials may be made useful to my neighbors?"

Mather donned his flowing robes and skullcap for the Thursday lecture that evening and preached from the book of Judges. Nancy miraculously recovered on the next day. "To our surprise this day," Mather wrote, "Dear Nancy revives, and her fever breaks and gives us hopes that she may yet return unto us." She was enfeebled but recuperated slowly alongside Sammy. The story was very different with Nibby, who was at that moment "still dangerously circumstanced."

On the Sabbath, September 10, Mather persisted in preaching on healing miracles from the Bible to remind his congregation that physical and spiritual cleansing were at hand. He chose the healing of the centurion's servant from the eighth chapter of the Gospel of Matthew:

When Jesus was entered into Capernaum, there came unto him a Centurion, beseeching him,
And said, "Master, my servant lieth sick at home of the palsy, and is greviously pained."
And Jesus said unto him, "I will come and heal him."
But the Centurion answered, saying, "Master, I am not worthy that thou shouldest come under my roof, but speak the word only, and my servant shall be healed."
"For I am a man also under the authority of another, and have soldiers under me; and I say to one, 'Go,' and he goeth, and to another, 'Come,' and he cometh, and to my servant, 'Do this,' and he doeth it."
When Jesus heard that, he marveled, and said to them that followed him, "Verily I say unto you, I have not found so great faith, even in Israel."

The pregnant Nibby's condition did not improve. In her weakened state, she prematurely delivered a daughter on Sunday, September 17. Having prepared symbolically named "groaning beer" and "groaning cakes" beforehand to sustain her guests, she sent her husband to fetch a midwife and six or seven of her closest intimates, including her healthy sister Nancy, to attend her for her first contractions, when she "grew smart." At this point, Daniel Willard would have been excluded from the female dominion and made to get supplies and wait nervously.

Male physicians such as William Douglass and Zabdiel Boylston were also absent from any stage of the delivery. Male doctors would assume control over obstetrics during a later period of history. For now, midwives were respected for their wealth of experience rather than their specialized learning. Friends and family who had borne children rounded out the community of women present at births to offer emotional support. Even though Nancy did not have any children of her own, she had been present at previous childbirths and offered the knowing support that Daniel could not.

The women encouraged Nibby to eat something light and walk a bit, but she was too weak. Herbal remedies passed down through tradition were provided to ease her contractions. When she was ready to deliver the baby, she either sat in the lap of another woman or squatted on a "midwife's stool" and leaned back into the arms of her attendants. Her moans and screams were much more muted and resigned than normal. After the baby girl was born amid relief and celebration, a lactating female nursed her newborn as was common. There were a number of interesting superstitions associated with the umbilical cord: a short one on males would lead to certain sexual inadequacies and a long one on females would breed immodesty. The women in this case were focused on Nibby and the baby's health.

Childbirth was dangerous enough to mother and child without a smallpox epidemic raging in the community. The prognosis for Nibby and her baby would have been grim if she had smallpox. More than half the babies born at this late stage of pregnancy would have been stillborn, and if they survived childbirth, half of those would die within a few days. Moreover, there was a high risk that the child would develop virulent hemorrhagic smallpox—the most deadly type—which was usually lethal. Fortunately, Nibby was immune, and so her child averted a deadly case of smallpox in the womb. However, once born, her daughter was now susceptible because the malicious *variola* was merciless toward the vulnerable very young and very old.

Her illness and childbirth exhausted the last of Nibby's reserves. "My lovely Nibby, who was delivered of a daughter on the Lord's Day, is now in dying circumstances," Mather observed. The female network cared for the infant while the physicians now cared for the mother. Mather visited his daughter's home every day and rarely left her side. Around Boston, the mothers were rarely absent from the bedsides of the thousands of sick.

While funeral bells tolled and the aggressive debate over inoculation raged between physicians, ministers, and printers, the housewives and mothers throughout Boston quietly tended their patients shut away inside their homes. The strained physicians of the town, when they were not engaged in recriminations and actually saw their patients, were simply too burdened by the sheer numbers of the ailing that they could not visit everyone.

The critical role that mothers and wives played as healers during the 1721 smallpox epidemic was an invisible one that was never recorded. It was so common in every home as to escape mention by diarists, correspondents, and recorders of the outbreak and inoculation controversy. But they showed that their understanding of the humors, caring bedside manner, purges, and herbal remedies were Galenic medical practices that were virtually indistinguishable from the male physicians of the town, even the university-educated Dr. William Douglass. The common story of the 1721 smallpox inoculation controversy centers on the men involved and generally ignores how women dealt with the crisis.

Throughout the epidemic, the women of Boston were also worn thin by their efforts. Women owned the primary responsibility for the homes in colonial Massachusetts. Largely restricted from any direct participation in public life, the home was their domain. Being a productive housewife was a demanding job. There were children to raise and educate, servants to manage, food to cook, clothes to sew, gardens to tend, and household items to purchase. Besides their own work that had to be completed, their husbands often called on them for aid as "deputy husbands" with the farming or business chores. Rather than feeling oppressed by their domestic spheres, they often took great pride in acquiring a reputation for being a good wife. They aspired to earn the praise of their husbands, other women, and God.

Women quietly played the roles they had naturally performed since time immemorial sitting at the bedsides of loved ones to care for them. They did not dramatically introduce any medical innovations, like the team of Reverend Mather and Dr. Boylston was trying to do. Nor did any newspaper or public body recognize their healing craft during the dreadful year. They did not write any pamphlets describing their efforts. But they were the unsung heroes of the 1721 smallpox epidemic.

During the late summer and early autumn of 1721, few women had a child, husband, or extended family member who resided with them who was not ill with smallpox—although the sick were primarily their children who lacked immunity. They had made up a bed for the pathetically small victims relatively close to the fire. However, they were careful not to put them too close to the fire, for smallpox was understood to be a hot-humor disease, according to humoral theory, and had to be balanced with cool elements. Patients suffered fever, aches, malaise, and restlessness. The characteristic rash appeared, followed by the raised pustules covering their bodies.

Throughout the ordeal, mothers were overcome with worry but did not show it. They smiled and kissed their children, adjusted their blankets, and fed them small amounts of food. They prayed for and with them. They read the Bible or some other book aloud and generally comforted them day and night, ignoring their own need for rest.

The mothers pulled out their recipe books and opened them on their wooden tables by the hearth. The book included all of their favorite family recipes that had been passed down through generations of female ancestors, whose names were inscribed as well. Recipes for medicines were side by side with those for cooking and baking. With these recipes in hand, the women harvested specific items from their herbal gardens, items that were used both to season food and heal sickness.

They brought the handful of herbs over to the table and crushed them by hand or ground them with a mortar and pestle. They added some other ingredients and then boiled the mixture over the fire, infusing it in liquid. Once they were satisfied with the concoction, they administered a few spoonfuls to the children or husbands, who raised their heads to take a mouthful.

The mothers and wives were not the only women who cared for their sick ones. Older daughters, kinfolk, friends, and neighbors sat with them and examined the sick, prepared medicines, and made meals. They supported each other with empathy and experience, sharing their knowledge, advice, and recipes. Young women learned the skills that they would need one day in their own households. All women were expected to reciprocate and aid other women when necessary. These small interdependent communities of women were hard pressed to offer each other help in the fall of 1721, when the demands placed on each of them in their own homes made it difficult to fulfill their informal obligations to each other.

Moreover, midwifery was not the only kind of medicine that women in colonial Massachusetts practiced. Women were paid to be nurses and were in great demand during the autumn of 1721. They were typically hired by the affluent to aid in the lying-in period after childbirth. But during the smallpox epidemic, particularly if a housewife was sick herself or just overwhelmed, nurses would sit at bedsides, prepare medicines, and complete the tasks that the good wives would do. During their stay, nurses usually became intimate with the family members they resided with due to the physical and spiritual proximity in which they worked.

Other women acted as doctors and were recognized as medical authorities and charged fees. Their numbers were fewer than the men who bore the title of doctor, but the women did not engage in the public debate over inoculation. Female doctors maintained smallpox hospitals in Boston and watched patients, diagnosed illnesses, prescribed meals and medicines, and provided constant care much as their male colleagues did.

Whether as mothers, wives, nurses, or "doctoresses," women cared for their patients as the pustules emerged. Many watched in horror as their loved ones suffered subcutaneous bleeding, which came from gums, eyes, and noses. The women tried in vain to draw out the smallpox into pustules before this happened with hot-humor remedies such as ginger in water so scalding hot that patients could barely stand it. This was the practice of the time because pus was viewed by classical medicine to be a desirable expulsion of vitiated blood. The women encouraged the emergence of pustules with the same method that doctors used: blistering a patient's skin. They were bedside to see that their efforts usually failed, and these patients died a horrible death.

Healers had to deal with the confluent sort of smallpox in which pustules converged into an oozing and stinking mass that others avoided, but the women faced bravely. Most of the patients who suffered this kind of smallpox quickly perished painfully. Mothers and wives would pour a few drops of water excruciatingly down scab-ridden and crusty throats. All the sufferers had their pustules dry up into scabs that fell off after about a week. Those who survived had unsightly scars but were alive. The women helped them during their convalescent period as they recovered their appetite and strength. Broths and posset were served to fortify them slowly. Sometimes, a final purge in the form of induced vomiting or an enema generated by a herbal mixture would be administered to the weakened patient to bring the humors back into balance. Afterward, any women who were helping a good wife would return to their homes.

Nearly two dozen Indians were among those who were dying of smallpox and generally left without a voice in the history of the epidemic. They were those who had assimilated into Puritan society after King Philip's War of 1675, proportionally one of the most destructive wars in American history. Puritan John Eliot had preached to the Indians in the mid-seventeenth century. He had studied native ways, learning their language and creating a dictionary that facilitated his translating the Bible into the Massachusetts language. In 1652 he organized an Indian College at Harvard to train them as ministers and adopt English ways. Moreover, he established fourteen "praying towns" in which the Indians adopted

European clothing, agriculture, and religion. The converted were admitted as full church members.

During King Philip's War, the praying-town residents were summarily rounded up and incarcerated on Deer Island in Boston Harbor. After the war, many of them were sold into slavery in the West Indies along with the prisoners of war. Hundreds remained, however, and lived among the Puritans. By that time, the Indian College at Harvard had closed, and the Indians' opportunities were limited. They became indentured servants and took up trades, some going to sea to earn a living while others worked on farms for wages. They were often impoverished and were recipients of poor relief.

Indians suffered tragic death rates of 75 to 90 percent to smallpox and other European diseases because they had no natural immunity. They responded to the outbreaks with their traditional healing cures. Like the English, they had an extensive knowledge of local plants, such as sassafras, ginseng, and witch hazel, to employ in common ailments. There was a prevailing belief that God had placed remedies for illnesses where they were native to certain areas around the world. The Puritans were particularly impressed by how the Indians dealt with rattlesnake bites. The Puritans and Indians often shared this knowledge with each other. The Indians also had a strong spiritual dimension to the healing cures employed by shamans and medicine men and women.

Indians often aggravated smallpox with one of their common cures, which was to fast, take a purging sweat, and then jump into an icy river. Some of the dozens who were sick in 1721 were converted Christians while others retained their native beliefs. Indeed, previous epidemics may have stirred conversions because they lost their faith in the shamans when they failed to cure the disease. Their religious reaction to the disease may have been different from their Puritan neighbors, but they suffered the same painful symptoms and the same agonizing deaths and sense of loss. They, like the Puritan women, were silent voices in the 1721 epidemic.

All Bostonians had one tragic thing in common: they experienced the common sense of loss and suffering. With hundreds dying, no one escaped the loss of a family member, a friend, a fellow worker, a servant, or a neighbor. As summer turned to autumn, funerals began to multiply in rapid profusion. The public debate continued but seemed at times muted because of the mourning. Although his own child died, Reverend Mather still had responsibilities as a pastor and had the poignant duty of delivering a funeral sermon at the New North Church for a pastor's wife who died of smallpox. It was among the first funerals that he and members of the gentry attended that fall.

Chapter Twelve
DEATH'S HEAD

Ordinarily Samuel Sewall would have spent an autumn day running his private merchant business or conducting the public's business. Sewall was one of Boston's prominent business elites and public servants. But in the autumn of 1721, he spent most of those days attending one or more funerals for people he knew. He was also an inveterate introspective diarist who recorded the great many funerals he attended, which provides a lens into the grief in Boston at this time as well as the funerary practices of the Puritans.

Sewall was born in England in 1652 and migrated to New England with his family in 1661, a year after the Stuart restoration. After receiving a classical education in languages and history, he trained for the ministry at Harvard. He studied diligently for seven long years at College Hall, earning a bachelor's degree and a master's of divinity. His master's thesis on original sin was composed and delivered orally in Latin at the commencement exercises in 1674. (The incoming class of 1678 included eleven-year-old Cotton Mather.)

Despite his lengthy training, young Sewall decided he was not cut out for the ministry because he was an awful preacher, and he proceeded to make his way into the world of business very quickly instead. His meteorite rise was due in no small part to his marrying Hannah Hull, the daughter of the fabulously wealthy merchant John Hull. Sewall received a generous dowry many times the average annual salary of ministers and became a junior partner in his father-in-law's business, handling complex accounting books and voluminous correspondence. Hull's diverse investments around the Atlantic included outfitting ships to carry tons of salted cod, molasses and rum, sugar and salt, chocolate, furs, books, and a wide variety of dry goods as part of the triangular trade between the colonies, England, and West Africa. Investments in mills, ironworks, and land rounded out Hull's mercantile activities. The port of Boston provided one of the best locations to participate in the trade networks and was only growing.

Sewall was a man of the world, but he was also a devout Puritan. The Bible was the literal word of God and the guide for moral conduct. He struggled with the interior of his soul as he scrupulously examined his faith, as did all young Puritans. He found it wanting, full of "sinfulness and hypocrisy," much like Cotton Mather and other young Puritans did during their conversion experiences. His self-reproach about his fallen nature was believed to be a necessary step in practicing the humility associated with being a member of the elect. Having experienced the grace of conversion in March 1677, he was admitted into Thomas Thacher's Third Church in the South End on the Common, along with another gentleman and two women. His piety was evidenced when he held private prayer meetings in his home, served his congregation as precentor because of his love of music, and had his children baptized. He decried the decline of the Puritan covenant and sternly applied his Puritan beliefs to society, condemning the wearing of wigs, the observance of Christmas, the flying of the cross on St. George's flag, and the youthful male fashion of long hair as sinful and idolatry.

Like Cotton Mather, Sewall was a member of the third generation who grappled with conserving the mission of the founding generation and kept a constant vigilance for any sign of decline. But Sewall was even more of a reactionary and railed against the slightest changes he witnessed. He often sought Mather's spiritual guidance on moral issues but then summarily ignored it when the minister counseled prudence over self-righteousness. Sewall's life represents the sometimes uneasy turmoil between traditional Puritanism and the cosmopolitanism of the rising Boston.

Sewall served the public good from a variety of positions befitting his social station. In 1681 he became a freeman voter and served as the colony's official printer, although he delegated the printing operation to Samuel Green. In 1683 the thirty-one-year-old Sewall won appointment to the Massachusetts General Court. He also served as a captain of the militia, an overseer of Harvard College, and several minor public offices, such as watchman, during which he enforced the nightly curfew.

Samuel Sewall was a highly respected businessman and civic leader who exemplified Boston worldliness and Puritan piety. If anyone epitomized the Protestant work and success ethic of a man blessed by God for his piety and hard work, it was Sewall.

Sewall continued in public service throughout his life and became entangled in two contentious episodes in Massachusetts history. In the first, he went to England in the fall of 1688 to aid Increase Mather in securing a new charter from the king. James II had revoked the old charter in 1684 after decades of autonomous behavior in the Massachusetts Bay Colony that ignored the wishes of the Crown. He was there just as the Glorious Revolution swept

William and Mary onto the throne while Boston mobs rushed into the streets to arrest the hated royal governor, Edmund Andros. Eventually the new monarchy granted a new charter, but its terms did not please many Puritans. It robbed independent-minded New Englanders of their tradition of self-government with the provision that the colonial governor would be appointed rather than elected. The new charter also granted the appalling principle of religious tolerance to all Christians except Catholics in a Puritan society that had banished and hanged dissenters.

More infamously, Sewall was appointed in 1692 to a special court that was called to handle the spate of witchcraft cases in Salem village. After several ministers (including Increase Mather), judges, and the governor questioned the use of spectral evidence (in which testimony was admitted as to spirits that influenced actions in the material world), the witchcraft trials resulted in the hanging of nineteen suspected witches and one wizard crushed to death. Sewall suffered great personal agony for his role in the Salem witch trials and publicly repented at the Third Church in January 1697. Because of the communal threat of individual sin, Puritans publicly confessed their sins to their congregations. Guided by Reverend Samuel Willard, Sewall desired "to take the blame and share of it, asking pardon of men, and especially desiring prayers that God, who has an unlimited authority, would pardon that sin and all other of his sins, personal and relative."

Only Sewall knew whether he ever truly felt that God had forgiven him for his role in the dreadful affair, but the merchant did not fear being punished for his thoughts on slavery. In 1700 Sewall wrote one of the first and most important antislavery tracts in early American history. In the tract he criticized both the slave trade and slavery itself in terms that Cotton Mather concurred. Sewall attacked the slave trade for lamentably tearing apart African families:

"In taking the Negroes out of Africa, and selling that here, that which God has joined together men do boldly rend asunder: men from their country, husbands from their wives, parents from their children. How horrible is the uncleanness, mortality, if not murder, that the ships are guilty of that bring great crowds of these miserable men and women."

Sewall then used Scripture to undermine the foundation of slavery that other Puritans comfortably utilized to support the practice. He argued that the patriarch Joseph was wrongfully sold into slavery by his brothers in Genesis 37; nor were Africans the descendents of Ham and condemned to slavery because they were from Ethiopia [Cush] and their "promised conversion ought to be prayed for." Sewall also quoted Leviticus 25, which enjoined Jews not to enslave each other. Answering those who posited that Africans were taken in just wars or that they were heathens who received the benefit of the gospel in Christian lands, he warned, "Evil must not be done, that good may come of it."

Besides using the Bible to condemn slavery, Sewall also asserted natural law principles of justice to bolster his argument. "It is most certain that all men, as they are the sons of Adam, are coheirs and have equal right unto liberty," he maintained. "For as much as liberty is in real value next unto life, none ought to part with it themselves, or deprive others of it," he continued. In short, Africans were human beings who were endowed by their Creator with life, liberty, and the right to determine their own destiny.

However enlightened Sewall's views on slavery may have been, his opinions on the new science that so inspired the imagination of the Mathers were reactionary. He did not read the latest philosophical works coming from Europe. In addition, Cotton Mather clearly disgusted Sewall by preaching about the Copernican paradigm from the pulpit. When Mather stated, "The sun is in the center of our system," Sewall uncomfortably wrote in his diary, "I think it inconvenient to assert such problems."

Sewall was no stranger to the tragedy of disease and death that overtook Boston in the fall of 1721. One small child after another of his had been carried away in pitifully small coffins for burial by the distraught father. Without a childhood immunity to the virus, *variola* had almost claimed the twenty-six-year-old Sewall just as he was launching his successful career. "Multitudes died" during the epidemic of 1678, and Sewall was "reported to be dead." He barely pulled through after lying in bed in agonizing pain and anguish for six weeks. When the town's population faced another epidemic, disease easily traveled with the English armies fighting the French and Indians during King William's War, and *variola* swept into the city and nearly killed three of Sewall's children. The widower had also buried two wives by the time the 1721 epidemic erupted, with his most recent wife dying the year before.

As the 1721 smallpox epidemic struck down hundreds, Sewall served as the chief justice of the Supreme Court of Judicature. His regal mansion was situated in South Boston, facing the town's main street, Cornhill, one block east of the Common and a short walk from his church and his governmental and mercantile activities at the Town House. He commanded a view of Boston Harbor from his rear and side windows, looking out at the ship masts that signified his great wealth in international trade. The exquisite home was conspicuously decorated with imported objects that displayed the status of the owner. His gardens provided herbs for the kitchen and fruits eaten or fermented into alcoholic beverages. Servants in stables and coach houses busily maintained his horses and carriage. The small servants' quarters housed British men and women rather than Africans. The Sewalls entertained guests frequently, providing a cornucopia of delicacies befitting a man of his wealth.

During the autumn of 1721, however, Sewall's social calendar was clear of pleasant dinners and social engagements. Instead, he spent much of his time attending the funerals of dear friends and acquaintances. His diary is an important record of the funerary beliefs and practices of the Puritans. As the death toll from smallpox climbed precipitously, there were more calls to Boston's burying places to inter the victims.

The Puritans had a unique perspective on death. They shared with other Christians a belief that Christ had died for their sins and would stand in divine judgment over one's soul in the afterlife. However, as Puritans heavily influenced by Calvinist theology, they developed a distinctive set of beliefs about death and mourning. Not surprisingly, they encountered death with a severe austerity that eliminated much of the emotion and ritual that comforted the living during their loss.

Many Puritans went to their deathbeds with a great deal of trepidation. Some may have been hypocrites, truly wailing at death because they now saw the state of their soul as clearly as God did. Even the saints cried because of doubts about their conversion and salvation. A lack of certitude was a proper expression of humility about their souls and further proof that the person was a saint. The wails of the unregenerate were too late to make much difference and would pale in comparison with the screams from the torture rooms of hell, where they would lament forever and their cries would fall on the deaf ears of a just God.

The living could do nothing to help them now. The papists attended masses, held holy days, and said prayers for the dearly departed whose souls were being cleansed of their sins in purgatory while they awaited final judgment. The Puritans inherited the Protestant Reformation's rejections of such notions as unscriptural and superstitious nonsense, not to mention wrapped up in the corruptions of indulgence selling.

John Calvin promulgated much different beliefs. "The souls of the faithful, after completing their term of combat and travail, are gathered into rest, where they await with joy the fruition of their promised glory; and thus all things remain in suspense until Jesus Christ appears as the Redeemer," he wrote. The unfaithful were "chained up like malefactors until the time when they are dragged to the punishment that is appointed for them." Such was the simple elegance of divine judgment—the faithful were rewarded, the sinners were punished. If it bred a certain indifference regarding the souls of the dead, it bore a wrenching introspective self-examination by the living.

An earlier generation of Puritans had seen the elaborate rituals of death—dressing in black, burying the dead with highly decorated gravestones, wailing over the departed with excessive emotional displays, and eulogizing the dead—as Catholic frauds. Puritan funerals were simpler affairs that reminded the living that death was ever-present as well as reminding them of the need for conversion. A governor might have some cannon fire at his funeral, but there was no mistaking that that was part of the civil ceremony. Later, they became much more formalized while still following certain ideas of Puritan theology. Perhaps the human need for ritual to mark certain occasions of life in particular ways overcame the desire to distance themselves from Roman Catholic practices. And these were accepted even by those conservatives who might normally bemoan any changes to the original practices of their fathers and grandfathers.

While family members helplessly watched loved ones painfully succumb to the awful disease that wracked their bodies, preparations for burial commenced. The Puritans who settled America would have agreed with the English nonconformist who wrote, "Thy body, when the soul is gone, will be an horror to all that behold it; a most loathsome and abhorred spectacle." In early eighteenth-century Boston, this view had evolved to include some embalming and related preparations of the body for interment.

However, after a contagious and disfiguring illness, embalming was omitted. A few years after the smallpox epidemic, Sewall buried his daughter Hannah and noted, "Now she cannot be emboweled," because of the distemper that killed her. Oppressive late summer heat and smallpox induced people to expedite the initial stages of their funeral rituals. Only a hardy family member would willingly wash and dress a crust-covered relation.

In normal times, the body would be laid out in the home and possibly in the church where the deceased had been a member. But during the epidemic in which victims filled the death rolls daily, some churches would have been overcrowded with corpses. Moreover, because of the prevailing view of miasma, the contagious bodies had to be buried as soon as possible.

Although the documentation does not always provide a comprehensive description of the burial practices of every individual who died in 1721, Sewall was attentive enough to show that most Puritan funerals followed a general pattern. Whatever shape the funerals and burials assumed, it was a tragic time for Bostonians.

In mid-September, the family of Francis Webb, a smallpox victim, sent funeral invitations to friends and family. The list of mourners included Sewall, who received his invitation in the form of a pair of gloves to be worn to the funeral. Ministers like Cotton Mather and important businessmen and public servants such as Sewall had quite a collection of gloves from all of the funerals they attended over the years. Indeed, some collections ran into the thousands, and doleful times like 1721 added considerably to the total. Because Sewall commanded respect as a high-ranking member of the community, he received an exquisite pair of finely crafted gloves. Those lower down on the social ladder received gloves of more middling quality.

Francis Webb was described as the "virtuous consort" of Reverend John Webb, the pastor of the New North Church. Cotton Mather had battled the installation of Webb at the church and then entangled himself in the controversial installation of Peter Thacher that led to the establishment of the New Brick Meetinghouse in the spring. All of that animosity was laid aside for the funeral of Webb's dear Francis.

Sewall accepted the invitation to attend the funeral, which followed the general pattern of Puritan funerals. As such, it reveals how survivors coped with the experience of so many of their loved ones dying and how they were laid to rest. By mid-September there had been scores of such grim occasions.

Francis Webb's funeral was on September 16. The New North Church bells tolled for close to a half-hour early that afternoon, summoning Sewall and other mourners to the Webb home for the funeral. The deep clanging echoed through somber city streets announcing yet another death in the North End. That month the sound of ringing bells was often joined by other church bells in a sad cacophony. Funeral attendees, mostly groups of families, with little ones struggling to catch up, walked soberly through the quiet city streets. The same epidemic that brought so many mourners out for funerals had shut down much of the normal traffic. Many who were attending to sick family members fought back tears when they heard the bells and thought they might be the next to organize a funeral.

The General Court met the week before the Webb funeral and empowered the Selectmen to regulate many aspects of funerals in Boston. Because "many persons in the town of Boston are visited with the smallpox and several have died of that distemper...the frequent ringing of bells at funerals [was] found very inconvenient and prejudicial." In other words, the tolling spread despondency and fear among the living. The court resolved, "No bells shall be tolled for the burial of persons that may die of that or any other distemper but what the Selectmen of the town shall order and direct." The Selectmen would also determine what time of the day funerals would be allowed to take place. The court threatened a fine against any who would dare to disobey the law.

When the Selectmen met four days later, the General Court outlined specific funeral regulations. "At each funeral there shall be but one bell tolled, and that but a first and a second time." Each time, the ringing was not to last for more than six minutes. During the month of September, bell ringing was limited to "between the hours of five and six in the afternoon." In the following months, the time was set back an hour. Blacks and Indians suffered tighter regulations and were allowed only one tolling each. Because of the fear that a gathering of so many people would proliferate the number of smallpox cases and "probably occasion the deaths of sundry persons," funeral processions were ordered "in carrying them to their graves, they shall pass the nearest way."

After the mourners arrived at the Webb home, they were ready to proceed a few blocks toward Mill's Pond to the North Burying Ground. They were adorned with mourning gloves, ribbons, and cloaks. One of the early funeral regulations banned the wearing of special black mourning scarves because such items as scarves, clothes, and blankets might carry the *variola* virus. Of course, it was likely that many of the gloves that had been sent by the family and frequently touched the mouth and face were similarly infected. Some Bostonians were not happy that the government attempted to control funeral rituals; others said good riddance to a very expensive custom. Either way, Sewall noted, "I think this is the first public funeral without scarves." He added, "Has a very good character," possibly indicating that he concurred with the banning of scarves.

Coffins were usually made of a very fine wood and lined with expensive cloth. The year of the deceased's passing was tradition-ally inscribed on the outside, which was usually covered with a mortcloth. During funerals for people of less means, members of the cortege would take turns as pallbearers, transporting the coffin to the burial place. For example, Sewall described another funeral at which he and three other pallbearers slipped napkins through the carrying rings of the coffin, lifted it a foot above the ground, and carried a girl "underhand by four." In cases where the deceased's family was wealthy, the coffin was placed atop a hearse and pulled by horse (which might be decked in symbols of mourning). When a fellow church member of means died that fall, Sewall and his son-in-law, William Cooper (who married his daughter Judith the year before and ministered at the Brattle Square Church), were among the prominent men who walked "next [to] the hearse" in a position of honor during the funeral.

Francis Webb's coffin was conveyed by hearse to the cemetery. Sewall and Cotton Mather and Increase Mather walked with Reverend John Webb and his family at the head of the procession. The rest of the assemblage followed behind two by two.

The coffin and hearse often had small pieces of paper pinned to them with scribblings of funeral verses. These frequently fluttered in the wind during the march to the burial site. Cotton Mather once commented that a coffin had so many scraps of paper pinned to it that it looked like a "paper winding sheet to lay him out."

During such a busy year for funerals, the processions passed other funeral processions in the street. Sewall witnessed a funeral for an African whose status after death, if not in life, was equal to the Europeans.

Finally, the mourners reached the North Burying Ground where Francis Webb was interred. Practically, this was not always an easy undertaking because snow fell in November and December, freezing the ground and making grave digging a grueling effort. Moreover, a fierce wintry gale could make the assembly temporarily miserable. "Great snow on the ground," Sewall wrote by a comfortable fire after one funeral.

Although Puritans had been iconoclasts against what they considered blasphemous headstones in England, the New England variety were becoming more elaborate by the time of the third generation. Death's-heads, hourglasses, Death's-scythes, and other reminders of mortality as well as crosses decorated the grave markers. Prayers had rarely been said over the dead, and displays of emotion were frowned upon, but now both were becoming increasingly important parts of the funeral ritual.

After the funeral, the assemblage returned to the Webb home for a feast of breads, meats, and cheeses laid out by the servants. Beer and hard cider were also served to wash down the food and fortify everyone's spirits. The conversation at the home can only be guessed at—surely people expressed condolences and shared news of the latest sufferers in the town. The poignant occasion was made even more depressing by the fact that everyone knew many more would soon die, including others gathered with them.

They received another tangible reminder of their mortality when they were given a funeral ring to mark the occasion. The gold rings could not be mistaken for any other ritual for they were carved with death's-heads in enamel, etched with skeletons, and inlaid with coffin-shaped gems. The expense became so prohibitive that the General Court stepped in a few years later to limit the practice.

Cotton Mather apparently waited until the Sabbath to preach a funeral sermon for Francis Webb. He chose to discuss Romans

14:7–8, in which Paul writes: "For none of us liveth to himself, neither doeth any die to himself. For whether we live, we live unto the Lord; or whether we die, we die unto the Lord; whether we live therefore, or die, we are the Lord's." For ninety minutes Mather expounded upon the idea of salvation by faith rather than works, or the Mosaic law. His listeners were to consider their own mortality and encouraged to submit their wills and open their hearts.

On the next Sabbath Mather's dear Nibby was still deathly ill. He titled his sermon "Our Cry unto the Glorious One to Undertake for Us When We Are under Oppressions." He was prepared to trust in God and submit to his will, "It being a time of heavy pressures." He donned his flowing robes and skullcap and entered the meetinghouse for the afternoon service with a heavy heart. The "dying circumstances of my lovely daughter, in conjunction with a variety of other trials" steered him toward preaching from Isaiah 38:14. Hezekiah, the king of Judah had recovered from an illness and sang: "Like a crane or a swallow, so did I chatter: I did mourn as a dove: mine eyes were lift up on high: O Lord, it hath oppressed me, comfort me."

Mather was so proud of his sermon that he transcribed the final part into his diary. The congregants probably stifled some sobs for loved ones who were ill.

I have two things to observe unto you. The one is, that it pleases the Holy One, to make my sorrows profitable to some few among his people. There are some few among the children of God who fare the better for my sorrows. And the view of this renders my sorrows in a measure welcome to me. The other is that a poor servant of God can assure you from his own happy experience that while he knows he has a Christ concerned for him, none of his distresses prove too heavy for him. He doesn't sink under the pressures, but can rise and soar and sing.... Oh! Prize the Christ for whom you hear our testimony.

After the sermon, Mather climbed down the steps from the pulpit and stood in front of the congregation. The minister stood there uncomfortably waiting for his son-in-law Daniel Willard to arrive with the newest granddaughter. Mather expected to receive the baby, hear her named publicly, and then baptize her in the name of the Father, Son, and Holy Ghost. The baby's name was to be the strange but apt "Resigned." Mather explained, "The newborn grandchild should have been brought forth to baptism in the afternoon, and the water stood ready for it." But there was no baby to baptize. Willard showed up and shared the dreadful news—little Resigned had died during the service. A shaken Mather exclaimed in his diary, "An uncommon occurrence!"

The public character of his personal travails exemplified Mather's lessons more than the eloquence of his sermons, or so he thought. The melancholy scene in Second Church testified to the imperative of faith in suffering. "Can I edify the flock more than by two such testimonies as I bore yesterday unto them?" he asked his journal.

His eyes were turned heavenward for strength: "What have I to support me under the pressures which the view of my dying daughter lays upon me? A glorious Christ! He is my life, he is my all. I feel what it is to live by the faith of the Son of God."

On Monday evening, Mather visited Nibby and saw that she was waning and did not have long to live. It was a morose business to pray with her and advise her to trust in her Savior. "To strengthen a dear child in the agonies of death is a sad work which I am again called unto." He came again the next night and witnessed her expected end. The nine o'clock bells had rung, chasing the few daring revelers who were out back home. An eerie silence settled over the North End. The Willard home was quiet except for sobs and the restless death throes of its mistress. "Between ten and eleven in the evening the dear child expired. A long and a hard death was the thing appointed for her," Mather wearily penned in his diary by candlelight that night.

Mather consoled his son-in-law the following day as they made arrangements for Nibby's funeral and sent out the customary black gloves. The aged minister offered his sagacity born of experience to the young man in this difficult period. "The condition of my widowed son-in-law, now calls for my singular cares, to befriend him, and advise him."

His faith bolstered his ability to cope with the wretched loss of more of his progeny. He had survived his eleventh child, but Nibby was headed to paradise where she would find greater joy than anything that could be imagined on earth. Moreover, Nibby's death provided the minister with an opportunity to witness to his flock on God's consolation to him during his time of trial. "How much may I serve the cause of piety and edify the people of God if I entertain the public with such sentiments as the faith and love of Christ has given me on such occasions as I have now before me!"

The grieving father stood on the pulpit at the Thursday lecture meeting, looking out over an expectant congregation. They knew what it was like to lose a child prematurely and empathized with his plight. Many had children who were sick with smallpox, and they were anxious about their survival. They needed spiritual guidance on how to endure the anguish. Mather's sermon was perhaps not what they expected from the minister.

Mather titled his sermon "The Holy Silence That Sad Things Are to Be Entertained Withal." He chose to lecture on Leviticus 10:3: "Then Moses said unto Aaron, This is it that the LORD spake, saying, 'I will be sanctified in them that come near me, and before all the people I will be glorified': but Aaron held his peace."

What was to be said when one had lost a "lovely daughter?" There were no lamentations to heaven, nor any angry questions placed before the Almighty regarding the ways of suffering. There was no loud wailing and tears. There was only the silence of grief. Quietly, a pious minister opened his heart and mind to the Lord.

Mather dutifully walked by his daughter's coffin to the North Burying Ground and hosted the feast afterward. His wife, daughter, son, and father sat silently in the Mather home, grieving and praying. The Friday after the funeral, Mather entered his study for a day of fasting and prayer "that I may humble myself before the Lord for all the sins which the death of my dear Nibby calls me to a repentance for." He prayed to "obtain mercy for the family that she has left behind her" and for his surviving children. He also prayed for strength in his social ministry during his daily visits to pervasive sick chambers in the North End.

As an additional succor to the suffering families of Boston, Mather republished his *Pastoral Letter to Families Visited with Sickness,* which had gone through printings during the 1703 smallpox epidemic and the 1713 measles outbreak. In addition to the release of the pamphlet, Mather joined forces with politicians and other public figures to relieve the strain of the epidemic. They wanted to ensure that the physical needs of the public were attended to as the harsh New England winter loomed. Suffering families did not need the additional burdens of attempting to figure out how they were going to keep their homes warm or put a meal on the table while they were attending to the sick.

Chapter Thirteen

LIFE-GIVING FIRES

In late September, light from the protracted summer evenings faded earlier, altering the time funeral bells were rung and sending the superstitious indoors to escape the night. More than 150 Bostonians had succumbed to the smallpox virus, and many hundreds were currently experiencing its symptoms. A chill seized the night air and would not relent, while the days were noticeably cooler. Farmers were reaping their harvests, going through the motions without the customary autumn feasts. They brewed cider and prepared foods for the dearth of the coming season. Snow would blanket the rolling New England hills soon. The innumerable ponds and lakes would ice over. A palpable quiet would settle over the land.

In the autumn of 1721, feared gripped Boston to such an extent that paralysis imperiled even the most basic facets of life. The death toll from smallpox was already high and continuing to rise. The thousands who were immune to the disease were nonetheless indirectly imperiled as well. There was an impending wood shortage that threatened to kill hundreds more in this northern port if the shortage was not solved. The total number of deaths caused by the smallpox epidemic might be catastrophic.

Wood was one of the most important commodities in New England life that shaped settlement patterns, trade, employment, shelter, and daily lives. It was the chief natural resource of New England and the lifeblood of the port city. Life could not survive without it.

Puritans and other New Englanders believed that the massive forests were evidence of God's bounty provided for those who worked hard to use it. They may have consumed the trees differently from the nomadic Indian tribes and not always efficiently, but they were also shrewd enough to use them wisely and profitably.

The Bostonians exploited trees for the international trade that characterized their important port. The towering white pines of Maine and New Hampshire soared one hundred to two hundred feet above the forest ground and had a girth of some four to six feet. They became a strategic resource at the center of the international colonial competition. They served as masts for the British naval vessels that ruled the seas, protecting a sprawling economic empire. Indeed, the *Seahorse* in Boston waters undoubtedly had such a mast.

White pine was also used by Boston artisans working at shipyards around the harbor. The pine was used for masts, while white oak was cut into planks for ships. The white oaken timbers were nailed together for the topsides of trading vessels owned by merchants and sea captains. The undersides of the ships were made of black oak, which was more resistant to the sea worms that bored holes in the hulls of ships, rendering them unfit. Pitch pine provided vital naval stores used on maritime vessels such as pitch, turpentine, and rosin. As many as twenty-five hundred trees might be used to create an oceangoing vessel.

The goods that crisscrossed the Atlantic were stored in barrels and thousand-pound hogsheads fashioned by coopers out of the same white oak. Salted Newfoundland cod and other fish, meats, raisins, cheeses, flour, Madeira wine, West Indian rum, Virginia tobacco, salt, and New England furs, among a bewildering variety of other goods, were packed in the sturdy oaken barrels and protected against the elements during sea voyages.

The businesses and homes of the city consumed great amounts of wood. Many of the public buildings, meetinghouses, and businesses were framed with wood. Almost every trade—bakers, blacksmiths, ironmongers, pewterers, and soap makers—used wood for fuel to create their products. Five cords of wood would produce 140 bushels of charcoal that would manufacture a ton of iron. A cord of wood was needed to make 11 bushels of sea salt.

Homes consumed voracious amounts of wood. Framed houses used a lot of wood in raising them, but so did newer brick homes because the clay was fired with wood. Roofs were shingled, and homes were sided with cedar. Home interiors often had white-pine flooring and red-oak wainscoting. Beds, benches, chairs, tables, and other household goods also were made of wood.

But by far the greatest consumers of wood inside the home were the massive New England hearths that burned it for fuel. What they lacked in efficiency, they made up for in size. These huge openings were often eight feet wide. Fires burned throughout the day and night, year round in New England. Wives and servants tended the cooking in the fireplaces. Meat was placed on spits and turned over the flames, water was boiled in kettles, and pies were baked in special ovens. A great variety of fireplace tools and cooking implements surrounded the hearth.

Besides cooking, fireplaces provided warmth. They were centrally located to distribute warmth evenly around the house. Some homes had more than one fireplace for this reason, and the expansive homes of wealthy merchants could contain eight fireplaces in different rooms. Hickory was burned for the best and hottest fires to sit by on a cold autumn night. Family members also sat by fires to spin, read a book, or do business accounts. Depending on size and usage, the average Boston home annually burned between fifteen and thirty cords of wood.

The first Puritan settlers denuded the forests rapidly, especially around Boston. As early as 1638, the city's inhabitants had to import firewood from the surrounding islands. Over the past century they had to transport the firewood over greater distances from farther forests. In the intervening decades, tens of millions of cords of wood were burned.

As a result, wood boats carried tons of wood to Boston and unloaded their cargoes at the Long Wharf or at one of the many private wharves around town. Private carters then distributed the wood by cart in nice weather or by sled over packed winter snow. In the 1720s as many as five hundred loads were hauled over the city streets on frigid days. Citizens spent a whopping £17,000 on this precious commodity yearly. The rising prices were becoming prohibitive for the poor who had to rely on charitable donations. Ministers such as Cotton Mather received part of their salaries in adequate supplies of firewood.

The smallpox epidemic threatened to do what the elements could not in hardy New England—stop the flow of wood transports. If it did so, most people's daily lives would be halted further and their lives put in additional danger.

As the death rate in Boston climbed in early September, the sloop men who brought wood to the city refused to come "to town with their boats by reason of the smallpox." The resulting firewood shortage would quickly escalate into a crisis as the winter came closer. Many artisans would have to close the few shops that remained open. People's hearths would go cold, affecting their diets and home heating. At this point in the year, it would be a great inconvenience; in winter, it would be deadly. The ensuing public crisis would compound the smallpox emergency. Cotton Mather and others commented on the impending dire situation. He was going to prod the Selectmen "to look for a seasonable supply of wood for the town."

The Selectmen clearly appreciated the importance of firewood deliveries and met to address the matter. They gave public notice to all who were unwilling to enter the town that special arrangements were available for their firewood to be transported to residents. The captains would be allowed to navigate to Castle Island where "their sloops or boats shall be brought up to Boston and immediately unloaded at such wharfs as the master or owner of the boats shall direct and appoint." The town even offered to pay for the piloting of the vessels between the island and Boston. "The charge of bringing up and carrying down the several vessels to and from the Castle," the Selectmen pledged, "to be born by the town of Boston." The owners of the wood or boats would still have "to pay the charge of unloading." But it was a great deal. Their fears of smallpox would be allayed, and they would still make a profit in the wood trade.

Puritanism had a strong social ethic and a long history of public regulation in New England. The social hierarchy obligated those on the upper end of the ladder to care for those below. Mather and the public officials wanted to ensure that their less-fortunate neighbors were provided for during the harsh New England winter. At the time, his pregnant daughter Nibby was dying and his son was recovering from the smallpox inoculation, but Mather took the time to write in his diary that he would work on firewood supplies "that the poor may not suffer for want of a convenient fuel in the approaching winter."

Although most captains were willing to dump their supplies of wood at Castle Island, some were wary of going anywhere near Boston and ended their shipments for the duration of the outbreak. This caused prices to soar. The indigent could not afford to buy any wood and probably resorted to begging or scavenging scraps in the streets. The issue came up again a few months later. Mather felt duty-bound to "address a letter to the Lieutenant Governor and other gentlemen of New Hampshire to obtain from their charity a considerable quantity of wood for the poor of this loathsome town under the necessities of the hard winter coming on."

Bostonians scraped by with enough firewood through December. The *variola* had excited mass hysteria and come close to closing off the town from the outside world. The efforts of the town's officials to keep those lines open meant that there was still a good chance that it could escape the confines of Boston into the Atlantic world.

Nevertheless, Mather was more concerned about those closer to home. He had pursued the public good with the practice of variolation and lobbied for supplies of firewood for the town. Now, Mather helped to dispense charity for those who were impoverished by the epidemic. Dependent wives and children lost many fathers to the disease. Parents who relied on the additional income provided by their children suffered monetarily. Artisans who depended on the labor of their apprentices had to seek other sources. Most shops were empty anyway. Goods usually transported to the brisk city trade lay still in merchant warehouses.

Boston ministers tried to meet the need among their congregants and the poor of the neighborhood. In common times and during emergencies, they received donations from the wealthy and took up collections for the less fortunate. Cotton Mather generously supported many families from his own meager salary. The Scot's Charitable Society was a philanthropic society that included the support of important figures such as Dr. William Douglass.

In the fall of 1721, ministers and wealthy benefactors increased their efforts to help the indigent. "I am furnished with money to be dispensed unto miserable families," Mather wrote. "My dear Greenwood supplies me with a sum for that purpose. I'll be as faithful and prudent a steward as I can." He did not want to mislead anyone into thinking he was responsible for the assistance. "Let it be declared that I am not myself the original bestower of the charity." Unrecorded by the pages of history were the many small charitable acts by neighbors and kin helping each other out—especially those with small children or aged parents—during the epidemic with money, food, firewood, and supplies.

Private collections for the poor, however, apparently did not match the need of the crisis. The government had a long history of dispensing aid from the public treasury and trying to solve the problem of poverty in the growing town. The problem was rife as was typical of a large urban port. Women were widowed and children were orphaned by the numbers of men who were annually lost in the dangerous profession of seafaring and fishing. Frontier wars such as the 1675 King Philip's War or the more recent King William's War with the French and Indians displaced large numbers of people from destroyed towns and sent them in droves to seek protection in Boston. Moreover, men were killed in proportions that would surpass almost all future wars. Regular epidemics and natural disasters created many more dependent poor people. Many undesirables were warned away not only for their religious heterodoxy but because they might enlarge the town's welfare rolls. The town built almshouses for the deserving poor who could not support themselves through no fault of their own. The able poor were seen as sinful in their idleness, and thrust into workhouses. Overseers were appointed to monitor the town and determine the needs of the poor residing in the neighborhoods.

On November 14, during the greatest part of the crisis, the General Court passed a bill for the succor of the poor. The representatives realized that the epidemic had forced many into poverty who normally would have been productive members of the community who could support themselves. "Whereas by reason of the smallpox so generally prevailing in the town of Boston, many persons are reduced to very great straits and necessitous circumstances, who otherwise would have been in a capacity to have subsisted their families in comfortable circumstances." The bill provided for the relief of the poor: "That the sum of one thousand pounds be allowed and paid out of the public treasury to the Selectmen and the Overseers of the poor of the town of Boston to be distributed among such persons as they shall account to stand in need of relief for the reasons aforesaid." The aid in this case was only for families suffering economically due to the epidemic, not a broad attempt to relieve poverty in the city.

The appointed persons presumably began interviewing residents, determining their needs, and dispensing the appropriated monies. Townspeople also received firewood supplies. They neither starved nor froze to death because of the private and public efforts of their fellow citizens, neighbors, church members, and representatives. The Puritan social ethic and Christian charity were alive and well in Boston in 1721. The people did not abandon each other to their fates or act only to save themselves. Although they were frightened, they bound themselves together and shared their destiny according to the will of God. They would need that courage and sense of community in the weeks to come, for the death toll rose rapidly.

Chapter Fourteen

"THE AFFLICTED STILL MULTIPLY"

Greater numbers were taking ill and dying as summer faded into autumn. While only a dozen people had expired in June and July, twenty-six died in August. While Francis Webb and Nibby Mather were dying of smallpox and a fever, *variola* had claimed 101 lives during the month of September. On September 23, Cotton Mather noted the rapid rise in the numbers who were ill: "The afflicted multiply fast enough. One day this week their condition obliged it, that my prayers were seventeen, on another day, twenty two." Only a week later, he continued, "The afflicted. Lord, how are they increased that affect me."

The virus survived outside the human body for weeks and was rife in people's clothing, bedding, and funeral gloves. The meetinghouses were full of infected people seeking solace but unknowingly infecting their fellow congregants with the disease. In late September the Selectmen had ordered several clerks to inspect each home and create an accounting of the sick and deceased. On October 2 both the *Boston Gazette* and *New England Courant* impartially published the findings.

The number who suffered smallpox in the common way numbered some 2,750 persons with 1,499 already recovered. More than 200 had already died, including 174 whites, 15 blacks, and 14 Indians.

On October 7, Mather recorded: "The afflicted still multiply upon me. The contagious distemper seems now at the height in my neighborhood. The number of the sick that had prayers asked for them in the bills at the Old North Church, on the last Lord's Day, was two hundred and two." Thirty-one more were soon added, causing Mather to state resignedly, "I am exceedingly tired, and have little time to study."

By October 8, the "number of persons in the bill for prayers on behalf of the sick of the smallpox in the Old North Church" had risen to a staggering 315. One week later, many of those were dead, but new cases rapidly replenished the numbers who were reported sick. Mather noted: "322 in the notes for the sick of the smallpox prayed for…. My prayers with the sick of the flock take up a very great part of my time." During the month of October, a mind-numbing 411 persons died of smallpox in Boston.

Hundreds died during the autumn, but thousands more were infected with smallpox in the common way. The overwhelming majority suffered the full effect of the disease and recovered. They were scarred and some were blinded by the disease, but they were all comforted by their mothers and wives and by private prayer and the comforting sermons of their ministers.

By the end of October the number of smallpox victims that were tended by skilled female healers and prayed for by Mather had decreased noticeably, even if still frighteningly high. By October 22 Mather noted in his diary, "The sick of the smallpox in the notes to be prayed for sunk to 180."

A few days later, the people of Boston went to their churches upon the tolling of the bells throughout the town at eleven o'clock

in the morning to thank God for his merciful lessening of the affliction of smallpox. The day of thanksgiving occurred on the normal
Thursday lecture day. Mather preached "How to Receive Good, and
How to Receive Evil at the Hand of God" on Job 2:10 to the North
Church congregants: "But he said unto her, Thou speakest like a
foolish woman: What? shall we receive good at the hand of God, and
not receive evil? In all this did not Job sin with his lips."

Mather reflected in his sermon about the benevolence of God's
mercy. Just when the people did not believe that they could handle
any more suffering, God heard their lamentations and relieved their
agony. His punishing hand had chastised his chosen people, and
their piety had been corrected and refined in the fire of the smallpox.
They were reminded to obey the sovereignty of the divine will in
blessings and punishments. As Mather wrote in his diary, "Shall I
not endeavor to show our people after what manner the praises of
the glorious God and his Christ are to be copiously and affectuously
celebrated? I do it this day, which is a day of general thanksgiving
throughout the province."

Mather himself felt overwhelmed by the suffering that he had
done so much to relieve among family, church members, and neighbors. His body and spirit were strained by his unremitting efforts,
and he became ill. "This day, towards the evening, a fever seized me
brought on me by colds taken in my night-visits, and by the poisons
of infected chambers." He knew he was immune to smallpox, so
he did not fear the disease but thought the miasma had sickened
him with fevers nonetheless. He was resigned even to death and
wondered, "Is my hour come? 'Tis welcome."

In the South End, Samuel Sewall was satisfied with the sermon
that was preached, but the dour reactionary was quite displeased
with a change that had taken place for the day of thanksgiving. He
complained that there was "but one sermon in most congregations

by reason of the distress of the smallpox." Such an unapproved change was unacceptable, and he privately railed, "Note. I think so great an alteration should not have been made without the knowledge and agreement of the councilors and other Justices in town met together for that purpose!" Smallpox or no, the ritual of the day of thanksgiving was not to be lightly tampered with, whatever the prudence of the measure. Indeed, Sewall might agree with an unstated proposition that the opportunity to thank God humbly after a time of punishment was not the time to alter the proper format for doing so. It was a time to flee to church as often as possible to repent.

Despite the innovation, the Puritans had evidently pleased God with their regeneration and humble gratitude. Although Cotton Mather had attested often to the divisions that split Boston over the inoculation debate and might have angered God, as of November 5, "the number of the sick in our bills now sunk to little more than 50." That was not much solace to those who lost loved ones. From the day of thanksgiving through December, Sewall attended fourteen funerals that he noted in his diary and "many more" that he did not document. He lost fellow church members, friends, college students with whom he had been acquainted, and fellow public servants. Although the number of smallpox deaths had fallen from the October high and the epidemic was waning, a staggering 249 persons died of the disease in November.

On November 2, a distressed Reverend Mather looked out over his congregation from the pulpit of his church. He saw the worn look on their faces brought on by sleepless nights attending to a dying child or spouse. Some had the vacant stare of mourning. They were numbed by the sheer weight of death around them. Mather alluded to Psalm 38 to offer solace to the grieving who could bear no more pain:

O Lord, rebuke me not in thine anger, neither chastise me
in thy wrath.

For thine arrows have light upon me, and thine hand lieth
upon me.

There is nothing sound in my flesh, because of thine anger:
neither is there rest in my bones because of my sin.

For mine iniquities are gone over mine head, and as a
weighty burden they are too heavy for me.

My wounds are putrefied, and corrupt because of my
foolishness.

I am bowed, and crooked very sore: I go mourning all the
day.

The psalm ends with a prayer: "Forsake me not, O Lord: be not thou far from me, my God. Haste thee to help me, O my Lord, my salvation." Although the minister would not have read the entire psalm during the service, there were probably few in attendance at that Thursday lecture who did not read it over and over again when they returned to their homes. Mather noted in his diary that he preached on that particular psalm because of "a loathsome disease."

Even though fewer were dying, the danger had not passed. On November 7, the members of the General Court were too afraid to meet in Boston and decided to convene in Cambridge: "Whereas the great and General Court…designed to have met at Boston…and inasmuch as the smallpox is in all parts of the town of Boston, and the greatest part of the members of this Court not having had the distemper forbids the session being held there, for which reason his Excellency issued out a proclamation that the session of the General Court should be held at Cambridge." Other regional courts soon followed the example of the General Court and repaired to safer locations where the smallpox was relatively contained.

On November 12, Cotton Mather wrote in his diary, "it being a dying time," he chose to give a sermon on Psalm 63:3 that Sunday. He reminded the congregation to yearn for God's salvation. Their bodies were longing for release from the suffering, and their souls were thirsting for solace. The answer, Mather explained, was found in the verse: "For thy loving kindness is better than life: therefore my lips shall praise thee."

On November 20, James Franklin printed a poem in the *New England Courant* that perfectly captured the suffering and anguish that Bostonians had endured:

> Now on the town an Angel flaming stands
> Grasping tremendous woes in his right hand,
> And in his left, a black and awful list
> Of all our crimes. And shall we dare persist
> In hostile deeds, t' incense an angry God,
> And stand the blows of his revenging rod?
> Stand clear ye fearless sons of vice, whose breasts
> With more than brutish folly are possessed,
> T' engage omnipotence!—His kindled darts
> Will chase and reach, and pierce your flinty hearts.
> See! Now th' infectious clouds begin to rise
> With sickly gloom, to veil the healthful skies:
> The thunder roars, the lightning flashes in our eyes.
> Then let him fight that will, my soul shall fly
> For speedy shelter from the storm so nigh:
> I'll hide me in love's chamber, till his rage
> Is overblown, and mercy mount the stage.
> Then of his sparing grace I'll gladly sing;
> My rescu'd life to him a thankful tribute bring.

By December, the *variola* was expiring. People died of smallpox that month, but the Selectmen reported that the death rate had returned to normal levels. The virus became a victim of its own success. It had infected a total of 5,889 people in a population of nearly 11,000, many of whom previously had the disease in another outbreak; 844 persons reportedly died during the epidemic. There were not enough human hosts for the virus to endure and it expired, having destroyed almost one thousand lives and the fabric of Puritan society. Its ends had nearly been achieved, although it failed in spreading it to other American seaports or the hinterland to any significant degree.

The Selectmen allowed the town to resume normal bell ringing for funerals. The Puritans wanted everyone to *momento mori* (remember death) as a matter of course while they examined their souls for conversion and repentance, so the bells would be allowed to toll. There was no more epidemic to make the politicians limit the macabre reminder. "In as much as the funerals at the present through the goodness of God are very much abated, and not many more than in a time of health," they ordered, "the aforesaid order is superseded, and the bells may be tolled for funerals as heretofore accustomed til further order of the Selectmen."

Cotton Mather was relieved by the cessation of the epidemic and saw it as an opportunity to stir his congregation's piety in thankfulness. "Considering the several classes of people in the flock, the great number that have recovered of a terrible distemper do particularly call for my consideration. And I would with adapted prayers and sermons, awaken them to glorify God their Savior with suitable returns of obedience to him." He reminded himself of the fact that his African servant awaited baptism. He would soon be distracted from this task once again.

The abating smallpox epidemic did not mean that all was quiet in Boston. The debate over inoculation had not quieted, and the newspaper and pamphlet war continued. Many townspeople were still resentful toward Mather and Zabdiel Boylston, especially because inoculations were continuing into the late autumn. Mather himself had incurred the hatred of many people for his role in the controversy. Some people sought to vent their frustration personally on the minister rather than pen some anonymous diatribe in the *New England Courant.* He was about to feel that wrath personally as enemies moved against him for supposedly endangering their lives when he introduced what was perceived to be a deadly new medical procedure. Although he did not know it, Mather's life was in danger.

Chapter Fifteen

"COTTON MATHER, YOU DOG, DAMN YOU!"

Cotton Mather felt chronically hassled throughout the late autumn as hundreds perished in Boston and thousands lay sick. The freeholders had decided against him and Boylston by voting against inoculated persons coming to town. Meanwhile, the interminable animosity against the procedure was expressed in sustained attacks upon him and Boylston. The divisions in the town persisted. The dispute, however, was not one that could be confined to the pages of a newspaper or pamphlet any longer. Mather passionately confronted James Franklin in the street. More ominously, there was a plot afoot to assassinate the Puritan minister.

Mather found the opposition to the inoculation experiment unintelligible. It had worked successfully scores of times while those who caught the disease in the common way had an atrocious death rate. Still, he would attempt to reason with the ignorant and persuade them to accept the plain truth. "The sottish errors and cursed clamors that fill the town and country, raging against the astonishing success of the smallpox inoculated," he wrote, "makes it seasonable for me to state the case and exhibit that which may silence the unreasonable people."

But Mather was close to the breaking point. Some people were assaulting his character unrelentingly. He took solace in the role his Savior played as the suffering servant and in the martyrs of the ancient church, which the Puritans sought to recapture in order to eradicate the errors of Roman Catholic medievalism. "This abominable town," he blasted with a string of alliteration, "treats me in a most malicious and murderous manner for my doing as Christ would have me to do in the saving of lives of the people from a horrible death. But I will go on in the imitation of my admirable Savior and overcome evil with good."

Mather was so irritated that he could barely restrain his anger. One day in early November he crossed paths with the insolent young newspaper editor James Franklin. Mather, "with an air of great displeasure," stopped Franklin and began screaming at him. "You make it your business in the paper called the *Courant* to vilify and abuse the ministers of the town." The minister's eyes were filled with rage, and spittle flew from his lips. Condemnation and threats followed. "There are many curses which await those that do so. The Lord will smite the loins of them that rise up against the Levites. I would have you consider of it. I have no more to say to you." And he stomped off. Everyone's nerves were stretched to the breaking point.

The Selectmen knew that there were people from Roxbury in Cotton Mather's home to receive inoculations. The officials had had enough of Zabdiel Boylston's risky procedure and Mather's collaboration in it. They certainly did not want to encourage people to come from all over the countryside as if under Indian attack, rushing to Boston to receive inoculations and possibly rekindle a diminishing epidemic.

The Selectmen stated that they were "credibly informed that many persons belonging to other towns are already come into this town, and have taken the infection of the smallpox, in the way of inoculation, but that as yet the infection has not operated upon them yet expect that in a few days it will." Moreover, the officials were concerned that "many others belonging to other towns intend to come to this town for the purpose aforesaid, and that they know how to come in and where, and what houses to use in spite of the town." The Selectmen empowered the justices of the peace and constables with warrants to search the town diligently, apprehend the outsiders, and "carry them to the respective towns to which they belong or to the province hospital" at Spectacle Island. The measures were an attempt to "keep them from infecting others."

Boylston apparently did not heed the word of the Selectmen. He performed more than a hundred inoculations during the month, including several prominent individuals, including ministers, a Harvard professor, and Samuel Sewall's grandson, Samuel Hirst. Even on November 29 Mather related to his diary that "several persons at this time under the smallpox inoculated. I must look on as my patients, and so, my relatives."

The Selectmen called several ministers to appear at a meeting and answer accusations that they were encouraging country people to come to Boston to be inoculated in violation of the law. "After some hot discourse on both sides," the ministers denied it with barefaced lies, knowing full well that they were continuing. One thing the public authorities failed to do was to arrest the inoculator who continually defied the law.

Boylston and Mather broke the law, perhaps believing they had a higher law to obey. If they did, they helped undermine the covenantal basis of Puritan society that respected the voluntary submission to law and authority. They were breaking the law in tandem: Boylston performing inoculations in Mather's home and certainly with his support elsewhere. Others were similarly preparing to violate the civil law as well as God's commandment against murder. There was a complete breakdown in law and order in Boston.

One person in Boston had had enough of the high and mighty Cotton Mather. He lorded his position over everyone, thinking he was better than everyone else. He was filled with rage that the fool minister was in league with the quack Boylston giving people smallpox. What they were doing just did not make sense. The resentment boiled for weeks, if not months, and was now about to explode.

The person must have nervously sat in his home, an assortment of odd materials spread out on the table. With quivering hands, the individual poured black powder into a spherical shape. Some liquid followed the powder into the metal ball. He probably feared that someone would knock on the door and discover what was going on.

The figure went over to a desk and grabbed a quill, some ink, and a few small pieces of parchment. He might have thrown a couple of the scraps away, dissatisfied that his feelings were properly conveyed. The individual choose his words carefully. The figure reached for a small cord of material and began to fasten it to the sphere.

Where had the individual secured the materials being assembled? Was he working alone or plotting with others? Was he goaded to act because of comments overheard in a tavern or direct conversation with some friends? Did he know Mather casually or was the minister a remote figure known only from the pages of the *New England Courant,* which dared to speak the truth about him? Was he young or old? black or white? rich or poor? Had loved ones and dear friends recently died from smallpox? How many funerals had he accompanied to a burying ground? Did he know one of the few victims of smallpox inoculation gone awry? These are all questions history leaves unanswered.

He probably sat staring at the black ball for some indeterminable amount of time. Minutes turned into hours. The last light of the setting sun had long ago faded and the nine o'clock curfew bells rung. Well past midnight he steeled his heart to act. The individual stepped furtively into the night. Even the drunken sailors who risked breaking the curfew had gone to their rooms. The night was quiet.

The Mather home on Ship Street was still in the morning hours before dawn. Three guests slept fitfully in the lodging room. Mather's nephew, Reverend Thomas Walter, had traveled from Roxbury with two gentlemen into Boston. Walter had risked the epidemic in order to "undergo the smallpox inoculat[ion], and so return to the service of his flock, which have the contagion begun among them." Walter was one of the cases that had prompted the authorities to stop people from coming to town for that purpose.

Dr. Boylston inoculated the three men on October 31. He later wrote that the three provided a great service to Roxbury because they related their successful inoculations to the town, and more than forty others followed them in seeking inoculations. Walter's symptoms recently commenced, his dreams haunted him as he faded in and out of sleep. Little did he know that a real specter was stalking him.

At roughly three o'clock in the morning on November 14, a figure probably stood in the shadows, staring at the windows of the home and planning his escape route. The metal of the bomb was cold to his touch, but a source of fire was brought into contact with the fuse. He hurled the weapon toward the house.

Shattered glass and the iron ball smashed onto the floor of Walter's bedroom and instantly awoke him and the others in the room. Mather came running into the room with his wife, his daughter Nancy, and his servants. The minister saw the sundered bomb lying in two pieces on the floor. He bent down to inspect it, seeing that "the granado was charged, the upper part with dried powder, the lower part with a mixture of oil of turpentine and powder and what else I know not."

Looking around the room, Mather deduced that the unexploded grenade "passing through the window, had by the iron in the middle of the casement such a turn given to it, that in falling on the floor, the fired wild-fire in the fuse was violently shaken out upon the floor without firing the granado."

Everyone present, especially Walter and his traveling companions, knew that they were lucky to be alive. After all, the "weight of the iron ball alone, had it fallen upon [Walter's] head, would have been enough to have done part of the business designed." But if it had detonated, it surely would have killed them. Mather thought that "upon its going off, it must have split, and have probably killed the persons in the room and certainly fired the chamber and speedily laid the house in ashes."

Interestingly, Mather picked up the broken pieces of the grenade to inspect it and found a piece of paper tied to the fuse with a string "that it might outlive the breaking of the shell." It was a dubious proposition that the parchment would survive the incendiary explosion, but the assailant wrote out the message and attached it anyway. It read, "Cotton Mather, you dog, damn you! I'll inoculate you with this, with a pox to you!"

Stunned, the minister led his extended family in a prayer of thanksgiving to be alive. "This night there stood by me the angel of the God, whose I am and whom I serve; and the merciful Providence of God my Savior so ordered it," Mather wrote in his diary later that day. He and Walter agreed to thank God in a special way for their surviving the attack. "My kinsman having received so great a deliverance, he shall not stir from me till we have contrived and resolved, some very special and signal service to be done by him for the Kingdom of God."

Mather looked through the window for the mysterious attacker, but the person was long gone. The minister had so many enemies he could hardly have guessed who might have done such a thing. No one in the house felt much like sleeping afterward and gathered to talk about it. Mather resolved to do something about it.

The minister met the following day with some members of the General Court assembled in Cambridge. They were afraid to come to Boston to investigate the attempted murder both because of the epidemic and because of the inoculations being performed at the crime scene. Mather explained what happened, and they responded by offering a reward to apprehend the "villain" responsible for the crime. They immediately voted the sum of fifty pounds to "such person or persons as shall discover the author of the above said wickedness, so that he be brought to exemplary justice." Despite the reward, the perpetrator was never discovered.

Mather also planned to meet with other ministers of the town and discuss how to calm the tempers and fears that led people to such violence. "Ought not the ministers of the town, to be called together that we may consider what may be our duty and most proper to be done upon the occasion of Satan let loose to possess the town?" They did not convene for quite some time, but what he failed to understand was how much he was contributing to the declining respect for the ministry by spearheading the inoculation movement.

Mather composed a newspaper story for the *Boston News-Letter* to prevent the "spreading false reports about the country." He stated ruefully that he was not asking himself "what good he could do," but now, "How shall I prevent others from doing evil?"

At North Church, Mather had the perfect forum for him to preach about the event and the wider controversy. On the Sunday after the attempted assassination, he rose on November 19 and delivered a sermon on Acts 27:23–24: "For there stood by me this night the Angel of God, whose I am, and whom I serve, saying, Fear not, Paul." He chose the passage "on the occasion of the astonishing deliverance, the last week, bestowed upon me."

Mather then discoursed on the "services done by the good Angels, for the servants of God. So I will bespeak more praises to God my Savior for the benefits of the angelic ministry, which alas are not enough thought upon."

With every word and the encouragement of his congregation, Mather felt vindicated in what he was doing. He became more convinced that he was about to become a martyr for Christ to the cause of inoculation. He returned to his study following the afternoon sermon and examined recent events.

Mather believed that he was in the right and doing the good he had pledged himself to practice. "I have been guilty of such a crime as this. I have communicated a never-failing and a most allowable method of preventing death and other grievous miseries by a terrible distemper among my neighbors. Every day demonstrates that if I had been hearkened to, many precious (and hundreds) had been saved."

His opponents had vilified him to such an extent that he would probably be killed for it. Indeed, he believed that he heard whispers condoning the action and expected another attempt on his life at any time: "The opposition to it has been carried on with senseless ignorance and raging wickedness. But the growing triumphs of truth over it throw a possessed people into a fury which will probably cost me my life. I have proofs that there are people who approve and applaud the action of Tuesday morning, and who give out words that though the first blow miscarried, there will quickly come another that shall do the business more effectually."

As Mather considered his impending martyrdom he did not recoil from it. "Now I am so far from any melancholy fear on this occasion that I am filled with unutterable joy at the prospect of my approaching martyrdom." He joyfully envisioned himself to be Christ on the cross or martyred in Rome like many ancient Christians and welcomed his death. "When I think on my suffering death for saving the lives of dying people, it even ravishes me with a joy unspeakable and full of glory." He was even strangely trying not to avert it. "I cannot help longing for the hour when it will be accomplished. I am even afraid almost of doing anything for my preservation. I have a Crown before me; and I now know by feeling, what I formerly knew only by reading, of the divine consolations with which the minds of Martyrs have been sometimes irradiated." Finally, he would much rather "die by such hands as now threaten my life," he thought, "than by a fever."

Mather pondered thoughts such as these for the rest of the week, culminating in the sermon "A Crucifixion with Christ" he delivered on the last Sunday in November on Galatians 2:20, which centered on Calvinist justification as well as crucifixion: "I am crucified with Christ, thus I live, yet not I now, but Christ liveth in me; and in that which I now live in the flesh, I live by the faith in the Son of God, who hath loved me, and given himself for me. I do not abrogate the grace of God, for if righteousness be by the Law, then Christ died without a cause."

Over the next few weeks, Mather oscillated between his feelings of martyrdom and practicing charity toward his would-be assassin. Perhaps his sermon of December 3 gave him pause for praying too much to die for his cause. He entitled the sermon "Our Desires and Our Groanings, Yea, the Hidden Desires Which Rise No Higher than Groanings, All Known unto the Glorious God." Prayers of desolation and cries for help largely replaced his desire for death when he turned to Psalm 38:9: "Lord, I pour my whole desire before thee, and my sighing is not hid from thee."

On the following Wednesday, while in his study, Mather mustered his strength to pray for the person who had bombed his home. He was ready to practice forgiveness as he had been called to do in Scripture. He made "particular supplications for the welfare of the unknown person who sought my death by the fired granado."

However, Mather could still not entirely abandon the feelings of persecution. Weeks later, he appealed to the example of Stephen the martyr in his prayers: "When the protomartyr Stephen had his countrymen crying and with a loud voice upon him, and stopping their ears, and running on him, and stoning of him, he was then so favored of Heaven, that he could say, 'Behold I see the heavens opened.' At this time, I am engaged in the methods of supplication and of meditation to seek such a favor that I am behold and see the heavens opened."

Mather met with other ministers in mid-January and offered a rather pathetic cry for attention. He read them a speech he had prepared. He whimpered that his life was dedicated to "doing Good" but "my opportunities to do good which have been to me the apple of my eye, have been strangely struck at. Odd occurrences have happened which have produced unaccountable combinations in all ranks of men to disable me for doing what I have most inclined unto."

Correctly, he described how the people of the town had disparaged him. Of course, he thought all of the attacks were nothing but lies and then disingenuously claimed that he had endured them silently when in reality he had prayed for a more moderate tongue. "The most false representations imaginable have been made of me, and of my conduct. And though I could easily have confuted the slanders and clamors, I have rather born them with silence, and been as the sheep is before the shearers, and as a man in whose mouth there are no reproofs. I hope I have known what it is to take pleasure in humiliations and annihilations."

But Mather could not tolerate the abuse any longer. Even worse, he averred that any further prospect of "doing Good" in Boston had been "almost entirely extinguished." He intimated that he was considering "doing Good" in "more distant places." He felt too harassed and believed he was entitled to more respect, so he was considering moving elsewhere. Practically inviting them to beg him to stay and give up his plans, he closed.

Reverend William Cooper pleasingly took the bait and quickly replied, "I hope the Devil don't hear you, sir!" Others joined in and convinced Mather not to leave his home and ministry in the port city.

In February, Mather and his fellow Boston ministers published a pamphlet titled *A Vindication of the Ministers of Boston, from the Abuses and Scandals, Lately Cast upon Them, in Diverse Printed Papers*. Their object was to defend themselves against the attacks published in James Franklin's *New England Courant*. They went on at some length, claiming the respect due to them as ministers of the Lord: "The sacred oracles of our blessed Savior everywhere charge us to treat the ministers of religion with a becoming esteem and veneration."

To their astonishment, "we see some in this place so daringly profane as to libel and lampoon these…servants of our blessed Jesus." It was unacceptably brazen folly and impudence in their view. If anyone wondered who they were referring to, the ministers stated, "Above all, we wonder at a weekly paper, which has been, and is now, published either designedly to affront the ministers, and render them odious; or else, it has hitherto wretchedly deviated from its ultimate intent, and been notoriously prostituted to that hellish servitude."

The abuse was sufficient to make "the most professed libertine blush." The attacks on the ministers were unwarranted because of all that they had done for the townspeople during the epidemic. They were "unshaken and constant" in fulfilling the duties of their offices. They prayed and delivered sermons and attended to the spiritual needs of the faithful. Their pastoral visits continued despite the general sickness. They offered relief in private conversations. Finally, they should be thanked rather than condemned for recommending "an instrument of saving many lives." The pamphlet contrasted the "blessed pastors" with those who were "given over to a penal hardness of heart."

Try as they might to save their declining prestige, every word that the ministers wrote confirmed that they no longer enjoyed the position they once held. They pushed back harder and harder, virtually damning those who dared to challenge their authority. They played into the hands of men like James Franklin who needed fodder for their attacks.

The smallpox epidemic had fortunately run its course. Mather's chief enemies were now embattled themselves as he fought to recover his prestige. Mather was going on the offensive to recover his lost personal and ministerial authority. But his bitter design against his perceived enemies did not help him to restore his influence and may have helped to ruin it. Mather had proven, with Boylston's help, that inoculation worked, saving hundreds of lives in the process. But he had staked his authority on the innovative procedure and gambled it away. The prestige that the ministers enjoyed one hundred years before could not recover from this controversy.

The public health crisis may have passed, but the debate over inoculation—or perhaps more precisely, the personal conflict among the primary actors—continued. Mather wrote about his intent to deal with James Franklin: "Warnings are to be given unto the wicked printer and his accomplices who every week publish a vile paper to lessen and blacken the ministers of the town and render their ministry ineffectual. A wickedness never paralleled anywhere upon the face of the earth!"

Chapter Sixteen

THE FINAL BOSTON INOCULATIONS

In the first half of 1722, with the inoculation controversy having descended into the gutter of incivility and name-calling, Judge Samuel Sewall's life had essentially returned to normal. He was involved in squabbles unrelated to the smallpox epidemic, but now that the health crisis was over, he also enjoyed several events that changed his life. By the end of the spring, however, his family would be thrust into the center of the final spasm of the inoculation debate.

Sewall visited Governor Samuel Shute on January 16, 1722, and presented him with a ring memorializing the horrible experience in Boston over the past six months and offering hope. It was inscribed with the Latin phrase *Post tenebras Lucem,* which reminded the governor that there was "light after the darkness of the smallpox" and of the visit by the prince of darkness.

Religious divisions in Puritan Boston could rarely stay buried for long, only obscured by a greater temporary emergency. Despite the policy of official toleration swept in by the Glorious Revolution, the presence of Anabaptists, Anglicans, and Quakers chronically stirred up doctrinal controversies. In January, Sewall and the other overseers of Harvard University met to consider Edward Wigglesworth for a professorship of divinity endowed by wealthy London merchant and college benefactor Thomas Hollis.

Hollis was an Anabaptist who believed in the baptism of adult believers only. Severely persecuted by other Protestant groups in Europe, Anabaptists faced hostility in colonial Massachusetts as well. The university overseers turned a wary eye toward Hollis's gift because he required that the candidates for the professorship could not be disqualified because of their Anabaptist faith, although he also mandated the person be "in communion with a church of Congregational, Presbyterians, or Baptists."

Sewall was willing to spurn the gift with such restrictions. He objected and desired "to have my dissent entered" for the record. "You shan't have it!" yelled the governor, and the debate ensued. Sewall believed the qualified donation was "a bribe to give my sentence in disparagement of infant baptism, and I will endeavor to shake my hands from holding it."

When the overseers questioned Wigglesworth on his beliefs, he answered that he assented to the "divine right of infant baptism." They were satisfied and two weeks later Wigglesworth was elected a professor of divinity at Harvard College.

More pleasantly, although perhaps even more nerve-wracking, Sewall was in love with Mary Gibbs. Sewall had lost his first wife, Hannah, in 1717, and a second wife, Abigail Tilley, in May 1720. He had courted Katharine Winthrop, the widow of Waitstill Winthrop, but to his dismay, she spurned him even after he offered her gifts and a proposal. Mary Gibbs had lost her husband in the 1702 smallpox epidemic.

Sewall and Gibbs had a quaint courtship combined with detailed negotiations. Sewall rode his carriage along the icy roads out to Newton to visit her every few days in January. Sewall tipped his hat to her like a gentleman; Mary responded with a matronly curtsy. On one visit he presented her with an orange, and he also arranged for her a proper visit to his mansion. Sewall took pride in his upright courtship, noting that a friend "complimented me respecting my courtship."

The pair had long since passed the age of youthful dowries and discussed what amounted to a prenuptial agreement, focusing on their individual wealth and how it would be distributed among their children. Once they cleared up the business end of their relationship, Sewall wrote her formally: "Your obliging answer harmonizes with the proposal mentioned in mine. These preliminaries being agreeably stated, I long now to see you." Before long, they were engaged.

On March 29, the couple's marriage was officiated by Sewall's son-in-law, Rev. William Cooper, at the Sewall mansion. There was no exchange of wedding rings or formal vows; they answered a single question by giving their assent. Puritan weddings were actually civic ceremonies. Ministers were not allowed to perform weddings until 1686, and this was done by order of the Crown.

The couple hosted a celebratory feast after the wedding. Sewall did not record whether he and his new wife were regaled with a bawdy charivari of obnoxious noise-making and ribald songs outside their bed chamber.

Life in Boston was returning to normal. In February, while the Sewalls' attention was diverted by their courtship, the town's Selectmen issued a statement informing the population that there were no known cases of smallpox in Boston. Trade resumed, and shops reopened for business. As spring came, ships from distant ports began arriving with decreasing consternation from a wary population. The Selectmen were glad to see "the inhabitants that went out of town to avoid that distemper are returned" and "our country neighbors daily coming into town" to trade their goods at the markets. Unfortunately for the young men at Harvard, they were going to have a greatly abbreviated summer vacation. Because the smallpox epidemic from the previous summer and fall had caused them to be "absent a great part of the year past," the General Court ordered them to remain on campus that they "may in some measure regain their lost time." The groans could probably be heard all the way in Boston. The horror of the smallpox epidemic receded in people's memories. The furor over inoculation quieted down, and resentments slowly gave way to charitable Christian forgiveness. For a time, that is.

During a chilly night in late March 1722, as spring was struggling to break the grip that winter held on Boston, a figure darted furtively through the darkness. He moved as stealthily as possible, considering his large frame. It was not another assassin with murder in his eyes, and he was carrying nothing deadlier than a few sheets of paper flapping in his hand. He headed toward a place well known to him: James Franklin's printshop. The individual glanced at the sheets by the moonlight and then slipped them under the door.

Apprentice Benjamin Franklin knew that his brother "would object to printing anything of mine in his paper if he knew it to be mine." So Franklin wrote his essay trying to "disguise my hand," and he "put it in at night under the door of the printing house."

In the morning, James read the sheet he stumbled across in the morning and was suitably impressed with the anonymous piece. He showed it to friends, who also liked it. Benjamin witnessed this and relished their praise as he feigned ignorance of its author. "They read it, commented on it in my hearing, and I had the exquisite pleasure of finding it met with their approbation and that in their different guesses at the author none were named but men of some character among us for learning and ingenuity." The essay was appropriately mocking of the authorities and fit in well with the *New England Courant*'s editorial standards. James decided to print it as well as the thirteen essays that followed.

The clever essays were simultaneously modeled after and satires of Cotton Mather's *Bonifacius: Essays to Do Good.* The sixteen-year-old Franklin brilliantly assumed the voice of a middle-aged widow. In the essays he argued for liberty and mocked authority as Franklin did throughout his public life, but these essays cannot be understood apart from the battle over inoculation.

After introducing his character in the first essay, Franklin stated his principle of doing good in "Dogood #2" with clear undertones of satirizing the ministry and government due to the recent newspaper wars. "Know then, I am an enemy to vice, and a friend to virtue. I am one of an extensive charity, and a great forgiver of private injuries: a hearty lover of the clergy and all good men, and a mortal enemy to arbitrary government and unlimited power."

In his fourth essay, published in mid-May, Franklin launched an assault on Harvard College, the colonial center for educating clergymen. The figure of Learning sat atop a stately and magnificent throne, writing out words on a sheet titled the *New England Courant.* Meanwhile, on her left were seated "several antique figures...Latin, Greek, Hebrew, etc." that were veiled in "*idleness,* attended with *ignorance.*" When Silence left the temple, she stated, "I reflected in my mind on the extreme folly of those parents, who, blind to their children's dullness, and insensible of the solidity of their skulls, because they think their purses can afford it, will needs send them to the temple of learning, where, for want of a suitable genius, they learn little more than how to carry themselves handsomely, and enter a room genteelly...and from when they return, after abundance of trouble and charge, as great blockheads as ever, only more proud and self-conceited." Surely Franklin had Reverend Mather in mind when he penned this essay.

The biting satires were further proof that the covenant and the traditional authority of the ministry and the government were under constant bombardment. The ministers were held up for mocking public criticism. In an age that was not known for an expansive free press, government authorities did not seek to censor the author and publisher of the Silence Dogood letters. The contrast with the covenant from a century before was stark.

On May 11, Dr. Zabdiel Boylston inoculated Samuel Sewall's nephew Samuel as well as the young merchant's wife and the three boys living in their household (two sons and an apprentice). They were taken into the home of blacksmith Joseph Hubbard for the duration of their convalescence. Another woman, Joanna Alford, was inoculated at her home and was left in the care of her husband, John.

These were Boylston's first inoculations since late February and his first in Boston since December, when the outbreak had generally expired. Whether Boylston believed the furor had expired and would not be rekindled, or whether he was driven to perform a procedure proven to save lives, he misjudged the community's ensuing response. Their reaction was predictably swift and severe.

In March, the assembly had passed a bill "to prevent the spreading of the infection of the smallpox by the practice of inoculation." This new regulation shows that even after the epidemic had passed and after inoculation had been established as a safer alternative to treating smallpox than the common way, the legislators still argued that it was a dangerous method of spreading the infection. In any event, the council negated the law, allowing Boylston to continue the practice legally. When young Samuel Sewall came to him to be inoculated, the doctor gladly started the practice again.

The Selectmen did not wait to ponder a right course of action. The body proclaimed that the "infection upon the operations taking effect may probably be communicated to others." This was a reasonable fear because Boylston never viewed the virus in inoculated patients as communicable and thus necessitating strict quarantine. His recent patients were rounded up from both the Sewall and Alford homes by the sheriff and town constables and taken to the hospital on Spectacle Island. The island hospital provided the quarantine that would prevent the disease from spreading, thus the Selectmen chose it as the "most suitable place for the reception and accommodation of those inoculated persons."

The Selectmen were not heartless and did not blame the patients for Boylston's actions. The politicians empowered the officers to impress nurses and other necessaries (such as herbal medicines and medical equipment) for the "accommodation, safety, and relief of the said persons." But to show their level of fear and desire to regulate the procedure closely, the General Court decreed that "the persons so inoculated shall not come up to the town of Boston during this present session of the General Assembly without leave first obtained."

That was not the end of it, however. Town officials hauled Boylston to a meeting and threatened him with prosecution. Public opinion was clearly against his practicing inoculation in the town. He was compelled to "solemnly promise to inoculate no more [people] without the knowledge and approbation of the authority of the town." In other words, he was not to practice inoculation at all.

But Boylston had reason to be pleased with himself. He had boldly inaugurated a practice that saved lives. While thousands suffered from smallpox and almost 900 had died, he had inoculated 242 persons and lost only 6 patients. It was a significantly lower death rate than the common way and might prove to be even more successful when others perfected the procedure. He had participated in one of the most innovative medical discoveries of the eighteenth century.

Thus the inoculation controversy ended.

Dr. William Douglass was beside himself with glee at the news of Boylston's censure. The rogue doctor and Cotton Mather had been under fire for several months. Douglass's ally, James Franklin, might still be embattled in the controversy, but Douglass emerged largely unscathed. He had fought for the better part of a year to ban this loathsome practice and reestablish his authority as the town's leading medical practitioner. He had refused to examine any evidence or oversee any inoculations, but he was not going to let a country physician or a minister rule the practice of medicine in Boston.

Douglass published his thoughts in his main forum, the *New England Courant,* raising several red herrings and engaging in numerous personal attacks to ruin his opponents' credibility. He linked the Salem witchcraft trials and the inoculation trials to paint his adversaries as credulous and murderous fools. He wrote: "Last January inoculation made a sort of exit, like the infatuation thirty years ago, after several had fallen victims to the mistaken notions of Dr. Mather and other learned clerks concerning witchcraft. But finding inoculation in this town, like the serpents in summer, beginning to crawl abroad again the last week, it was in time, and effectually crushed in the bud, by the Justices, Selectmen, and the *unanimous* vote of a general town-meeting."

Such were Douglass's public writings. In private, he wrote to a fellow scientist: "To speak candidly for the present, [treatment for smallpox] seems to be somewhat more favorably received by inoculation than received the natural way." He had opposed inoculation because he was not convinced of its safety and raised "great heats" against its practitioners. In the silence of his own mind, and confiding only in a distant friend, he admitted that inoculations had been successful—even as he stubbornly asserted otherwise publicly.

James Franklin attacked the colonial authorities one too many times as the strokes of his brush of defiance were painted too broadly. The authorities finally pushed back and showed him the limits of their tolerance for his freewheeling attacks on the colony's established institutions, which they saw as subversive of both the public order and the social covenant. The surprising thing was that they allowed him to continue to pillory the societal establishment as long as they did.

On June 11, James published a phony letter to the editor that he himself had penned. In it he criticized the authorities for not sufficiently prosecuting its hunt for the pirates who raided the New England coasts. He derided their efforts, writing, "'Tis thought he will sail sometime this month, if wind and weather permit."

The council instantly hauled James in for questioning. They learned about his subterfuge in printing the letter and ruled that his satire was "a high affront to this government." He was imprisoned for this offense without a trial.

Boston's "public gaol" was a neglected and dilapidated structure, with several inmates previously escaping after a sharp push against the door. James, however, did not attempt to break out. He petitioned the council for his release, humbly expressing his regret for his "indiscretion and indecency…for all which he entreats the court's forgiveness and praying a discharge from the stone prison where he is confined." He had a signed statement from a doctor attesting that the prison was adversely affecting James's health. With the greatest of irony, it was signed by Dr. Zabdiel Boylston.

Benjamin Franklin was called in for questioning regarding his brother's offenses. Benjamin reported that he was "taken up and examined before the Council, but though I did not give them any satisfaction, they contented themselves with admonishing me and dismissed me, considering me perhaps as an apprentice who was bound to keep his master's secrets."

For the next two weeks James remained confined, and his brother published the *Courant*. Benjamin included more Dogood essays, which continued satirically taking Boston's ministers to task. The "hypocritical pretenders to religion" were more dangerous than the openly profane, Dogood posited. The author distrusted "a religious man in power, though he may be a good man; he has many temptations to propagate *public destruction* for *personal advantages*." The most dangerous hypocrites in the commonwealth were those public servants who left "*the gospel for the sake of the law*: a man compounded of law and gospel, is able to cheat a whole country with his religion, and then destroy them under *color of law*." You will know them by their fruits, Dogood advised, for we "must judge of men by the whole of their conduct." And in this, Franklin found them wanting.

Battling a common enemy did not preclude animosity between the Franklin brothers in their unequal relationship of apprentice and master. The relationship turned sour when Franklin revealed his authorship of the Dogood essays: it did "not quite please him, as he thought, probably with reason, that it tended to make me too vain." The revelation was the ostensible cause of the conflict that allowed seething resentments to come to the surface. In short, Franklin believed that his brother was lording his apprenticeship over him and had "demeaned me too much." James also beat Franklin physically. Their father was drawn into the awkward situation to mediate and apparently sided with the younger brother. Franklin regretted his apprenticeship and wished for "some opportunity of shortening it, which at length offered in a manner unexpected."

In the meantime, James resumed publishing the *Courant*. For the next few months he could not resist criticizing the authorities and eventually ran afoul of them again. He praised Christmas (which Puritans did not celebrate because of its pagan origins) and lauded the Yale faculty members who had converted to Anglicanism. On January 14, 1723, perhaps remembering the phrasing of Silence Dogood, James wrote in his paper: "Whenever I find a man full of religious can and pellaver, I presently suspect him of being a knave. Religion is indeed the principal thing, but too much of it is worse than none at all. The world abounds with knaves and villains, but of all knaves, the religious knave is the worst; and villainies acted under the cloak of religion are the most execrable."

The General Court assembled again to decide upon the fate of the printer who tended to "mock religion and bring it into disrespect." In addition, James disturbed "His Majesty's government, and peace and good order." He was ordered to submit all of his articles to a censor for prior approval or "James Franklin, the printer and publisher thereof, be strictly forbidden by this court to print or publish the *New England Courant*." The town had finally acted against James for his insolence, but by then it was too late for ministerial authority. Moreover, the independent-minded printer summarily ignored the edict.

The court sent the sheriff to arrest the seditious printer. James, understanding the seriousness of the charges, caught wind of his impending arrest and went into hiding. He surreptitiously met with his brother Benjamin and hatched a plan to continue publishing his mouthpiece of dissent. James contrived to grant his brother freedom from the rest of his term of labor so that he might be allowed to publish the *Courant*, because it was only James who had been banned. James coerced Benjamin to sign a secret indenture that continued his term for its original duration, but he foolishly believed that the authorities would endorse this deception against their decrees. As Benjamin observed later, "A very flimsy scheme it was."

When renewed tensions tore at the Franklin brothers' relationship, Benjamin resolved to "assert my freedom" and escape. He rightly guessed that James "would not venture to produce the new indentures" to enforce them in court. But James was hardly powerless to impede his brother's freedom. When James caught wind of Franklin's intent, "he took care to prevent my getting employment in any other printing-house of the town, by going round and speaking to every master, who accordingly refused to give me work." James had the economic strings to pull, and he used them to bind his brother.

With a bit of self-puffery regarding his infamy in the community, Franklin later claimed that he had "made myself a little obnoxious to the governing party…that my indiscreet disputations about religion began to make me pointed at with horror by good people as an infidel or atheist." The young man was not constantly under public scrutiny, but it was true that his association with his irreverent brother made him suspect in the eyes of many.

Franklin formulated a shrewder design to escape than his brother had made to keep him bound. The young man sold his growing book collection to raise some money. Enlisting the help of a friend, Franklin went to a ship captain and explained that he had "got a naughty girl with child, whose friends would compel me to marry her." The knowing sea captain smiled at the predicament, having encountered the same problem many times in his long experience in countless ports. He agreed to slip the young man quietly out of Boston.

Before he covertly departed Boston, Franklin was called on by an improbable host. He dutifully went to the Ship Street home with some misgivings, considering the events of the last two years.

After he knocked on the door, a servant led him into one of the finest personal libraries in America. It was also a place of piety where countless prayers and supplications had been given during the smallpox epidemic. The master of the house, Cotton Mather, greeted the suddenly deferential young man pleasantly if gravely. The two discussed matters privately for some time. Franklin recounted, "I had been some time with him in his study, where he condescended to entertain me, a very youth, with some pleasant and instructive conversation." The minister indicated that all was magnanimously forgiven in the recent war of words that had played themselves out in public.

When they completed their conversation in the library, Mather escorted the young man out through a narrow side passage. The minister suddenly called out, "Stoop, stoop!" But Franklin did not hear Mather and banged his head on a low beam. Mather genially moralized to the young man about the virtue of humility: "Let this be a caution to you not always to hold your head so high. Stoop, young man, stoop—as you go through the world—and you'll miss many hard thumps." It was Mather's way of "hammering instruction into one's head."

The seventeen-year-old Franklin embarked on the vessel without letters of recommendation, no names of any printers who might take him on, and "very little money in my pocket." Not to be deterred, he landed at New York and boldly went to the printing shop of William Bradford, the city's only printer. The kindly old man could not take on Franklin but suggested he continue on to Philadelphia, where he might find employment at the printshop of Bradford's son, who had recently lost his assistant.

Franklin booked passage to Perth Amboy, New Jersey, but the sloop was battered by a squall and violently driven toward Long Island. During the storm, a drunken passenger was thrown overboard, and the muscular youth from Boston reached into the water and "drew him up so that we got him in again." As the sloop lay at anchor, riding out the storm, the boat was pounded by the surf, the spray soaking everything on board. Damp, miserable, and hungry, the passengers and crew slept fitfully that night and were barely comforted by a "bottle of filthy rum."

The howling winds finally abated, and a makeshift sail replaced the one tattered in the storm. After the vessel resumed its voyage to Perth Amboy, Franklin became feverish. He crashed in a bed as soon as he went ashore. A deep sleep and great draughts of water healed him, and he was recovered sufficiently to walk fifty miles to Burlington to catch a boat on the Delaware River to Philadelphia. He tramped along in a driving rain and started to regret his decision and "wish I had never left home." He cut a miserable figure and was questioned at an inn about being "some runaway servant"—which he was—but he was evasive and left the next morning.

After another day of walking and a stopover at an inn with a thoughtful, well-read host, he arrived at Burlington. He had missed the regularly scheduled boat to Philadelphia and was compelled to accept the invitation of a kind matron to board him. While walking along the river in the twilight, he spied a boat and learned it was headed for his destination. Because the winds were still, the sturdy youth helped to row the boat for several hours. In the chill and darkness of the autumn night, the boat put in to shore, and the travelers built a fire. At sunrise, they saw that they were closer to Philadelphia than they had believed and rowed to the wharf at Market Street. After purchasing three large, puffy rolls, two of which he tucked under his arms while he chewed on the third, the ambitious youth passed by his future wife as he began to make inquiries about employment at the printing shops.

No one knew that this youth would one day make a vast fortune by printing in America's rising capital, which allowed him to retire early and serve humanity as a statesman and scientist. He would become the most famous American in the world, renowned for his scientific achievements. In celebrated meetings with the iconic figures of European philosophy and science, Benjamin Franklin was hailed as the epitome of the Enlightenment.

Interestingly, Franklin became a fervent advocate of inoculation. In 1730 another smallpox epidemic in Boston was quickly transmitted to New York and Philadelphia. Less than a decade after the Franklin brothers had been mouthpieces of opposition to inoculation, Benjamin sought to dispel rumors that inoculation was a dangerous, risky procedure that did not work. In the *Pennsylvania Gazette,* he reported on inoculations and editorialized, "The first patient of note is now upon recovery, having had none but the most favorable symptoms during the whole course of the distemper, which is mentioned to show how groundless all those reports are that have been spread through the province to the contrary." Franklin published proof from Boston to substantiate his case: "There is an account published of the numbers of persons inoculated in Boston in the month of March, amounting to seventy-two; of which two only died, and the rest have recovered perfect health. Of those who had it in the common way, 'tis computed that one in four died."

Franklin suffered the grievous loss of one of his children, Francis Folger Franklin, to smallpox. He wrote: "In 1736, I lost one of my sons, a fine boy of four years old, by the smallpox taken in the common way. I long regretted bitterly and still regret that I had not given it to him by inoculation. This I mention for the sake of parents, who omit that operation on the supposition that they should never forgive themselves if a child died under it; my example showing that the regret may be the same either way, and that therefore the safer should be chosen."

Franklin inoculated his daughter a few years after this tragedy. Adopting the arguments of his ministerial opponents in 1721, he told the readers of *Poor Richard's Almanac* in 1737, "It now begins to be thought *rash* to hazard taking it in the common way, by which one in seven is generally lost; and *impious* to reject a method discovered to mankind by God's good Providence, whereby 99 in 100 are saved."

Even Dr. William Douglass, after all the contention during the 1721 smallpox outbreak, came to accept the efficacy of inoculations. After he opened his mind and examined the evidence, he grudgingly admitted that the procedure worked. In 1730 he wrote a pamphlet titled *A Practical Essay Concerning the Smallpox* in which he discussed the use of preparatory mercuric regimes that would become an established part of inoculation for decades. He soon became an inoculator himself, later calling the practice "a very considerable and most beneficial improvement." Douglass deserves credit for establishing the first medical society in the American colonies in 1736 and for advocating the creation of the modern profession by requiring formal education and licensing. That same year, he conducted the first clinical study of scarlet fever (ahead of his European contemporaries), emulating the methods of Dr. Boylston during the smallpox epidemic of 1721.

One of the persons Franklin later met in Europe was none other than Dr. Zabdiel Boylston. In 1724 the doctor traveled to England to discuss variolation at the Royal Society. In a letter to the society, Cotton Mather introduced Boylston with effusive praise: "Perhaps the princes and princesses themselves if informed of such a one coming to London may not be unwilling to take some cognizance of a person so distinguished by an operation of so much consequence." Boylston was elected to that august scientific body in May 1726, and in the same year he published a pamphlet titled *An Historical*

Account of the Smallpox Inoculated in New England, a pioneering clinical study in the use of medical statistics in which he determined that fewer persons died from inoculation than in the common way. Boylston lectured on smallpox inoculation at the Royal Society as well as at the Royal College of Physicians.

While he was in London, Boylston encountered Benjamin Franklin, who was there to purchase printing supplies at the behest of Pennsylvania governor William Keith. The governor had duped the credulous young man into believing he would receive patronage and credit for his ambitions to become a printer. Boylston supposedly gave some money to the desperate Franklin. Though he found employment in a London printshop, he was profligate in his spending, wasting it on a number of frivolities.

Cotton Mather died in 1728, eulogized as a man of piety and great learning in scientific endeavors. Benjamin Colman said of him:

> His name is like to live a great while among us in his printed work; but yet these will not convey to posterity, nor give to strangers, a just idea of his real worth and great learning of the man. His works will indeed inform all that read them of his great knowledge and singular piety, his zeal for God, and holiness and truth; and his desire of the salvation of precious souls; but it was conversation and acquaintance with him, in his familiar and occasional discourses and private communications, that discovered the vast compass of his knowledge and the projections of his piety; more than I have sometimes thought than all his pulpit exercises. Here he excelled, here he shone; being exceeding communicative, and bringing out of his treasury things new and old, without measure. Here it is seen how his wit, and his fancy, his invention, his quickness of thought, and ready apprehension were all consecrated to God.

But Colman was wrong. The greatness of Mather's mind and science has generally been lost to history. His popular historical reputation is that of a sad caricature of a zealous witch hunter. His accomplishments of the early American Enlightenment went largely unnoticed by future generations and completely overshadowed by the upstart youth he once battled over smallpox inoculation.

Benjamin Franklin was the man who was renowned for snatching "lightning from the sky and the scepter from tyrants," which made the "name of Franklin like that of Newton, immortal." Franklin has come to embody the American character like no other historical figure. His autobiography has been the model for young Americans for centuries. His rise to greatness, inventiveness, energy, and pluck in the pursuit of wealth, science, and independence has endured as the quintessential American society. He may have been on the wrong side of history briefly during the 1721 smallpox episode, but he had a democrat's irreverent inability to bow down to any man—aristocrat, monarch, or even a Puritan minister.

In this terrible epidemic that killed nearly one thousand people and the fierce inoculation debate that rent Puritan society in its largest city, the ministerial authority of the Puritans was also a victim. Cotton Mather (and Zabdiel Boylston) proved that inoculation worked, but that proof came at a very great price. For decades Puritan ministers had been suffering a declining credibility to shape people's lives and crumbling deference. With every insult printed in the town's newspapers, with every rumor uttered in the street, the people of Boston began to lose respect for their ministers. Even when they defended themselves, the ministers were entrenched in a public controversy in which there could be no winners. The inoculation controversy was the defining moment for the destruction of the one-hundred-year-old covenant.

But this important caution aside, we should realize that the inoculation controversy was fundamentally not based on religious arguments. As we dig deeper, this episode of the Enlightenment reveals something critically important about the eighteenth century. Two men, both scientists, butted heads over a medical practice that was a scientific solution, not a religious answer, to the smallpox epidemic in Boston. The argument shifted subtly from the religious worldview of the seventeenth century to the science of the Enlightenment.

The drama that unfolded in 1721 spelled a death knell for the Puritan experiment. Already undermined by growing worldliness, declining piety, and religious diversity, the authority of its ministers and the cogency of its social covenant were decimated by the furious broadsides of the Boston newspapers. The torch of enlightenment passed from highly educated ministers to a new generation of scientists and thinkers, such as Benjamin Franklin.

In the coming decades, Puritan thought heavily influenced the republican ideology of the American Revolution. Its emphasis on the public good, virtue, and covenantal theology was consistent with the classical republican ideals of ordered liberty and the compact theory of government. During the Revolutionary War, Americans and their leaders voluntarily covenanted with each other and with God to defend their sacred liberties. But the republican vision also assumed an increasingly secular character that focused on republican government and liberties rather than a covenanted Puritan society governed by the Ten Commandments. Perhaps more important, the American Revolution unleashed a fundamental revolution against all vestiges of social hierarchy and monarchy. This democratic revolution of social forces was rooted upon the principle of equality and self-governance.

Americans would no longer step out of the way of their "betters" or defer to someone because of his or her station in society. Americans moved westward, eagerly sought out opportunities for social mobility, and pursued wealth and profit in an industrial-izing society. The republican moment in which the altered Puritan covenant helped to create the American Revolution passed quickly, giving way to the tide of democratic forces. The archetype for the American character through the centuries would be Benjamin Franklin, not Cotton Mather.

CONCLUSION

In 1962 Thomas Kuhn postulated in his book *The Structure of Scientific Revolutions* that revolutionary theories and discoveries in science are initially resisted by scientific communities bound to a particular way of thinking—a paradigm. Kuhn argued that the scientific community "often suppresses fundamental novelties." Paradigm shifts, in which revolutionary changes in scientific thinking occur, are only gradually accepted by scientists. But, he continued, "the very nature of normal research ensures that novelty shall not be suppressed for very long."

The 1721 smallpox epidemic and inoculation controversy in Boston epitomized Kuhn's thesis. The doctors of the town resisted an innovative medical practice because their traditional medical ideas and practices originated in the ancient world. Even though Aristotle, Hippocrates, and Galen were increasingly challenged by advancements during the scientific revolution and Enlightenment, allegiance to these ancient thinkers died hard. The doctors in Boston had good reason for caution as the practitioners experimented somewhat haphazardly and without taking reasonable precautions. But they refused to engage the scientific method by testing an unproven hypothesis. They also made fundamentalist religious arguments that confounded the debate and muddied the issue of science and religion. Finally, they accepted the paradigm shift that inoculation presented in humanity's struggle against smallpox.

It was a Puritan minister and one lone doctor who stood up to the medical establishment and boldly continued the practice in the face of vehement medical and popular opposition. They defended their experiments with religious arguments steeped in eighteenth-century natural law consistent with Puritan belief. But their arguments were primarily that inoculation was a sound and efficacious medical practice, and they followed the scientific method to test their theory.

It was the hidebound and haughty Dr. William Douglass who fought the practice tooth and nail, and a man of God who bravely proved that inoculation worked and saved many lives. Cotton Mather scorned those who clung tenaciously to their scientific presuppositions and refused to examine new views. He once criticized a Florentine scientist who declined to look through Galileo's telescope because "he was afraid that then his eyes would from ocular demonstrations, make him stagger concerning the truth of Aristotle's principles, which he was resolved he would never call in question."

Indeed, we cannot escape the overwhelming evidence from this dramatic story that Douglass and most of Boston's physicians acted unscientifically throughout the entire contest. They refused to examine evidence, withheld scientific literature that contradicted their arguments, manufactured testimony that they probably knew was false, argued from racist premises, and used personal attacks to defeat their opponents. Contrarily, Cotton Mather and Zabdiel Boylston examined the findings in scientific journals, confirmed them with those who knew about the procedure, and tested the procedure repeatedly and successfully through experiments that proved their hypothesis.

Still, the inoculation crisis of 1721 helps to show that the history of Western science has followed a progressive march. If we take a more expansive view of the events of 1721, we can clearly see how scientific discoveries occurred and incrementally increased scientific knowledge in the eighteenth century. Mather and Boylston stood "on the shoulders of giants," to use Isaac Newton's often-quoted phrase. They did not have an "aha!" moment but simply introduced into the American colonies what had already been practiced elsewhere. It was communicated from the periphery of Europe through contact between different cultures. Although the West has often appropriated scientific ideas from around the globe without acknowledging their origin, Mather always credited his sources. When the ideas were transmitted to Western Europe, they were then spread easily within the scientific community through international journals. This community was committed to the new ideas of an enlightened age in which scientists would unlock the mysteries of the universe. So the pair of Bostonians was initiating a practice from abroad that had a long history of success. Within a few decades, the doctors in the West accepted the practice and were able to improve upon it with the discovery of vaccination. Even then, however, it was discovered by a bit of serendipity when Edward Jenner developed a vaccine from cowpox after he noticed that milkmaids were immune to inoculation. But we can trace the discovery of vaccination from the introduction of inoculation by Cotton Mather in America and Lady Mary Wortley Montagu in England and its subsequent widespread adoption by physicians in those places. Jenner's vaccination eventually led to the elimination of the disease from humanity and saved millions of lives, and Mather deserves to share in the credit for this accomplishment.

The inoculation controversy shows us that we cannot blithely continue to make the simplistic and wrong assumption that religion has been an impediment to the progress of modern science and reason throughout the centuries. Moreover, the idea of a conflict between science and religion is a product of the dogmatic and shrill voices on both sides that demonize their opponents and garner media attention. Unexpectedly, an episode from Puritan Massachusetts helps us to debunk those who would pit science against religion. One historian of science has succinctly summarized their reconciliation that might have a great deal of relevance for our debates in the public square today:

> Between the knowledge of God revealed in the Bible and natural knowledge obtained by rational, experimental means there was an essential unity, as both derived ultimately from God. Natural knowledge was, then, a partial manifestation of the mind of God. There was no conflict between science and religion, nor were there any controversies of this nature either in colonial America or in the homeland. To the adherent of this natural theology, as it soon became known, experimental science was an instrument of theology whereby man might enlarge his knowledge of God's laws and the wonders of God's universe.

Thus we might introduce a little sanity and tolerance into our discussions of the pursuit of truth and the relationship of faith and reason, accepting the obvious fact that many scientific persons are people of faith and many religious people readily accept the majestic truths about the universe that science has revealed.

BIBLIOGRAPHY

PRIMARY SOURCES

NEWSPAPERS

Boston Gazette

Boston News-Letter

New England Courant

PAMPHLETS

Boylston, Zabdiel. *An Historical Account of the Small-Pox Inoculated in New England, upon All Sorts of Persons, Whites, Blacks, and of All Ages and Constitutions.* London: S. Chandler, 1726; Boston: S. Gerrish, 1730.

Colman, Benjamin. *Some Observations on the New Method of Receiving the Smallpox by Engrafting or Inoculation, in New England.* Boston, 1721.

Cooper, William. *A Letter to a Friend in the Country.* Boston, 1721.

Douglass, William. *The Abuses and Scandals of Some Late Pamphlets in Favor of Inoculation of the Smallpox.* Boston, 1722.

———. *A Dissertation Concerning Inoculation of the Smallpox. Giving Some*

Account of the Rise, Progress, Success, Advantages, and Disadvantages of Receiving the Smallpox by Incisions. Boston, 1730.

———. *Inoculation of the Smallpox as Practiced in Boston.* Boston, 1722.

———. *A Practical Essay Concerning the Smallpox.* Boston, 1730.

Greenwood, Isaac. *A Friendly Debate, or a Dialogue between Academicus, and Sawny and Mundungus, Two Eminent Physicians about Some of Their Late Performances.* Boston, 1722.

A Letter from One in the Country, to his Friend in the City: In Relation to their Distresses Occasioned by the Doubtful and Prevailing Practice of the Inoculation of the Smallpox. Boston, 1721.

Mather, Cotton. *An Account of the Method and Success of Inoculating the Smallpox in Boston in New England.* Boston, 1722.

———. *A Pastoral Letter, to Families Visited with Sickness from Several Ministers of Boston, at a Time of Epidemical Sickness Distressing of the Town.* 3rd impression. Boston, 1721.

———. *Some Account of What Is Said of Inoculating or Transplanting the Smallpox by the Learned Dr. Emmanuel Timonius and Jacobus Pylarinus.* Boston: S. Gerrish, 1721.

———. *A Vindication of the Ministers of Boston from the Abuses and Scandals, Lately Cast upon Them, in Diverse Printed Papers.* Boston, 1722.

Mather, Increase. *Several Reasons Proving that Inoculation or Transplanting the Smallpox, is a Lawful Practice, and That It Has Been Blessed by God for the Saving of Many a Life.* Boston, 1721.

Sewall, Samuel. *The Selling of Joseph: A Memorial.* Boston: Green and Allen, 1700.

Williams, John. *An Answer to a Later Pamphlet, entitled, A Letter to a Friend in the Country, Attempting a Solution of the Scruples and Objections of a Conscientious or Religious Nature, Commonly Made Against the New Way of Receiving the Smallpox.* Boston, 1722.

———. *Several Arguments Proving That Inoculating the Smallpox Is Not Contained in the Law of Physick, Either Natural or Divine, and Therefore Unlawful.* Boston, 1721.

PUBLISHED SOURCES

Allison, Robert J., ed. *Olaudah Equiano, The Interesting Narrative of the Life of Olaudah Equiano: Written by Himself.* Boston: Bedford Books, 1995.

Bradford, William. *Of Plymouth Plantation.* Mineola, NY: Dover, 2006.

Franklin, Benjamin. *Benjamin Franklin's Autobiography.* Edited by J. A. Leo Lemay and P. M. Zall. New York: Norton, 1986.

Isaacson, Walter, ed. *A Benjamin Franklin Reader.* New York: Simon and Schuster, 2005.

Jacob, Margaret C. *The Enlightenment: A Brief History with Documents.* Boston: Bedford Books, 2001.

Kittredge, George L. "Some Lost Works of Cotton Mather." *Proceedings of the Massachusetts Historical Society* 45 (1911–1912): 418–79.

Labaree, Leonard, ed. *The Papers of Benjamin Franklin.* 39 vols. New Haven: Yale University Press, 1959–2008.

Lemay, J. A. Leo, ed. *Benjamin Franklin: Autobiography, Poor Richard, and Later Writings.* New York: Library of America, 1987.

The Letters and Papers of Cadwallader Colden, 1711–1729. 7 vols. New York: New York Historical Society, 1917–1923.

Massachusetts General Court. *The Acts and Resolves, Public and Private, of the Province of the Massachusetts Bay, 1720–1726.* 21 vols. Boston: Wright and Potter, 1902.

Mather, Cotton. *Diary of Cotton Mather.* Collections of the Massachusetts Historical Society, 7th ser., nos. 7–8. 2 vols. Boston: Massachusetts Historical Society, 1911–1912.

A Report of the Record Commissioners of the City of Boston, Selectmen Minutes, 1715–1729. Boston, 1885.

Silverman, Kenneth, ed. *Selected Letters of Cotton Mather.* Baton Rouge: Louisiana State University Press, 1971.

Thomas, M. Halsey, ed. *The Diary of Samuel Sewall, 1674–1729.* 2 vols. New York: Farrar, Straus, and Giroux, 1973.

Warner, Michael, ed. *American Sermons: The Pilgrims to Martin Luther King, Jr.* New York: Library of America, 1999.

Yazawa, Mel, ed. *The Diary and Life of Samuel Sewall.* Boston: Bedford Books, 1998.

BOOKS AND ARTICLES

Bailyn, Bernard. *The Ideological Origins of the American Revolution.* Cambridge, MA: Harvard University Press, 1967.

———. *New England Merchants in the Seventeenth Century.* Cambridge, MA: Harvard University Press, 1955.

Barry, John M. *The Great Influenza: The Story of the Deadliest Pandemic in History.* New York: Penguin, 2004.

Beall, Otto T. Jr., and Richard H. Shyrock. *Cotton Mather: First Significant Figure in American Medicine.* Baltimore: Johns Hopkins University Press, 1954.

Bercovitch, Sacvan. *The American Jeremiad.* Madison: University of Wisconsin Press, 1978.

———. *The Puritan Origins of the American Self.* New Haven: Yale University Press, 1975.

Berkin, Carol. *First Generations: Women in Colonial America.* New York: Hill and Wang, 1996.

Berlin, Ira. *Many Thousands Gone: The First Two Centuries of Slavery in North America.* Cambridge, MA: Harvard University Press, 1998.

Black, Jeremy. *The British Seaborne Empire.* New Haven: Yale University Press, 2004.

Blake, John B. *Public Health in the Town of Boston, 1630–1822.* Cambridge, MA: Harvard University Press, 1959.

———. "The Inoculation Controversy in Boston: 1721–1722." *New England Quarterly* 25 (December 1952): 489–506.

Bobrick, Benson. *Wide as the Waters: The Story of the English Bible and the Revolution It Inspired.* New York: Simon and Schuster, 2001.

Bolster, W. Jeffrey. *Black Jacks: African American Seamen in the Age of Sail.* Cambridge, MA: Harvard University Press, 1997.

Bonomi, Patricia U. *Under the Cope of Heaven: Religion, Society, and Politics in Colonial America.* New York: Oxford University Press, 1986.

Boorstin, Daniel. *The Americans: The Colonial Experience.* New York: Vintage, 1958.

Brands, H. W. *The First American: The Life and Times of Benjamin Franklin.* New York: Anchor, 2000.

Breen, T. H. *The Character of the Good Ruler: Puritan Political Ideas in New England, 1630–1730.* New York: Norton, 1970.

———. *Puritans and Adventurers: Change and Persistence in Early America.* New York: Oxford University Press, 1980.

Breitwieser, Mitchell Robert. *Cotton Mather and Benjamin Franklin: The Price of Representative Personality.* Cambridge: Cambridge University Press, 1984.

Bridenbaugh, Carl. *Cities in the Wilderness: The First Century of Urban Life in America, 1625–1742.* 2nd ed. New York: Knopf, 1955.

Brock, C. Helen. "The Influence of Europe on Colonial Massachusetts Medicine." In *Medicine in Colonial Massachusetts.* Edited by Frederick S. Allen Jr. Boston: Colonial Society of Massachusetts, 1980.

———. "North America, A Western Outpost of European Medicine." In *The Medical Enlightenment of the Eighteenth Century.* Edited by Andrew Cunningham and Roger French. Cambridge: Cambridge University Press, 1990.

Brown, Richard D. "The Healing Arts in Colonial and Revolutionary Massachusetts: The Context for Scientific Medicine." In *Medicine in Colonial Massachusetts.* Edited by Frederick S. Allen Jr. Boston: Colonial Society of Massachusetts, 1980.

Burnham, John C. *What Is Medical History?* Cambridge: Polity, 2005.

Bushman, Richard L. *From Puritan to Yankee: Character and the Social Order in Connecticut, 1690–1765.* Cambridge, MA: Harvard University Press, 1967.

———. *King and People in Provincial Massachusetts.* Chapel Hill: University of North Carolina Press, 1985.

Bynum, William. *The History of Medicine: A Very Short Introduction.* Oxford: Oxford University Press, 2008.

Calloway, Colin G. *New Worlds for All: Indians, Europeans, and the Remaking of Early America.* Baltimore: Johns Hopkins University Press, 1997.

Carrell, Jennifer Lee. *The Speckled Monster: A Historical Tale of Battling Smallpox.* New York: Penguin, 2003.

Cassedy, James H. "Church Record-Keeping and Public Health in Early New England." In *Medicine in Colonial Massachusetts.* Edited by Frederick S. Allen Jr. Boston: Colonial Society of Massachusetts, 1980.

———. *Medicine in America: A Short History.* Baltimore: Johns Hopkins University Press, 1991.

Chaplin, Joyce E. *The First Scientist: Benjamin Franklin and the Pursuit of Genius.* New York: Basic Books, 2006.

Christianson, Eric H. "The Medical Practitioners of Massachusetts, 1630–1800: Patterns of Change and Continuity." In *Medicine in Colonial Massachusetts.* Edited by Frederick S. Allen Jr. Boston: Colonial Society of Massachusetts, 1980.

Christianson, Gale, E. *Isaac Newton.* Oxford: Oxford University Press, 2005.

Clark, Ronald W. *Benjamin Franklin: A Biography.* New York: Random House, 1983.

Cohen, I. Bernard. *Benjamin Franklin's Science.* Cambridge, MA: Harvard University Press, 1990.

Collinson, Peter. *The Reformation: A History.* New York: Modern Library, 2003.

Commager, Henry Steele. *The Empire of Reason: How Europe Imagined and America Realized the Enlightenment.* London: Phoenix Press, 2000.

Conroy, David W. *In Public Houses: Drink and the Revolution of Authority in Colonial Massachusetts.* Chapel Hill, NC: University of North Carolina Press, 1995.

Crane, Verner W. *Benjamin Franklin and a Rising People.* Boston: Little, Brown, 1954.

Cronon, William. *Changes in the Land: Indians, Colonists, and the Ecology of New England.* New York: Hill and Wang, 1983.

Darnton, Robert. *George Washington's False Teeth: An Unconventional Guide to the Eighteenth Century.* New York: Norton, 2003.

———. *The Great Cat Massacre and Other Episodes in French Cultural History.* New York: Vintage, 1984.

Demos, John. *A Little Commonwealth: Family Life in Plymouth Colony.* Oxford: Oxford University Press, 1970.

Dixon, Thomas. *Science and Religion: A Very Short Introduction.* Oxford: Oxford University Press, 2008.

Dow, George Francis. *Everyday Life in the Massachusetts Bay Colony.* New York: Dover, 1935.

Dray, Philip. *Stealing God's Thunder: Benjamin Franklin's Lightning Rod and the Invention of America.* New York: Random House, 2005.

Duffy, John. *Epidemics in Colonial America.* Baton Rouge: Louisiana State University Press, 1953.

———. *From Humors to Medical Sciences: A History of American Medicine.* 2nd ed. Urbana: University of Illinois Press, 1993.

Dunn, Richard. *Puritans and Yankees: The Winthrop Dynasty of New England, 1630–1717.* New York: Norton, 1962.

Estes, J. Worth. "Therapeutic Practice in Colonial New England." In *Medicine in Colonial Massachusetts.* Edited by Frederick S. Allen Jr. Boston: Colonial Society of Massachusetts, 1980.

Evans, Richard J. *Death in Hamburg: Society and Politics in the Cholera Years, 1830–1910.* New York: Penguin, 1987.

Fenn, Elizabeth. *Pox Americana: The Great Smallpox Epidemic, 1775–1782.* New York: Hill and Wang, 2001.

Finger, Stanley. *Doctor Franklin's Medicine.* Philadelphia: University of Pennsylvania Press, 2006.

Fischer, David Hackett. *Albion's Seed: Four British Folkways in America.* New York: Oxford University Press, 1989.

Fitz, Reginald H. "Zabdiel Boylston, Inoculator, and the Epidemic of Smallpox in Boston in 1721." *Bulletin of the Johns Hopkins Hospital* 22 (1911): 315–327.

Fortune, Brandon Brame, and Deborah J. Warner. *Franklin and His Friends: Portraying the Man of Science in Eighteenth-Century America.* Washington, DC: Smithsonian Institution, 1999.

Francis, Richard. *Judge Sewall's Apology: The Salem Witch Trials and the Forming of an American Conscience.* New York: HarperCollins, 2005.

Gaustad, Edwin S. *Benjamin Franklin.* Oxford: Oxford University Press, 2006.

Gay, Peter. *The Enlightenment: The Rise of Modern Paganism*. New York: Norton, 1966.

Gifford, George E., Jr. "Botanic Remedies in Colonial Massachusetts, 1620–1820." In *Medicine in Colonial Massachusetts*. Edited by Frederick S. Allen Jr. Boston: Colonial Society of Massachusetts, 1980.

Gleick, James. *Isaac Newton*. New York: Pantheon, 2003.

González-Crussi, F. *A Short History of Medicine*. New York: Modern Library, 2007.

Green, James N. "Benjamin Franklin, Printer." In *Benjamin Franklin: In Search of a Better World*. Edited by Page Talbott. New Haven: Yale University Press, 2005.

Greene, Lorenzo Johnston. *The Negro in Colonial New England, 1620–1776*. New York: Columbia University Press, 1942.

Gribbin, John. *The Fellowship: Gilbert, Bacon, Harvey, Wren, Newton, and the Story of a Scientific Revolution*. New York: Overlook Press, 2005.

Grob, Gerald N. *The Deadly Truth: A History of Disease in America*. Cambridge, MA: Harvard University Press, 2002.

Hall, David D. *The Faithful Shepherd: A History of the New England Ministry in the Seventeenth Century*. Chapel Hill: University of North Carolina Press, 1972.

———. *Worlds of Wonder, Days of Judgment: Popular Religious Belief in Early New England*. Cambridge, MA: Harvard University Press, 1989.

Hall, Michael G. *The Last American Puritan: The Life of Increase Mather*. Middletown, CT: Wesleyan University Press, 1988.

Hawke, David Freeman. *Everyday Life in Early America*. New York: Harper and Row, 1988.

Herman, Arthur. *How the Scots Invented the Modern World*. New York: Three Rivers Press, 2001.

———. *To Rule the Waves: How the British Navy Shaped the Modern World*. New York: HarperCollins, 2004.

Himmelfarb, Gertrude. *The Roads to Modernity: The British, French, and American Enlightenments*. New York: Knopf, 2004.

Hochschild, Adam. *Bury the Chains: Prophets and Rebels in the Fight to Free an Empire's Slaves*. Boston: Houghton Mifflin, 2005.

Hof, Ulrich Im. *The Enlightenment: An Historical Introduction.* Oxford: Blackwell, 1994.

Hopkins, Donald R. *The Greatest Killer: Smallpox in History.* Chicago: University of Chicago Press, 1983.

Houston, Alan. *Benjamin Franklin and the Politics of Improvement.* New Haven: Yale University Press, 2008.

Innes, Stephen. *Creating the Commonwealth: The Economic Culture of Puritan New England.* New York: Norton, 1995.

Isaacson, Walter. *Benjamin Franklin: An American Life.* New York: Simon and Schuster, 2003.

———. "What Benjamin Franklin Means for Our Times." In *Benjamin Franklin: In Search of a Better World.* Edited by Page Talbott. New Haven: Yale University Press, 2005.

Johnson, Steven. *The Ghost Map: The Story of London's Most Terrifying Epidemic—and How It Changed Science, Cities, and the Modern World.* New York: Riverhead, 2006.

Jordan, Winthrop D. *White over Black: American Attitudes Toward the Negro, 1550–1812.* New York: Norton, 1968.

Kelly, John. *The Great Mortality: An Intimate History of the Black Death, the Most Devastating Plague of all Time.* New York: HarperCollins, 2005.

Kemp, Peter. *The British Sailor: A Social History of the Lower Deck.* London: J. M. Dent & Sons, 1970.

Ketcham, Ralph L. *Benjamin Franklin.* New York: Washington Square Press, 1966.

King, Lester S. *Medical Thinking: A Historical Preface.* Princeton: Princeton University Press, 1982.

———. *The Medical World of the Eighteenth Century.* Chicago: University of Chicago Press, 1958.

———. *Transformations in American Medicine: From Benjamin Rush to William Osler.* Baltimore: The Johns Hopkins University Press, 1991.

Kittredge, George Lyman. "Cotton Mather's Election into the Royal Society." *Publications of the Colonial Society of Massachusetts* 14 (1912): 81–114.

————. "Further Notes on Cotton Mather and the Royal Society." *Publications of the Colonial Society of Massachusetts* 14 (1913): 281–292.

Krider, E. Philip. "Benjamin Franklin's Science." In *Benjamin Franklin: In Search of a Better World*. Edited by Page Talbott. New Haven: Yale University Press, 2005.

Kuhn, Thomas S. *The Copernican Revolution: Planetary Astronomy in the Development of Western Thought*. New York: Vintage, 1957.

————. *The Structure of Scientific Revolutions*. 2nd ed. Chicago: University of Chicago Press, 1970.

Labaree, Benjamin W. *Colonial Massachusetts: A History*. Millwood, NY: KTO Press, 1979.

Landsman, Ned C. *From Colonials to Provincials: American Thought and Culture, 1680–1760*. Ithaca: Cornell University Press, 1997.

LaPlante, Eve. *Salem Witch Judge: The Life and Repentance of Samuel Sewall*. New York: HarperCollins, 2007.

Lemay, J. A. Leo. *The Life of Benjamin Franklin, Volume 1: Journalist, 1706–1730*. Philadelphia: University of Pennsylvania Press, 2006.

————. "The Life of Benjamin Franklin." In *Benjamin Franklin: In Search of a Better World*. Edited by Page Talbott. New Haven: Yale University Press, 2005.

Lepore, Jill. *The Name of War: King Philip's War and the Origins of American Identity*. New York: Vintage, 1998.

Levin, David. *Cotton Mather: The Young Life of the Lord's Remembrancer, 1663–1702*. Cambridge, MA: Harvard University Press, 1978.

————. "Giants in the Earth: Science and the Occult in Cotton Mather's Letters to the Royal Society." *William and Mary Quarterly*, 3rd ser., vol. 4 (October 1988): 751–770.

Lindberg, David C., and Ronald L. Numbers. *God and Nature: Historical Essays on the Encounter between Christianity and Science*. Berkeley, CA: University of California Press, 1986.

————. *When Science and Christianity Meet*. Chicago: University of Chicago Press, 2003.

Lockridge, Kenneth A. *A New England Town: The First Hundred Years.* New York: Norton, 1970.

Lopez, Claude-Anne, and Eugenia W. Herbert. *The Private Franklin: The Man and His Family.* New York: Norton, 1975.

Lovelace, Richard F. *The American Pietism of Cotton Mather: Origins of American Evangelicalism.* Grand Rapids, MI: Wm. B. Eerdmans, 1979.

Lowance, Mason I., Jr. *Increase Mather.* New York: Twayne, 1974.

Lutz, Donald S. *The Origins of American Constitutionalism.* Baton Rouge: Louisiana State University Press, 1988.

Mapp, Alf J., Jr. *Three Golden Ages: Discovering the Creative Secrets of Renaissance Florence, Elizabethan England, and America's Founding.* Lanham, MD: Madison House, 1998.

May, Henry F. *The Enlightenment in America.* New York: Oxford University Press, 1976.

McNeill, William H. *Plagues and Peoples.* New York: Anchor Books, 1977.

Melton, James Van Horn. *The Rise of the Public in Enlightenment Europe.* Cambridge: Cambridge University Press, 2001.

Middlekauff, Robert. *Benjamin Franklin and His Enemies.* Berkeley, CA: University of California Press, 1996.

———. *The Mathers: Three Generations of Puritan Intellectuals, 1596–1728.* Berkeley, CA: University of California Press, 1971.

Miller, Perry. *Errand into the Wilderness.* New York: Harper and Row, 1964.

———. *The New England Mind: From Colony to Province.* Cambridge, MA: Harvard University Press, 1953.

———. *The New England Mind: The Seventeenth Century.* Cambridge, MA: Harvard University Press, 1939.

Minardi, Margot. "The Boston Inoculation Controversy of 1721–1722: An Incident in the History of Race." *William and Mary Quarterly,* 3rd ser., 61 (January 2004): 47–76.

Morgan, Edmund S. *Benjamin Franklin.* New Haven: Yale University Press, 2002.

———. *The Genuine Article: A Historian Looks at Early America.* New York: Norton, 2004.

——. *The Puritan Dilemma: The Story of John Winthrop.* Boston: Little, Brown, 1958.

——. "The Puritan Ethic and the American Revolution." *William and Mary Quarterly*, 3rd Series, vol. XXIV, no. 1. (January, 1967): 3–43.

——. *The Puritan Family: Religion and Domestic Relations in Seventeenth-Century New England.* New York: Harper and Row, 1944.

——. *Visible Saints: The History of a Puritan Idea.* Ithaca: Cornell University Press, 1963.

Morison, Samuel Eliot. *The Intellectual Life of Colonial New England.* New York: New York University Press, 1956.

——. *The Maritime History of Massachusetts, 1783–1860.* New York: Houghton Mifflin, 1921.

——. *Three Centuries of Harvard, 1636–1936.* Cambridge, MA: Harvard University Press, 1936.

Nicolson, Adam. *God's Secretaries: The Making of the King James Bible.* New York: HarperCollins, 2003.

Outram, Dorinda. *The Enlightenment.* Cambridge: Cambridge University Press, 1995.

Pennack, William. *War, Politics, and Revolution in Provincial Massachusetts.* Boston: Northeastern University Press, 1981.

Philbrick, Nathaniel. *Mayflower: A Story of Courage, Community, and War.* New York: Viking, 2006.

Piersen, William D. *Black Yankees: The Development of an Afro-American Subculture in Eighteenth-Century New England.* Amherst: The University of Massachusetts Press, 1988.

Porter, Roy. *Blood and Guts: A Short History of Medicine.* New York: Norton, 2002.

——. *The Creation of the Modern World: The Untold Story of the British Enlightenment.* New York: Norton, 2000.

——. *The Enlightenment.* London: Macmillan, 1990.

——. *The Greatest Benefit to Mankind: A Medical History of Humanity.* New York: Norton, 1997.

Powell, J. H. *Bring Out Your Dead: The Great Plague of Yellow Fever in Philadelphia in 1793*. New York: Time, 1964.

Rediker, Marcus. *Between the Devil and the Deep Blue Sea: Merchant Seamen, Pirates, and the Anglo-American Maritime World, 1700–1750*. Cambridge: Cambridge University Press, 1987.

Reiss, Oscar. *Medicine in Colonial America*. Lanham, MD: University Press of America, 2000.

Risjord, Norman K. *Representative Americans: The Colonists*. 2nd ed. Lanham, MD: Rowman and Littlefield, 2001.

Robbins, Caroline. *The Eighteenth-Century Commonwealthman*. Indianapolis: Liberty Fund, 1959.

Rodger, N. A. M. *The Wooden World: An Anatomy of the Georgian Navy*. New York: Norton, 1986.

Shryock, Richard Harrison. *Medicine in America: Historical Essays*. Baltimore: Johns Hopkins University Press, 1966.

Silverman, Kenneth. *The Life and Times of Cotton Mather*. New York: Columbia University Press, 1984.

Smith, Billy G. "Benjamin Franklin, Civic Improver." In *Benjamin Franklin: In Search of a Better World*. Edited by Page Talbott. New Haven: Yale University Press, 2005.

Sobel, Dava. *Galileo's Daughter: A Historical Memoir of Science, Faith, and Love*. New York: Penguin, 2000.

Srodes, James. *Franklin: The Essential Founding Father*. Washington, DC: Regnery, 2002.

Staloff, Darren. *The Making of an American Thinking Class: Intellectuals and Intelligentsia in Puritan Massachusetts*. New York: Oxford University Press, 1998.

Stannard, David E. *The Puritan Way of Death: A Study in Religion, Culture, and Social Change*. Oxford: Oxford University Press, 1977.

Stark, Rodney. *For the Glory of God: How Monotheism Led to Reformations, Science, Witch-Hunts, and the End of Slavery*. Princeton: Princeton University Press, 2003.

Stearns, Raymond Phineas. *Science in the British Colonies of America.* Urbana: University of Illinois Press, 1970.

Stout, Harry S. *The New England Soul: Preaching and Religious Culture in Colonial New England.* New York: Oxford University Press, 1986.

Strandness, T. B. *Samuel Sewall: A Puritan Portrait.* East Lansing, MI: Michigan State University Press, 1967.

Tannenbaum, Rebecca J. *The Healer's Calling: Women and Medicine in Early New England.* Ithaca: Cornell University Press, 2002.

Taylor, Alan. *American Colonies: The Settling of North America.* New York: Penguin, 2001.

Thomas, Keith. *Religion and the Decline of Magic.* New York: Charles Scribner's Sons, 1971.

Tomalin, Claire. *Samuel Pepys: The Unequalled Self.* New York: Vintage, 2002.

Tucker, Jonathan B. *Scourge: The Once and Future Threat of Smallpox.* New York: Grove Press, 2001.

Ulrich, Laurel Thatcher. *Good Wives: Image and Reality in the Lives of Women in Northern New England, 1650–1750.* New York: Vintage, 1980.

Van Doren, Carl. *Benjamin Franklin.* New York: Penguin, 1938.

Van de Wetering, Maxine. "A Reconsideration of the Inoculation Controversy." *New England Quarterly* 58 (March 1985): 46–67.

Waldstreicher, David. *Runaway America: Benjamin Franklin, Slavery, and the American Revolution.* New York: Hill and Wang, 2004.

Walters, Kerry S. *Benjamin Franklin and His Gods.* Urbana: University of Illinois Press, 1999.

Warden, G. B. "The Medical Profession in Boston." In *Medicine in Colonial Massachusetts.* Edited by Frederick S. Allen Jr. Boston: Colonial Society of Massachusetts, 1980.

Weinberger, Jerry. *Benjamin Franklin Unmasked: On the Unity of His Moral, Religious, and Political Thought.* Lawrence: University Press of Kansas, 2005.

Whitehill, Walter Muir. *Boston: A Topographical History.* Cambridge, MA: Harvard University Press, 1959.

Wigglesworth, Michael C. "Surgery in Massachusetts, 1620–1800." In *Medicine in Colonial Massachusetts*. Edited by Frederick S. Allen Jr. Boston: Colonial Society of Massachusetts, 1980.

Winship, Michael P. "Prodigies, Puritanism, and the Perils of Natural Philosophy: The Example of Cotton Mather." *William and Mary Quarterly*, 3rd ser., vol. 1 (January 1994): 92–105.

Winslow, Ola Elizabeth. *A Destroying Angel: The Conquest of Smallpox in Colonial Boston*. Boston: Houghton, Mifflin, 1974.

———. *Meetinghouse Hill, 1630–1783*. New York: Norton, 1952.

———. *Samuel Sewall of Boston*. New York: Macmillan, 1964.

Witham, Larry. *A City Upon a Hill: How Sermons Changed the Course of American History*. New York: HarperOne, 2007.

Wood, Betty. *The Origins of American Slavery: Freedom and Bondage in the English Colonies*. New York: Hill and Wang, 1997.

Wood, Gordon S. *The Americanization of Benjamin Franklin*. New York: Penguin, 2004.

———. *The Radicalism of the American Revolution*. New York: Vintage, 1991.

Wright, Donald R. *African Americans in the Colonial Era: From African Origins through the American Revolution*. Arlington Heights, IL: Harlan Davidson, 1990.

Wright, Esmond. *Franklin of Philadelphia*. Cambridge, MA: Harvard University Press, 1986.

Wright, Louis B. *The Cultural Life of the American Colonies*. New York: Harper and Row, 1962.

Zuckerman, Michael. *Peaceable Kingdoms: New England Towns in the Eighteenth Century*. New York: Norton, 1970.

ENDNOTES

xi *He joined the international, cosmopolitan conversation:* James Van Horn Melton, *The Rise of the Public in Enlightenment Europe* (Cambridge, MA: Cambridge University Press, 2001).

xiii *he idealistically sought to serve:* The above information about Cotton Mather can be found in Kenneth Silverman, *The Life and Times of Cotton Mather* (New York: Columbia University Press, 1984), 42, 69–73, 227–60, 308. Other significant biographies include David Levin, *Cotton Mather: The Young Life of the Lord's Remembrancer, 1663–1703* (Cambridge, MA: Harvard University Press, 1978), and Robert Middlekauff, *The Mathers: Three Generations of Puritan Intellectuals, 1596–1728,* rev. ed. (Berkeley, CA: University of California Press, 1999).

xiii *The American Enlightenment:* Examples of this trend include Henry Steele Commager, *The Empire of Reason: How Europe Imagined and America Realized the Enlightenment* (London: Phoenix Press, 2000), as well as an outstanding study of the American founding and Enlightenment and its differences from the French and British Enlightenment by Gertrude Himmelfarb, *The Roads to Modernity: The British, French, and American*

Enlightenments (New York: Knopf, 2004), and Henry F. May, *The Enlightenment in America* (Oxford: Oxford University Press, 1976), whose index includes no mention of Cotton Mather or the Puritans.

xiv *hardly different from Galileo Galilei:* Dava Sobel, *Galileo's Daughter: A Historical Memoir of Science, Faith, and Love* (New York: Penguin, 1999), and Rodney Stark, *For the Glory of God: How Monotheism Led to Reformations, Science, Witch-Hunts, and the End of Slavery* (Princeton: Princeton University Press, 2003), 121–99, are but two recent examples.

xiv *The idea of warfare between science and religion:* David C. Lindberg and Ronald L. Numbers, eds., *God and Nature: Historical Essays on the Encounter between Christianity and Science* (Berkeley and Los Angeles: University of California Press, 1986), 1–14; and David C. Lindberg and Ronald L. Numbers, eds., *When Science and Christianity Meet* (Chicago: University of Chicago Press, 2003), 1–5.

xiv *that the Puritans rejected science and reason is demonstrably false:* See Daniel Boorstin, *The Americans: The Colonial Experience* (New York: Vintage, 1958), 243–65. Alf J. Mapp Jr. launches a devastating critique of the Puritans and science in a chapter titled "Science Enslaved" in *Three Golden Ages: Discovering the Creative Secrets of Renaissance Florence, Elizabethan England, and America's Founding* (Lanham, MD: Madison Books, 1998), 315–51. Important balanced correctives to this view include Ned C. Landsman, *From Colonials to Provincials: American Thought and Culture, 1680–1760* (Ithaca, NY: Cornell University Press, 1997), and Raymond Phineas Stearns, *Science in the British Colonies of America* (Urbana: University of Illinois Press, 1970), 3–18.

xiv *They would be recognized as enlightened men:* Margaret C. Jacob, *The Enlightenment: A Brief History with Documents* (Boston: Bedford Books, 2001); and Roy Porter, *The Enlightenment* (London: Macmillan, 1990).

xvii *"Religion has been disgraced":* William Bradford, *Of Plymouth Plantation* (1920; repr., Mineola, NY: Dover, 2006), 3.

xvii *with a "prosperous wind":* Ibid., 41.

xviii *"It pleased God":* Ibid.

xviii *"forced to hull for many days":* Ibid., 41–42.

 xix *"discontented and mutinous speeches":* Ibid., 49.

  xx *The laws would be drawn:* Nathaniel Philbrick, *Mayflower: A Story of Courage, Community, and War* (New York: Viking, 2006), 40–42.

  xx *This political covenant:* Donald S. Lutz, *The Origins of American Constitutionalism* (Baton Rouge: Louisiana State University Press, 1988), 19, 24, 26.

  xx *These elect experienced:* Perry Miller, *Errand into the Wilderness* (New York: Harper and Row, 1956), 60–66.

  xx *The ministers were beholden to:* Perry Miller, *The New England Mind: The Seventeenth Century* (Cambridge, MA: Harvard University Press, 1939), 435–37.

 xxi *each family was considered a "little commonwealth":* T. H. Breen, *The Character of the Good Ruler: Puritan Political Ideas in New England, 1630–1730* (New York: Norton, 1970), 271.

 xxi *They voluntarily assumed:* John Winthrop, "A Model of Christian Charity," in *American Sermons: The Pilgrims to Martin Luther King, Jr.,* ed. Michael Warner (New York: Library of America, 1999), 41–42; and Larry Witham, *A City Upon a Hill: How Sermons Changed the Course of American History* (New York: HarperOne, 2007), 18–19.

xxii *The cleavages that were gradually undermining the covenant:* Perry Miller, *The New England Mind: From Colony to Province* (Cambridge, MA: Harvard University Press, 1953), 172–383; and Breen, *Character of the Good Ruler,* 88–89, 134–53.

  1 *It was probably hiding:* Peter Kemp, *The British Sailor: A Social History of the Lower Deck* (London: J. M. Dent & Sons, 1970), 45.

  1 *They efficiently completed their tasks:* N. A. M. Rodger, *The Wooden World: An Anatomy of the Georgian Navy* (New York: Norton, 1986), 72–74.

  2 *these palliatives did little:* Ibid., 61, 68–71.

2 *Although life at sea was difficult:* Kemp, *British Sailor,* 47–48, 67, 78; and Marcus Rediker, *Between the Devil and the Deep Blue Sea: Merchant Seamen, Pirates, and the Anglo-American Maritime World, 1700–1750* (Cambridge: Cambridge University Press, 1987).

2 *They were freeborn men:* Rodger, *Wooden World,* 114–15.

2 *they enjoyed their service aboard the* Seahorse: Ibid., 159–60.

3 *Even if they were generally relegated to jobs:* W. Jeffrey Bolster, *Black Jacks: African American Seamen in the Age of Sail* (Cambridge, MA: Harvard University Press, 1997), 32.

3 *"I liked this little ship very much":* Olaudah Equiano, *The Interesting Narrative of the Life of Olaudah Equiano: Written by Himself,* ed. Robert J. Allison (Boston: Bedford Books, 1995), 77.

3 *It would not be difficult:* Elizabeth A. Fenn, *Pox Americana: The Great Smallpox Epidemic of 1775–1782* (New York: Hill and Wang, 2001), 15.

4 *The infected cells:* Donald R. Hopkins, *The Greatest Killer: Smallpox in History* (Chicago: University of Chicago Press, 1983), 3–5.

5 *European explorers brought it:* Jonathan B. Tucker, *Scourge: The Once and Future Threat of Smallpox* (New York: Grove Press, 2001), 5–6; William H. McNeil, *Plagues and Peoples* (New York: Anchor Books, 1977), 45; and Hopkins, *Greatest Killer,* 13.

6 *a better place to contaminate:* Samuel Eliot Morison, *The Maritime History of Massachusetts, 1783–1860* (Boston: Houghton Mifflin, 1921), 17–18.

7 *Dockyard workers:* Rodger, *Wooden World,* 42–43.

7 *Their tolerance endeared:* Ibid., 137–44, 188–204.

8 *He was fully contagious:* Hopkins, *Greatest Killer,* 4; and Fenn, *Pox Americana,* 16–19.

8 *Spires were frowned upon:* Ola Elizabeth Winslow, *Meetinghouse Hill, 1630–1783* (New York: Norton, 1952), 55.

8–9 *"robbing its stones for ballast":* Walter Muir Whitehill, *Boston: A Topographical History* (Cambridge, MA: Harvard University Press, 1959), 20–21.

9 *outward-bound sea captains:* Carl Bridenbaugh, *Cities in the Wilderness: The First Century of Urban Life in America, 1625–1742* (New York: Knopf, 1955), 86, 241.

9 *Boston's legislators chose:* Bridenbaugh, *Cities in the Wilderness,* 401.

10 *At least one carried an infectious disease:* Jennifer Lee Carrell, *The Speckled Monster: A Historical Tale of Battling Smallpox* (New York: Penguin, 2003), 131–32, 413–16.

11 *They walked:* Rediker, *Between the Devil and the Deep Blue Sea,* 11.

11–12 *Young ladies dressed:* Bridenbaugh, *Cities in the Wilderness,* 170–172; and David Freeman Hawke, *Everyday Life in Early America* (New York: Harper and Row, 1988), 109–14.

12 Seahorse's *sailors had visited:* Bridenbaugh, *Cities in the Wilderness,* 170–172.

12 *At the intersection:* Whitehill, *Boston,* 26.

13 *Bakers supplied biscuits:* Bridenbaugh, *Cities in the Wilderness,* 36–37, 42–43, 191.

13 *In any of these establishments:* Ibid., 41–42, 188.

13 *John Foster, Samson Waters, and Samuel Sewall:* Whitehill, *Boston,* 27–28.

14 *A fine line separated:* Bernard Bailyn, *The New England Merchants in the Seventeenth Century* (Cambridge, MA: Harvard University Press, 1955), 96–141.

14 *There was a leveling spirit:* Bridenbaugh, *Cities in the Wilderness,* 97, 256.

14–15 *Within a few years:* Bailyn, *New England Merchants,* 97–98; and Bridenbaugh, *Cities in the Wilderness,* 210.

15 *Bothersome swine and packs of dogs:* Bridenbaugh, *Cities in the Wilderness,* 19, 21–22, 44.

16 *seamen who lived at sea for months:* Ibid., 17, 156, 159, 162–63, 167–68, 238–39.

16 *A number of very respectful taverns:* Ibid., 109–11, 265–66.

16–17 *A Puritan minister complained:* David W. Conroy, *In Public Houses:*

Drink and the Revolution of Authority in Colonial Massachusetts (Chapel Hill: University of North Carolina Press, 1995), 51.

17 *"I have seen certain taverns"*: Bridenbaugh, *Cities in the Wilderness,* 272.

17 *"A proud fashion"*: Bailyn, *New England Merchants,* 141.

17–18 *One minister worried:* Bridenbaugh, *Cities in the Wilderness,* 226.

18 *A disgusted Cotton Mather:* Ibid., 227–28.

18 *The town's watchmen:* Whitehill, *Boston,* 26.

19 *The piteous sailor became:* Hopkins, *The Greatest Killer,* 4; and Fenn, *Pox Americana,* 16–19.

19 *"Purple spots, the bloody and parchment pox"*: Silverman, *Life and Times of Cotton Mather,* 337–38.

21 *He instantly recognized: A Report of the Record Commissioners of the City of Boston, Selectmen Minutes, 1715–1729* (Boston, 1885), 81.

22 *Englishmen (and other Europeans) carried the disease:* McNeill, *Plagues and Peoples,* 182–221.

22 *Puritan Miles Standish reported:* Hopkins, *The Greatest Killer,* 234–35.

22 *"The natives, they are near all dead"*: Tucker, *Scourge,* 11.

22 *In 1631, a passenger reported:* John Duffy, *Epidemics in Colonial America* (Baton Rouge: Louisiana State University Press, 1953), 43.

23 *"The Indians…fell sick of smallpox"*: Bradford, *Of Plymouth Plantation,* 172–73.

23 *One observer noted:* John B. Blake, *Public Health in the Town of Boston, 1630–1822* (Cambridge, MA: Harvard University Press, 1959), 3.

23–24 *"Our healthful days are at an end"*: Ibid., 4.

24 *Young Cotton Mather wrote:* Ibid., 20.

24 *"Thacher's pamphlet was notable"*: Duffy, *Epidemics in Colonial America,* 46–47.

25 *Smallpox raged anew in 1702 and 1703:* Ibid., 48–49.

25 *Selectmen were:* David Hackett Fischer, *Albion's Seed: Four British Folkways in America* (Oxford: Oxford University Press, 1989), 196–99.

25 *"distemper may now be onboard that ship"*: *Report of the Record Commissioners,* 81.

26 *the town had experience with smallpox epidemics:* Ibid.

26 *Quarantine was the most widely used countermeasure:* Ola Elizabeth Winslow, *A Destroying Angel: The Conquest of Smallpox in Colonial Boston* (Boston: Houghton Mifflin, 1974), 28.

26 *When the crew showed: Report of the Record Commissioners*, 76.

26–27 *two "prudent persons" were appointed:* Ibid., 81.

27 *a red flag bearing the inscription "God have mercy on this house":* Winslow, *Destroying Angel*, 44.

27 *Clark returned to town: Report of the Record Commissioners*, 82.

27 *They arranged for a local captain:* Ibid.

27 *the town reimbursed Robert Orange:* Massachusetts General Court, *The Acts and Resolves, Public and Private, of the Province of the Massachusetts Bay, 1720–1726*, 21 vols. (Boston: Wright and Potter, 1902), 10:105.

28 *in several homes around Boston, the residents felt: Boston News-Letter*, May 15, 1721.

28 *"There are now eight persons sick": Boston Gazette*, May 22, 1721.

28 *"The grievous calamity of the smallpox":* Cotton Mather, *Diary of Cotton Mather*, Collections of the Massachusetts Historical Society, 7th ser., nos. 7–8, 2 vols. (Boston: Massachusetts Historical Society, 1911–1912), 2:620.

28 *Because of the prevailing medical wisdom:* Otho T. Beall Jr. and Richard H. Shryock, *Cotton Mather: The First Significant Figure in American Medicine* (Baltimore: Johns Hopkins University Press, 1954), 101.

29 *Supervisors would be empowered: Report of the Record Commissioners*, 82.

29 *the Selectmen enforced a law:* Ibid., 59.

29 *Northern black codes:* Winthrop D. Jordan, *White over Black: American Attitudes Toward the Negro, 1550–1812* (New York: Norton, 1968), 71.

29 *"We have had but one person taken sick of smallpox": Boston News-Letter*, May 29, 1721.

30 *It was adjourned on June 1:* M. Hasley Thomas, ed., *The Diary of Samuel Sewall, 1674–1729* (New York: Farrar, Straus, and Giroux, 1973), 980.

30 *The charter granted after the Glorious Revolution:* Breen, *Character of the Good Ruler*, 197–98.

30 *Fleeing to the environs of an isolated farm:* Duffy, *Epidemics in Colonial America,* 17.

30 *God was:* David D. Hall, *Worlds of Wonder, Days of Judgment: Popular Religious Belief in Early New England* (Cambridge, MA: Harvard University Press, 1989), 71, 74, 78, 80.

31 *Puritans believed they suffered affliction for their sins:* Silverman, *Life and Times of Cotton Mather,* 58–59.

31 *Cries to turn from sin:* Sacvan Bercovitch, *The American Jeremiad* (Madison: University of Wisconsin Press, 1978), 1–35; and Middlekauf, *The Mathers,* ix–x.

32 *"The entrance of the smallpox":* Mather, *Diary of Cotton Mather,* 2:621–22.

33 *His grounds had lovely gardens:* Silverman, *Life and Times of Cotton Mather,* 289–90.

33 *"The time of year arrives":* Mather, *Diary of Cotton Mather,* 2:620–21.

34 *Besides the quiet hours spent in contemplation:* Silverman, *Life and Times of Cotton Mather,* 262–63.

34 *Mather nevertheless managed:* Levin, *Cotton Mather,* 1, 10.

35 *He was thoroughly prepared for Harvard:* Silverman, *Life and Times of Cotton Mather,* 7–15.

35 *They engaged modern scientific texts:* Samuel Eliot Morison, *Three Centuries of Harvard, 1636–1936* (Cambridge, MA: Harvard University Press, 1936), 22–36.

35 *He was largely self-taught in the subject:* Beall and Shryock, *Cotton Mather,* 9–11.

36 *He had fits of melancholy:* Levin, *Cotton Mather,* 32–39.

36 *One minister warned:* Miller, *The New England Mind: The Seventeenth Century,* 386.

37 *Increase reminded his son:* Levin, *Cotton Mather,* 40–41.

37 *The reassured young man:* Ibid., 41.

37 *the "unaccountable cloud and load" lifted from him:* Norman K. Risjord,

Representative Americans: The Colonists, 2nd ed. (Lanham, MD: Rowman and Littlefield, 2001), 201–2.

37 *he preferred cosmopolitan Boston:* Silverman, *Life and Times of Cotton Mather,* 27.

38 *Scientifically they embraced:* Landsman, *From Colonials to Provincials,* 61.

38 *It was Cotton Mather who stated that "we are born in an age of light":* Silverman, *Life and Times of Cotton Mather,* 94.

38 *"Nature and nature's laws":* Ulrich Im Hof, *The Enlightenment: An Historical Introduction* (Oxford: Blackwell, 1994), 3–4.

38 *"Ideas," he delighted:* Silverman, *Life and Times of Cotton Mather,* 249.

39 *These laws were discoverable:* John Gribbin, *The Fellowship: Gilbert, Bacon, Harvey, Wren, Newton, and the Story of a Scientific Revolution* (New York: Overlook Press, 2005), 51, 77–80, 115–119, 185–86, 234–35.

39 *when Mather harmonized the study of nature with religion:* Miller, *The New England Mind: The Seventeenth Century,* 76, 211; and Stark, *For the Glory of God,* 123, 163, 198–99.

39 *he called the appearance of Halley's comet:* Michael G. Hall, *The Last American Puritan: The Life of Increase Mather* (Middletown, CT: Wesleyan University Press, 1988), 158–70.

40 *Modern science would eventually undermine:* Keith Thomas, *Religion and the Decline of Magic* (New York: Charles Scribner's Sons, 1971), 285–352, 665–66; and James Gleick, *Isaac Newton* (New York: Pantheon, 2003), 99–106.

40 *they were also interpreted:* Hall, *Worlds of Wonder, Days of Judgment,* 58–60, 71–80, 106–7.

40 *"another would be published":* Landsman, *From Colonials to Provincials,* 31–36, 42–45, 66.

41 *Members of the Mathers' Second Church:* Miller, *The New England Mind: The Seventeenth Century,* 207–8.

41 *These studies were:* Stearns, *Science in the British Colonies of America,* 90.

42 *the society was to compile:* Ibid., 88–91.

42 *the society sent out its journal:* Ibid., 96–116.

42 *The Royal Society was "well-pleased":* Silverman, *Life and Times of Cotton Mather,* 244–54.

42 *Its purpose was to establish:* Stearns, *Science in the British Colonies of America,* 155–56.

43 *Americans were not unsophisticated:* Silverman, *Life and Times of Cotton Mather,* 41–42.

43 *Mather had high hopes:* Mather, *Diary of Cotton Mather,* 2:610.

43 *"small acknowledgment unto an invaluable friend":* Cotton Mather to John Winthrop, April 17, 1721, *Selected Letters of Cotton Mather,* comp. Kenneth Silverman (Baton Rouge: Louisiana State University Press, 1971), 335–36.

44 *Congregations could:* Edmund S. Morgan, *Visible Saints: The History of a Puritan Idea* (Ithaca: Cornell University Press, 1963), 25–28.

44 *A disgruntled Increase Mather:* Silverman, *Life and Times of Cotton Mather,* 225.

44 *vindictively planned to "take my farewell":* Mather, *Diary of Cotton Mather,* 2:616.

44 *"how easily and cheerfully we endure their departure":* Ibid., 2:617–18.

44–45 *"The wicked spirit manifested by them":* Ibid., 2:621.

45 *"fear the contagion":* Ibid., 2:628.

45 *Mather lamented:* Silverman, *Life and Times of Cotton Mather,* 268–69.

45 *His father was worried:* Ibid., 292–93.

46 *Mather bewailed to his diary:* Ibid., 307–8.

46 *Mather blamed himself:* Mather, *Diary of Cotton Mather,* 2:611.

46 *"cast out the Devil":* Ibid., 2:612.

46 *"My bowels are troubled for him":* Ibid., 2:615.

46 *Sammy entered Harvard:* Silverman, *Life and Times of Cotton Mather,* 269–70, 290–91, 308.

47 *She may have been immune:* Ibid., 267, 270, 324–25.

47 *"My two children have their terrors":* Mather, *Diary of Cotton Mather,* 2:622.

47 *"Oh! What shall I do"*: Ibid., 2:627.

47 *"I must cry to heaven"*: Ibid., 2:621.

47–48 *"on this occasion called unto sacrifices"*: Ibid., 2:621.

48 *"My two children have their terrors"*: Ibid., 2:622.

48 *Sammy raced home from Cambridge*: Ibid., 2:626.

48 *prayed "especially on the behalf of my two children"*: Ibid., 2:633.

48 *He asked humbly for "a direction of heaven"*: Ibid., 2:629–30.

48 *He considered them*: Betty Wood, *The Origins of American Slavery: Freedom and Bondage in the English Colonies* (New York: Hill and Wang, 1997), 109.

48 *"I must use my best endeavors"*: Mather, *Diary of Cotton Mather*, 2:603.

49 *In such close proximity*: Bolster, *Black Jacks*, 11–12, 27–28; Jordan, *White over Black*, 66; Wood, *Origins of American Slavery*, 94, 107, 109; and Donald R. Wright, *African Americans in the Colonial Era: From African Origins through the American Revolution* (Arlington Heights, IL: Harlan Davidson, 1990), 71, 110.

49 *Christian slave owners*: Wood, *Origins of American Slavery*, 105–6.

49 *In his essay* Negro Christianized: Jordan, *White over Black*, 201.

49 *"Their complexion sometimes"*: Ibid., 258.

49–50 *"They are kept only as horses or oxen"*: Ibid., 190.

50 *By experiencing a conversion to Christ*: Ibid., 131–32.

50 *"I must on this occasion"*: Mather, *Diary of Cotton Mather*, 2:624.

52 *The Puritan Bible*: Adam Nicolson, *God's Secretaries: The Making of the King James Bible* (New York: HarperCollins, 2003), xii; and Benson Bobrick, *Wide as the Waters: The Story of the English Bible and the Revolution It Inspired* (New York: Simon and Schuster, 2001), 253–54.

52 *The great eye signified*: Fischer, *Albion's Seed*, 118–24.

53 *Their power was able to*: Miller, *The New England Mind: The Seventeenth Century*, 286–362, 297.

53 *One minister summed up the purpose*: Ibid., 297.

53 *One listener was disgusted*: Ibid., 353.

54 *Examples, similies, and comparisons:* Ibid., 332–33, 356.

54 *The Puritans believed in "visible saints":* Peter Collinson, *The Reformation: A History* (New York: Modern Library, 2003), 62.

54 *one observer amusingly described the effect as:* Fischer, *Albion's Seed,* 120–24.

55 *"Because of the destroying Angel":* Mather, *Diary of Cotton Mather,* 2:623.

56 *The smallpox epidemic:* Ibid., 2:625.

59 *"We all came into the world":* Silverman, *Life and Times of Cotton Mather,* 228.

60 *"put upon him the name of Onesimus":* Mather, *Diary of Cotton Mather,* 1:579.

60 *Mather allowed Onesimus to work:* Silverman, *Life and Times of Cotton Mather,* 264–65.

61 *"showed me in his arm the scar":* Cotton Mather to Dr. John Woodward, July 12, 1716, in George L. Kittredge, "Some Lost Works of Cotton Mather," *Proceedings of the Massachusetts Historical Society* 45 (1911– 1912): 422.

61 *"I was first instructed by it":* Ibid., 423, 431.

61 *Mather was not content:* Cotton Mather, *Some Account of What Is Said of Inoculating or Transplanting the Smallpox by the Learned Dr. Emmanuel Timonius and Jacobus Pylarinus* (Boston: S. Gerrish, 1721), 9.

61 *"It is now become a common thing":* Cotton Mather, *An Account of the Method and Success of Inoculating the Smallpox in Boston in New England* (Boston, 1722), 1–2; and Mather, *Some Account of What Is Said of Inoculating or Transplanting the Smallpox,* 9.

61 *Mather always credited his slaves:* Margot Minardi, "The Boston Inoculation Controversy of 1721–1722: An Incident in the History of Race," *William and Mary Quarterly* 3rd ser., 61 (January 2004): 47–76.

62 *Douglass was an intellectual man:* Stearns, *Science in the British Colonies of America,* 477–84.

62 *"We are not much better":* William Douglass to Cadwallader Colden, February 20, 1721, *The Letters and Papers of Cadwallader Colden, 1711–1729.* 7 vols. (New York: New York Historical Society, 1917–1923), 1:114.

62 *Douglass apparently thought enough of Mather:* Kittredge, "Some Lost Works of Cotton Mather," 419–27.

62 *It was not the first time that authentic reports:* John B. Blake, "The Inoculation Controversy in Boston: 1721–1722," *New England Quarterly* 25 (December 1952): 489–90.

63 *Those who were inoculated:* Because it is primarily Mather's understanding of the Timonius article in which we are interested, I have used Mather's summary to describe the procedure as it was practiced in Constantinople. Mather's summary was honest and accurate. See Mather, *Some Account of What Is Said of Inoculating or Transplanting the Smallpox,* 1–4; and Mather, *An Account of the Method and Success of Inoculating the Smallpox in Boston,* 2–4.

63 *His microscope revealed:* Roy Porter, *The Greatest Benefit to Mankind: A Medical History of Humanity* (New York: Norton, 1997), 224–25.

64 *Animalcules were transmitted:* Beall and Shryock, *Cotton Mather,* 87–92.

64 *"It begins now to be vehemently suspected":* Cotton Mather, "Angel of Bethesda," in ibid., 87–92, 161.

64 *Mather was one of the earliest proponents:* Beall and Shryock, *Cotton Mather,* 87–92; and Roy Porter, *Blood and Guts: A Short History of Medicine* (New York: Norton, 2002), 86.

64 *Later, he experienced great anguish:* Mather, *Diary of Cotton Mather,* 1:451.

64–65 *He compared losing a child:* Levin, *Cotton Mather,* 141.

65 *"save more lives than Dr. Sydenham":* Cotton Mather to Dr. John Woodward, July 12, 1716, in Kittredge, "Some Lost Works of Cotton Mather," 422.

65 *"Nature, in the production of diseases":* Porter, *Greatest Benefit to Mankind,* 203–4, 229–30.

66 *"If I should live to see the smallpox again":* Cotton Mather to Dr. John Woodward, July 12, 1716, in Kittredge, "Some Lost Works of Cotton Mather," 422.

66 *Mather either read it:* Kittredge, "Some Lost Works of Cotton Mather," 419–27.

66 *Both descriptions included:* Mather, *Some Account of What Is Said of Inoculating or Transplanting the Smallpox,* 5–6; and Mather, *An Account of the Method and Success of Inoculating the Smallpox in Boston,* 5–7.

69 *the "grievous calamity" of smallpox had entered Boston:* Mather, *Diary of Cotton Mather,* 2:620–21.

69–70 *On June 6, Mather prepared an "Address to the Physicians of Boston":* Blake, "The Inoculation Controversy in Boston," 491–92.

70 *inoculation should not be attempted:* Beall and Shryock, *Cotton Mather,* 182.

70 *he conceded that this untested procedure:* Kittredge, "Some Lost Works of Cotton Mather," 428.

71 *"Shall I give it unto the booksellers?":* Mather, *Diary of Cotton Mather,* 2:627–28.

71 *"I write a letter unto the physicians":* Ibid., 2:628.

71 *"I now lay before you":* Winslow, *Destroying Angel,* 48.

72 *He chose to speak:* Mather, *Diary of Cotton Mather,* 2:678.

73 *Because there was smallpox at Harvard:* *Boston News-Letter,* June 22, 1721.

73 *He set up Boston's largest apothecary shop:* Winslow, *A Destroying Angel,* 40–42.

73 *he mundanely dispensed:* Silverman, *Life and Times of Cotton Mather,* 340.

74 *Hope within the town of "preventing the further spread of it":* Zabdiel Boylston, *An Historical Account of the Small-Pox Inoculated in New England, upon All Sorts of Persons, Whites, Blacks, and of All Ages and Constitutions* (London: S. Chandler, 1726; Boston: S. Gerrish, 1730), 2; and Blake, "The Inoculation Controversy in Boston," 492.

74 *Fevers and disease developed inside the body:* Porter, *Greatest Benefit to Mankind,* 57–60.

75 *Nevertheless, he decided to risk it:* Ibid., 60.

75 *Boylston wrote that he "chose to make it":* Boylston, *Historical Account of the Small-Pox Inoculated in New England,* 2.

75 *He followed his instructions:* Mather, *Account of the Method and Success of Inoculating the Smallpox in Boston,* 9–10.

75 *He monitored them:* Porter, *Greatest Benefit to Mankind,* 56–61, 229–30.

76 *The patients were all presently as "hale and strong":* Boylston, *Historical Account of the Small-Pox Inoculated in New England,* 3–4; and Mather, *Account of the Method and Success of Inoculating the Smallpox in Boston,* 10.

76 *There was communal responsibility:* Bridenbaugh, *Cities in the Wilderness,* 206–13.

77 *His whole body was wracked:* Boylston, *Historical Account of the Small-Pox Inoculated in New England,* 6.

77 *The confluent form of smallpox:* Fenn, *Pox Americana,* 18–20.

77 *When the blood was raging:* Porter, *Greatest Benefit to Mankind,* 75.

77 *Even though the Enlightenment doctor William Harvey had revolutionized:* F. González-Crussi, *A Short History of Medicine* (New York: Modern Library, 2007), 138–41.

77 *Cheever endured a great deal of agony for nothing:* Boylston, *Historical Account of the Small-Pox Inoculated in New England,* 6–7.

77 *Boylston again concluded:* Ibid., 7.

77–78 *he then welcomed three older townspeople:* Ibid., 7–8.

79 *"The said report is a scandalous and ridiculous falsehood":* Boston Gazette, June 27, 1721.

79 *"Some under grievous consternation":* Mather, *Diary of Cotton Mather,* 2:630–31.

79 *His flock must be directed and comforted:* Ibid., 2:630–31.

79 *The devout minister supplicated himself:* Ibid., 2:629–30.

79 *He relished the occasion to preach:* Massachusetts General Court, *Acts and Resolves,* 10:89.

80 *God's mercy would follow:* Miller, *The New England Mind: From Colony to Province,* 19–26.

81 *"We have seen that there is a gracious and merciful God":* Boston *News-Letter,* July 10, 1721; and Sewall, *Diary of Samuel Sewall,* 981.

81–82 *"In a few weeks more":* Boston *Gazette,* July 15, 1721; and *Boston News-Letter,* July 17, 1721.

82 *Cotton Mather was quite pleased and called it "an unspeakable consolation":* Mather, *Diary of Cotton Mather,* 2:631–32.

82 *"The Destroyer, being enraged":* Ibid., 2:632.

83 *He asked God for help:* Ibid., 2:633.

83 *"The cursed clamor of a people":* Ibid., 2:632.

83 *"I then gave a public invitation":* Boylston, *Historical Account of the Small-Pox Inoculated in New England,* 4.

83–84 *In other instances:* Mather, *Account of the Method and Success of Inoculating the Smallpox in Boston in New England,* 12.

84 *The "enraged physicians" who "raised a storm":* Ibid., 10.

84 *The doctors published a warning:* Ibid., 11.

85 *A Puritan minister called on him:* Mather, *Some Account of What Is Said of Inoculating or Transplanting the Smallpox,* preface, 10.

85 *They "severely reprimanded him":* Mather, *Account of the Method and Success of Inoculating the Smallpox in Boston in New England,* 11.

85 *"Whatever is done against the order":* Edmund S. Morgan, *The Puritan Family: Religion and Domestic Relations in Seventeenth-Century New England* (New York: Harper and Row, 1944), 9–20.

86 *His fortitude in even attempting inoculation:* Boylston, *Historical Account of the Small-Pox Inoculated in New England,* 5.

86 *"As far as I can find strength for it":* Mather, *Diary of Cotton Mather,* 2:633.

86 *Mather turned his Bible to Psalm 78:63:* Ibid., 2:679.

86–87 *A young man in the flock:* Ibid., 2:633.

89 *some of his kinsfolk "languish under great fear":* Ibid., 2:634.

89 *"The monstrous and crying wickedness":* Ibid.

90 *The chaos obliged him "in the fear of the divine judgments":* Ibid.

91 *Douglass called for criminal prosecution: Boston News-Letter,* July 24, 1721.

91 *This was a reasonable view of Puritan faith:* Ibid.

91 *He continued his prayer to "give me to see my opportunities":* Mather, *Diary of Cotton Mather,* 2:635.

92 *If the other doctors of the town: Boston Gazette,* July 27, 1721.

93 *The doctors were correctly using a discovery:* Ibid.

93 *The ministers flatly maintained:* Ibid.

94 *he "took little notice of the inhibition":* Mather, *Account of the Method and Success of Inoculating the Smallpox in Boston in New England,* 14.

94 *The doctor continued to mix:* Boylston, *Historical Account of the Small-Pox Inoculated in New England,* 8–12.

94–95 *Boylston complained that many:* Mather, *Account of the Method and Success of Inoculating the Smallpox in Boston in New England,* 14.

95 *He also employed the sixth commandment:* Ibid., 15.

96 *Tension would only build:* Miller, *The New England Mind: From Colony to Province,* 246–376.

96 *"It is the hour and power of darkness":* Mather, *Diary of Cotton Mather,* 2:636–37.

97 *Printer James Franklin:* H. W. Brands, *The First American: The Life and Times of Benjamin Franklin* (New York: Anchor, 2000), 20–21.

98 *The family rented a house:* Gordon S. Wood, *The Americanization of Benjamin Franklin* (New York: Penguin, 2004), 17; and Carl Van Doren, *Benjamin Franklin* (New York: Penguin, 1938), 5–8.

98 *After a few years education:* Walter Isaacson, *Benjamin Franklin: An American Life* (New York: Simon and Schuster, 2003), 21.

98 *The printers there churned out:* Dorinda Outram, *The Enlightenment* (Cambridge: Cambridge University Press, 1995), 22–23.

99 *Seeing that his son:* Isaacson, *Benjamin Franklin,* 16–20.

99 *He patiently walked his son:* Benjamin Franklin, *Benjamin Franklin's Autobiography,* ed. J. A. Leo Lemay and P. M. Zall (New York: Norton, 1986), 8–9.

99–100 *James Franklin's timing was perfect:* Isaacson, *Benjamin Franklin,* 21–22.

100 *He ate the small meals quickly:* Franklin, *Autobiography,* 8–9, 12–13.

100 *He bridled under:* Ibid., 9–10.

100–101 *"Often I sat up":* Ibid., 10.

101 *The painstaking work:* Ibid., 11–12.

101 *He was becoming disagreeable:* Ibid., 11–13.

102 *He might have taught:* Ibid., 11–14.

102 *James sought to break free:* Wood, *Americanization of Benjamin Franklin,* 20–21.

103 *Less funny was the danger: New England Courant,* August 7, 1721.

104 *"Ours shall be in summer":* Ibid.

104–105 *"Long had the rulers prudent care":* Ibid.

109 *"Sir, your argument do stink":* John Williams, *Several Arguments Proving That Inoculating the Smallpox Is Not Contained in the Law of Physick, Either Natural or Divine, and Therefore Unlawful* (Boston, 1721), 6, 13.

109 *"By inoculation, the smallpox":* Ibid., 3.

109 *"In the hot weather":* Ibid., 5.

110 *The conclusion was inescapable:* Ibid., 5–6, 10.

110 *"One single apothecary": A Letter from One in the Country, to His Friend in the City, in Relation to Their Distresses Occasioned by the Doubtful and Prevailing Practice of the Inoculation of the Smallpox* (Boston, 1721), 3.

110 *"To spread a mortal contagion":* Ibid., 3–4.

110 *"Two or three years hence":* Mather, *Account of the Method and Success of Inoculating the Smallpox in Boston in New England,* 22.

111 *the patients had acquired an immunity:* Mather, *Some Account of What Is Said of Inoculating or Transplanting the Smallpox,* 11.

111 *The procedure was performed:* Ibid., 14–17.

111–112 *"there is less of metaphor in our account":* Mather, *Account of the Method and Success of Inoculating the Smallpox in Boston in New England,* 8.

112 *John Williams mocked:* Williams, *Several Arguments Proving That Inoculating the Smallpox Is Not Contained in the Law of Physick,* 19.

112 *"Every age of the world":* A Reply to the Objections Made Against Taking the Smallpox in the Way of Inoculation from Principles of Conscience in a Letter to a Friend in the Country (Boston, 1721), 13.

112 *"The question is not":* Williams, *Several Arguments Proving That Inoculating the Smallpox Is Not Contained in the Law of Physick,* 7.

112–113 *Although the ministers:* Miller, *The New England Mind: The Seventeenth Century,* 310.

113 *They constantly cited scripture:* Ibid., 20.

113 *It was held to be a "horrid violation":* Williams, *Several Arguments Proving That Inoculating the Smallpox Is Not Contained in the Law of Physick,* 1.

114 *Averting the stroke of smallpox:* Ibid., 4–5.

114 *"Lord, we have sinned":* A Letter from One in the Country, 5–6.

114 *Another noted that the "lawless, ungaurged" practice:* Ibid., 5–6; and Williams, *Several Arguments Proving That Inoculating the Smallpox Is Not Contained in the Law of Physick,* 12.

114 *If Bostonians "walk contrary to God":* Williams, *Several Arguments Proving That Inoculating the Smallpox Is Not Contained in the Law of Physick,* 6.

114–115 *The opponents of inoculation:* Ibid., 13.

115 *Cotton Mather probably had a hand:* Cotton Mather, *A Vindication of the Ministers, from the Abuses and Scandals, Lately Cast upon Them, in Diverse Printed Papers* (Boston, 1722).

115 *They contented themselves:* Mather, *Some Account of What Is Said of Inoculating or Transplanting the Smallpox,* 20.

115 *Christians should "humbly give thanks":* Ibid., 15.

115 *Why could they not "lawfully make use":* A Reply to the Objections Made Against Taking the Smallpox in the Way of Inoculation from Principles of Conscience in a Letter to a Friend in the Country (Boston, 1721), 6.

115 *But he is a murderer:* Ibid., 12.

115–116 *the Puritan God had predestined:* Ibid., 11.

116 *"What is there of the hand or power of man":* Ibid., 7.

116 *"As to the divinity":* Mather, *Some Account of What Is Said of Inoculating or Transplanting the Smallpox,* 17.

116 *"What will they have to answer for":* Ibid., 22.

117 *many thousands had in fact died:* Ibid., 18–20.

117 *"To bring sickness upon one's self":* A Reply to the Objections Made Against Taking the Smallpox in the Way of Inoculation, 3–4.

117 *Expecting God to grant them:* Ibid., 4.

117 *He believed them to be:* William Douglass, *Inoculation of the Smallpox as Practiced in Boston* (Boston, 1722), 6–7; and Minardi, "The Boston Inoculation Controversy of 1721–1722," 62–66.

118 *The same credulous minister:* Douglass, *Inoculation of the Smallpox,* 6–7; and Minardi, "The Boston Inoculation Controversy of 1721–1722," 62–66.

118 *To show how much the inoculators were tricked:* A Letter from One in the Country, 2, 4, 8; and Williams, *Several Arguments Proving That Inoculating the Smallpox Is Not Contained in the Law of Physick,* 14.

118 *"A merciful God has taught":* Mather, *Some Account of What Is Said of Inoculating or Transplanting the Smallpox,* 9.

118–119 *Douglass would have to give up:* Ibid., 21.

119 *The people who practiced the inoculation:* Williams, *Several Arguments Proving That Inoculating the Smallpox Is Not Contained in the Law of Physick,* 10.

119 *Williams was a "sorry tobacconist":* Silverman, *Life and Times of Cotton Mather,* 356–59.

122 *His father comforted him:* Mather, *Diary of Cotton Mather,* 2:635.

122 *"If he should after all die":* Ibid., 2:635.

122–123 *"If I should suffer this operation":* Ibid.

123 *He looked heavenward:* Ibid., 2:635–36.

123 *With his children, kinsmen, and parishioners worried:* Ibid., 2:636–37.

124 *Dr. Boylston was not the physician:* Ibid., 2:637–38.

124 *He set aside his selfish inclinations:* Ibid., 2:639.

125 *"The eruption proceeds":* Ibid., 2:639–40.

125 *He was now personally confronting:* Ibid., 2:641.

126 *He prayed that Sammy may "come gold out of the fire":* Ibid., 2:643–45.

127 *It was particularity rare:* Fischer, *Albion's Seed,* 73, 83; and Silverman, *Life and Times of Cotton Mather,* 348.

127 *She presented her father:* Silverman, *Life and Times of Cotton Mather,* 290.

127 *Roughly 3 percent of women died during childbirth:* Carol Berkin, *First Generations: Women in Colonial America* (New York: Hill and Wang, 1996), 26.

127 *But they concurrently felt great joy:* Laurel Thatcher Ulrich, *Good Wives: Image and Reality in the Lives of Women in Northern New England, 1650–1750* (New York: Vintage, 1980), 126, 131, 135.

128 *"I have other children":* Mather, *Diary of Cotton Mather,* 2:640.

128 *Nancy was "very hazardously circumstanced":* Ibid., 2:641.

128 *"My Savior seems to multiply":* Ibid., 2:640.

128 *He again lamented his current lot:* Ibid., 2:643.

129 *"I am called unto repeated sacrifices":* Ibid., 2:645.

129 *She was enfeebled but recuperated slowly:* Ibid., 2:645.

129 *"still dangerously circumstanced":* Ibid., 2:645.

130 *Daniel Willard would have been excluded:* Ulrich, *Good Wives,* 126–35; and Berkin, *First Generations,* 33–35.

130 *she had been present at previous childbirths:* Ulrich, *Good Wives,* 132.

130 *The women in this case:* Ibid., 126–35.

131 *her daughter was now susceptible:* Fenn, *Pox Americana,* 21–22.

132 *They aspired to earn the praise:* Ulrich, *Good Wives,* 9–14, 37, 43, 54, 61–68.

133 *They read the Bible:* Rebecca J. Tannenbaum, *The Healer's Calling:*

Women and Medicine in Early New England (Ithaca: Cornell University Press, 2002), 17–22.

133   *the women harvested specific items:* Ibid., 23–24.

133   *they administered a few spoonfuls:* Ibid., 26–27.

134   *These small interdependent communities of women:* Ibid., 33, 49.

134   *nurses usually became intimate:* Ibid., 114–17.

134   *Female doctors maintained smallpox hospitals:* Ibid., 118–25.

134–155   *This was the practice of the time:* Porter, *Greatest Benefit to Mankind,* 59.

135   *They were bedside:* Fenn, *Pox Americana,* 16; and Tannenbaum, *Healer's Calling,* 34.

135   *Afterward, any women:* Fenn, *Pox Americana,* 18–20; and Tannenbaum, *Healer's Calling,* 34.

136   *The converted were admitted:* Colin G. Calloway, *New Worlds for All: Indians, Europeans, and the Remaking of Early America* (Baltimore: Johns Hopkins University Press, 1997), 75–77, 83.

136   *They were often impoverished:* Alan Taylor, *American Colonies: The Settling of North America* (New York: Penguin, 2001), 199–203.

136   *The Indians also had a strong spiritual dimension:* Boorstin, *The Americans,* 211; and Calloway, *New Worlds for All,* 25–32.

137   *They, like Puritan women, were silent voices:* Calloway, *New Worlds for All,* 33–38, 74.

137   *It was among the first funerals:* Mather, *Diary of Cotton Mather,* 2:647.

139   *His master's thesis on original sin:* Eve LaPlante, *Salem Witch Judge: The Life and Repentance of Samuel Sewall* (New York: HarperCollins, 2007), 75–77.

140   *The port of Boston provided:* Ibid., 91–92.

140–141   *He decried the decline:* Ola Elizabeth Winslow, *Samuel Sewall of Boston* (New York: Macmillan, 1964), 56–58, 62–63, 86–89.

141   *Sewall's life represents:* Richard Francis, *Judge Sewall's Apology: The Salem Witch Trials and the Forming of an American Conscience* (New York: HarperCollins, 2005), 257; and Winslow, *Samuel Sewall,* 90.

141 *He also served as captain:* LaPlante, *Salem Witch Judge,* 19–21.

141 *If anyone epitomized the Protestant work:* Stephen Innes, *Creating the Commonwealth: The Economic Culture of Puritan New England* (New York: Norton, 1995), 5–38.

141 *he went to England in the fall of 1688:* LaPlante, *Salem Witch Judge,* 101–17.

142 *The new charter also granted:* Taylor, *American Colonies,* 278–82.

142 *Sewall desired "to take the blame":* LaPlante, *Salem Witch Judge,* 199–200; and Francis, *Judge Sewall's Apology,* 83–182.

143 *"In taking the Negroes out of Africa":* Samuel Sewall, *The Selling of Joseph: A Memorial* (Boston: Green and Allen, 1700).

143 *Answering those who posited that Africans:* Ibid.

143 *Africans were human beings:* Ibid.

143 144 *When Mather stated:* LaPlante, *Salem Witch Judge,* 205.

144 *The widower had also buried:* Ibid., 62, 97, 123, 244–46.

144 *"befitting a man of his wealth":* Ibid., 12.

146 *If it bred a certain indifference:* David E. Stannard, *The Puritan Way of Death: A Study in Religion, Culture, and Social Change* (Oxford: Oxford University Press, 1977), 99–100.

146 *And these were accepted:* Ibid., 100–110, 117, 122.

147 *In early eighteenth-century Boston:* Ibid., 100, 110–11.

147 *Only a hardy family:* Samuel Sewall, 2:1020–21.

148 *The lower down on the social ladder:* Stannard, *Puritan Way of Death,* 112.

149 *The court threatened a fine:* Massachusetts General Court, *Acts and Resolves,* 10:114.

149 *"they shall pass the nearest way":* Ibid., 87, 114.

149–150 *"I think this is the first public funeral":* Sewall, *Diary of Samuel Sewall,* 2:983; and Stannard, *Puritan Way of Death,* 112.

150 *Sewall described another funeral:* Sewall, *Diary of Samuel Sewall,* 2:984–85.

150 *When a fellow church member of means died:* Ibid., 2:985.

150 *Sewall and Cotton Mather and Increase Mahter walked:* Ibid.

150 *Cotton Mather once commented:* Stannard, *Puritan Way of Death,* 112.

150 *Sewall witnessed a funeral:* Sewall, *Diary of Samuel Sewall,* 2:984.

151 *"Great snow on the ground":* Ibid., 2:985.

151 *Prayers had rarely been said:* Stannard, *Puritan Way of Death,* 115–17.

151 *The expense became so prohibitive:* Ibid., 113–15.

152 *He was prepared to trust in God:* Mather, *Diary of Cotton Mather,* 2:679.

152 *The "dying circumstances":* Ibid., 2:648.

153 *"An uncommon occurrence!"* Ibid.

153 *"Can I edify the flock":* Ibid.

153 *"What have I to support me":* Ibid.

154 *"Between ten and eleven in the evening":* Ibid., 2:649.

154 *"The condition of my widowed son-in-law":* Ibid.

154 *"How much may I serve the cause of piety":* Ibid.

154 *"The Holy Silence That Sad Things Are to Be Entertained Withal":* Ibid., 2:649, 679.

155 *Quietly, a pious minister:* Ibid., 2:648.

155 *He also prayed for strength:* Ibid., 2:649–50.

158 *They may have consumed the trees:* William Cronon, *Changes in the Land: Indians, Colonists, and the Ecology of New England* (New York: Hill and Wang, 1983), 109–12.

158 *the* Seahorse *in Boston waters:* Hawke, *Everyday Life in Early America,* 144; and Cronon, *Changes in the Land,* 110.

158 *As many as twenty-five hundred trees:* Hawke, *Everyday Life in Early America,* 14, 143.

159 *Salted Newfoundland cod:* George Francis Dow, *Everyday Life in the Massachusetts Bay Colony* (New York: Dover, 1935), 149.

159 *Almost every table:* Ibid., 120–42.

159 *A cord of wood:* Hawke, *Everyday Life in Early America,* 143.

159 *Beds, benches, chairs, tables, and other household goods:* Ibid.

160 *The rising prices were becoming prohibitive:* Bridenbaugh, *Cities in the Wilderness,* 11–12, 151, 311.

161 *The ensuing public crisis: A Report of the Record Commissioners of the City of Boston, Selectmen Minutes, 1715–1729* (Boston, 1885), 88–89.

161 *He was going to prod the Selectmen:* Mather, *Diary of Cotton Mather,* 2:646.

161 *Their fears of smallpox: Report of the Record Commissioners of the City of Boston,* 88–9.

161–162 *"that the poor may not suffer":* Mather, *Diary of Cotton Mather,* 2:646.

162 *Mather felt duty-bound:* Ibid., 2:655–56.

163 *The Scot's Charitable Society:* Bridenbaugh, *Cities in the Wilderness,* 233–35.

163 *"Let it be declared":* Mather, *Diary of Cotton Mather,* 2:653.

164 *Overseers were appointed:* Bridenbaugh, *Cities in the Wilderness,* 75–81, 233–35.

164 *"Whereas by reason of the smallpox":* Massachusetts General Court, *Acts and Resolves,* 10:123.

165 *"The afflicted multiply fast enough":* Mather, *Diary of Cotton Mather,* 2:648.

165 *"The afflicted":* Ibid., 2:650.

166 *More than 200 had already died: Boston Gazette,* October 2, 1721; and *New England Courant,* October 2, 1721.

166 *"I am exceedingly tired":* Mather, *Diary of Cotton Mather,* 2:652.

166 *"number of persons in the bill for prayers":* Ibid., 2:652.

166 *"322 in the notes for the sick":* Ibid., 2:653.

166 *"The sick of the smallpox in the notes":* Ibid., 2:654.

167 *"How to Receive Good, and How to Receive Evil":* Ibid., 2:680.

167 *"Shall I not endeavor to show our people":* Ibid., 2:654.

167 *He was resigned even to death:* Ibid.

168 *It was a time to flee to church:* Sewall, *Diary of Samuel Sewall,* 2:984.

168 *"the number of the sick in our bills now sunk":* Mather, *Diary of Cotton Mather,* 2:656.

168 *He lost fellow church members, friends, college students:* Sewall, *Diary of Samuel Sewall,* 2:984–86.

169 *"a loathsome disease":* Mather, *Diary of Cotton Mather,* 2:680.

169 *"Whereas the great General Court":* Massachusetts General Court, *Acts and Resolves,* 10:120.

170 *"it being a dying time":* Mather, *Diary of Cotton Mather,* 2:680.

170 *"Now on the town an Angel flaming stands":* New England Courant, November 20, 1721.

171 *Its ends had nearly been achieved:* Blake, "The Inoculation Controversy in Boston," 496.

171 *"In as much as the funerals":* Report of the Record Commissioners of the City of Boston, 92.

171 *"Considering the several classes of people":* Mather, *Diary of Cotton Mather,* 2:662.

173–174 *"The sottish errors and cursed clamors":* Ibid., 2:656.

174 *"This abominable town":* Ibid., 2:655.

174 *Mather, "with an air of great displeasure," stopped Franklin: New England Courant,* November 27, 1721. Franklin wrote that the scene occurred some three weeks before he reported on it.

175 *The measures were an attempt: Report of the Record Commissioners of the City of Boston,* 90–91.

175 *He performed more than a hundred inoculations:* Blake, "The Inoculation Controversy in Boston," 494.

175 *Mather related to his diary that "several persons":* Mather, *Diary of Cotton Mather,* 2:661.

175 *"After some hot discourse":* Blake, "The Inoculation Controversy in Boston," 495.

177 *He later wrote that three:* Mather, *Diary of Cotton Mather,* 2:657; and Boylston, *Historical Account of the Smallpox Inoculated in New England,* 20.

178 *"the granado was charged":* Mather, *Diary of Cotton Mather,* 2:657–58.

178 *Mather deduced that the unexploded grenade "passing through the window"*: Ibid.

178 *Mather thought that "upon its going off"*: Ibid.

178 *"Cotton Mather, you dog"*: Ibid.

178–179 *"My kinsman having received"*: Ibid.

179 *the perpetrator was never discovered:* Massachusetts General Court, *Acts and Resolves,* 10:124.

179 *They did not convene:* Mather, *Diary of Cotton Mather,* 2:658.

179 *He was not asking himself "what good he could do":* Ibid.

180 *He chose the passage "on the occasion":* Ibid., 2:680.

180 *Mather then discoursed on the "services done by the good angels":* Ibid., 2:659.

180 *"I have been guilty of such a crime":* Ibid.

180–181 *"The opposition to it has been carried":* Ibid.

181 *he would much rather "die by such hands":* Ibid., 2:659–60.

181 *Mather pondered thoughts:* Ibid., 2:680.

181–182 *"Our Desires and Our Groanings":* Ibid.

182 *He made "particular supplications":* Ibid., 2:663.

182 *"When the protomartyr Stephen":* Ibid., 2:669.

182 *his life was dedicated to "doing Good":* Ibid., 2:670.

182–183 *"The most false representations":* Ibid., 2:671.

183 *Others joined in and convinced Mather:* Ibid.

183 *"The sacred oracles":* Mather, *Vindication of the Ministers of Boston,* 1.

183–184 *the ministers stated: "Above all, we wonder at a weekly paper":* Ibid., 3.

184 *The pamphlet contrasted the "blessed pastors":* Ibid., 4–6, 12–13.

185 *"Warnings are to be given":* Mather, *Diary of Cotton Mather,* 2:663.

187 *It was inscribed with the Latin phrase* Post tenebras lucem: Sewall, *Diary of Samuel Sewall,* 2:989.

188 *In January, Sewall and the other overseers:* Morison, *Three Centuries of Harvard,* 66–69.

188 *The university overseers turned a wary eye:* Sewall, *Diary of Samuel Sewall,* 2:987–89.

188 *Sewall believed the qualified donation:* Ibid.

188 *They were satisfied and two weeks later:* Ibid.

188 *Mary Gibbs had lost her husband:* LaPlante, *Salem Witch Judge,* 244–50.

189 *noting that a friend "complimented me":* Sewall, *Diary of Samuel Sewall,* 2:993.

189 *"Your obliging answer":* Samuel Sewall to Mrs. Mary Gibbs, in ibid., 2:991.

189 *Sewall did not record:* Fischer, *Albion's Seed,* 81.

189–190 *The Selectmen were glad to see: Report of the Record Commissioners of the City of Boston,* 96.

190 *the General Court ordered them to remain on campus:* Massachusetts General Court, *Acts and Resolves,* 10:175.

191 *James decided to print it:* Franklin, *Autobiography,* 15.

191 *"Know then, I am an enemy to vice":* "Silence Dogood #2," in *A Benjamin Franklin Reader,* ed. Walter Isaacson (New York: Simon and Schuster, 2005), 13.

191–192 *"I reflected in my mind":* "Silence Dogood #4," in *Benjamin Franklin Reader,* 15–17.

192 *Another woman, Joanna Alford, was inoculated: Report of the Record Commissioners of the City of Boston,* 97.

192 *When young Samuel Sewall came to him:* Blake, "The Inoculation Controversy in Boston," 497–98.

193 *The politicians empowered the officers: Report of the Record Commissioners of the City of Boston,* 97–98.

193 *"the persons so inoculated":* Massachusetts General Court, *Acts and Resolves,* 10:161.

193 *He was compelled to "solemnly promise":* Boston Gazette, May 21, 1722.

194 *"Last January inoculation made a sort of exit": New England Courant,* May 21, 1722.

195 *In the silence of his own mind:* William Douglass to Cadwallader Colden, May 1, 1722, *The Colden Papers,*1:141–44.

195 *"'Tis thought he will sail sometime":* New England Courant, June 11, 1722.

195 *ruled that his satire was "a high affront to this government":* Massachusetts General Court, *Acts and Resolves,* 10:167.

195 *Boston's "public gaol" was a neglected:* Bridenbaugh, *Cities in the Wilderness,* 74–75, 224–25, 384–85.

195 *With the greatest of irony, it was signed by Dr. Zabdiel Boylston:* Massachusetts General Court, *Acts and Resolves,* 10:174.

195–196 *Benjamin reported that he was "taken up and examined":* Franklin, *Autobiography,* 16.

196 *Franklin found them wanting:* "Silence Dogood #9," in *Benjamin Franklin Reader,* 22–24.

196 *Franklin regretted his apprenticeship:* Franklin, *Autobiography,* 15–16.

197 *He praised Christmas:* David Waldstreicher, *Runaway America: Benjamin Franklin, Slavery, and the American Revolution* (New York: Hill and Wang, 2004), 48.

197 *"Whenever I find a man":* New England Courant, January 14, 1723.

197 *the independent-minded printer:* Brands, *The First American*, 31.

198 *"A very flimsy scheme it was":* Franklin, *Autobiography,* 16.

198 *James had the economic strings to pull:* Ibid., 16–17.

198 *The young man was not constantly under public scrutiny:* Ibid.

198 *He agreed to slip the young man:* Ibid., 17.

199 *"I had been some time with him":* Benjamin Franklin to Samuel Mather, July 7, 1773, in Leonard Labaree, ed., *The Papers of Benjamin Franklin,* 39 vols. (New Haven: Yale University Press, 1959–2008), 20:287.

199 *The minister indicated that:* Various authors have ascribed the timing of this meeting differently. David Waldstreicher argues that it occurred before Franklin left Boston in *Runaway America,* 53–54, while H. W. Brands holds that it took place during a subsequent visit to his home town in *The First American,* 53–54. Franklin specifically told Samuel Mather that the meeting occurred in 1723.

199 *It was Mather's way of "hammering instruction"*: Benjamin Franklin to Samuel Mather, July 7, 1773, in *Papers of Benjamin Franklin,* 20:287.

200 *Damp, miserable, and hungry:* Franklin, *Autobiography,* 17–18.

200 *He cut a miserable figure:* Ibid., 18–19.

201 *The first patient of note:* Duffy, *Epidemics in Colonial America,* 34.

201 *"There is an account published":* Stanley Finger, *Doctor Franklin's Medicine* (Philadelphia: University of Pennsylvania Press, 2006), 57.

201–202 *"In 1736, I lost one of my sons":* Franklin, *Autobiography,* 83.

202 *he told the readers of* Poor Richard's Almanac *in 1737:* Finger, *Doctor Franklin's Medicine,* 60.

202 *That same year, he conducted the first clinical study:* William Douglass to Cadwallader Colden, February 17, 1736, *Colden Papers,* 2:146–47; John Duffy, *From Humors to Medical Sciences: A History of American Medicine,* 2nd ed. (Urbana: University of Illinois Press, 1993), 24, 39; and Stearns, *Science in the British Colonies of America,* 480.

202 *In a letter to society, Cotton Mather introduced Boylston:* Stearns, *Science in the British Colonies of America,* 411.

203 *Boylston lectured on smallpox inoculation:* Ibid., 437; and Beall and Shryock, *Cotton Mather,* 108.

203 *Though he found employment in a London printshop:* Winslow, *Destroying Angel,* 70; and Wood, *Americanization of Benjamin Franklin,* 25–29.

203–204 *"His name is like to live a great while":* Levin, *Cotton Mather.*

204 *Benjamin Franklin was the man who was renowned:* Philip Dray, *Stealing God's Thunder: Benjamin Franklin's Lightning Rod and the Invention of America* (New York: Random House, 2005), 92, 139; Joyce E. Chaplin labels Franklin the "first scientific American" in *The First Scientific American: Benjamin Franklin and the Pursuit of Genius* (New York: Basic Books, 2006).

205 *Its emphasis on public good, virtue, and convenantal theology:* Edmund S. Morgan, "The Puritan Ethic and the American Revolution," *William and Mary Quarterly,* 3rd Series, XXIV, no. 1 (January, 1967): 3–43.

205 *During the Revolutionary War, Americans and their leaders:* Bernard Bailyn, *The Ideological Origins of the American Revolution* (Cambridge, MA: Harvard University Press, 1967), 32–33.

205 *This democratic revolution:* Gordon S. Wood, *The Radicalism of the American Revolution* (New York: Vintage, 1991).

207 *Kuhn argued that the scientific community "often suppresses":* Thomas S. Kuhn, *The Structure of Scientific Revolutions,* 2nd ed. (Chicago: University of Chicago Press, 1970), 5.

208 *He once criticized a Florentine scientist:* Miller, *The New England Mind: The Seventeenth Century,* 221–22.

209 *Jenner's vaccination eventually led:* Porter, *Greatest Benefit to Mankind,* 275–77.

210 *"Between the knowledge of God":* Stearns, *Science in the British Colonies of America,* 160.

ABOUT
THE AUTHOR

Tony Williams taught history and literature for ten years after earning degrees in American history from Syracuse University and Ohio State University. He is the author of *Hurricane of Independence* and is currently a full-time author who lives in Williamsburg, Virginia, with his wife and children.

photo credit: Paul Harrison

NOTE TO READER

I have modernized the quotations from the sources for purposes of clarity and readability. All of the dates assume the beginning of the calendar year on January 1, rather than the contemporary March, which held sway until England and the American colonies changed their calendar in 1752. Finally, all the biblical quotations were taken from the Geneva Bible translation of 1561/1599, which was used by the Puritans.

INDEX